Chomsky's Minimalism

Chomsky's Minimalism

Pieter A. M. Seuren

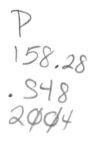

UNIVERSITY PRESS

2004

OXFORD
UNIVERSITY PRESS

Oxford New York

Auckland Bangkok Buenos Aires Cape Town Chennai
Dar es Salaam Delhi Hong Kong Istanbul Karachi Kolkata
Kuala Lumpur Madrid Melbourne Mexico City Mumbai Nairobi
São Paulo Shanghai Taipei Tokyo Toronto

Copyright © 2004 by Oxford University Press, Inc.

Published by Oxford University Press, Inc.
198 Madison Avenue, New York, New York 10016

www.oup.com

Oxford is a registered trademark of Oxford University Press

Library of Congress Cataloging-in-Publication Data
Seuren, Pieter A. M.
Chomsky's minimalism / Pieter A. M. Seuren.
p. cm.
Includes bibliographical references and index.
ISBN 0-19-517305-8; 0-19-517306-6 (pbk.)
1. Minimalist theory (Linguistics) 2. Generative
grammar. 3. Chomsky, Noam. I. Title.
P158.28.S48 2004
415'.0182—dc22   2003017662

Cover picture "Landscape with mountain chapel," oil painting (1924)
by Albert Carel Willink, Collection Museum Boymans
Van Beuningen, Rotterdam, © Sylvia Willink, Amsterdam.

2 4 6 8 9 7 5 3

Printed in the United States of America
on acid-free paper

Preface

This book has a history that goes back to about 1970, when I began to feel dissatisfied with the direction taken by Chomsky and his followers toward what was called "autonomous syntax" at the time, away from "generative semantics," the form of grammar I favored. That feeling of dissatisfaction has increased considerably over the years. I wrote against autonomous syntax in 1972 and could, of course, have written against it again, were it not that the quick succession of different versions in which this program of grammar writing kept being presented made it impossible to keep up with the most recent developments at any given time, unless one was prepared to make that one's main occupation, which I was not.

Now, however, with the publication of Chomsky's *The Minimalist Program* in 1995, the situation appears to have stabilized and the focus of attention has shifted from theorizing about grammar writing to the loftier level of methodological reflection. Besides being the presentation of yet another version of Chomsky's ideas of what a grammar is, *The Minimalist Program* is also the statement of a program of research guided by what are described as "minimalist principles." This shift to methodology makes it possible to transcend discussions on the value of specific details of grammatical analysis, which, though valuable and necessary, tend to fail to affect wider issues of how human language as a whole is to be viewed and analyzed. Chomsky's recent statements on these wider issues of methodology make it possible to operate at a more appropriate level, where the real battle between paradigms can be decided.

Unsurprisingly, this book is highly critical of Chomsky's views, which are, in the end, dismissed as basically misguided and intellectually irrelevant. It is also critical of his academic conduct, however, especially when he appears to appropriate central notions from generative semantics, the school of thought he has, for the past thirty years, opposed in all possible ways. Given Chomsky's status in the discipline and beyond, it is important that the historical, methodological, and empirical issues at play should be discussed explicitly and with maximal clarity. This book is meant as a contribution to that discussion.

Quite a few people have looked over my shoulder as I was writing this book, helping me in all sorts of ways. Rudie Botha and Gerard Kempen deserve special mention in this respect. But above all I wish to thank Paul Postal and Geoff Pullum, who read the prefinal version of the text with particular care and made many useful suggestions. They will detect the result of their effort in the text at hand. I must also thank the Russian Academy of Sciences, especially Igor Boguslavsky of the Moscow Institute for Information Transmission Problems, for enabling me to write part of this book as a guest in their institute.

Contents

Chomsky's Minimalism

1

Introduction

1.1 Stated aim

This book is a sustained argument purporting to show that Noam Chomsky's latest version of his linguistic theory, recently published as *The Minimalist Program* (MP) (Chomsky 1995), though presented as the crowning achievement of the Chomskyan version of generative grammar, is in fact the clearest possible demonstration that that version is fundamentally flawed. The MP is not so much the crowning achievement as the undoing of the development started by Chomsky during the late 1960s, when he decided to dissociate himself from what was then the natural continuation of the new paradigm of transformational generative grammar. That paradigm had been set into motion by Leonard Bloomfield during the 1920s and taken further by Zellig Harris during the 1940s and 1950s. In the early 1960s, when meaning began to be taken seriously again, transformational generative grammar transformed itself into a new version, known at the time as generative semantics. At first, Chomsky was sympathetic to this new development. Yet, for reasons that have never been clarified, he turned against it around 1968 and reverted to a strictly syntax-based or, as it is called in this book, a "random-generator" view of language. A quick succession of different varieties of this random-generator view then saw the light of day, ending in the MP, which shows more clearly than any of its predecessors the untenability and internal contradictions of the entire approach.

In the chapters ahead we will see that Chomsky's book *The Minimalist Program* is a sad example of spurious science, as it fails to satisfy basic scientific criteria, such as respect for data, unambiguous formulations, falsifiability, and also, on a different level, simple good manners. Apart from that, however, even if the book had been properly written, the ideas put forward do not pass muster, no matter how badly or how well presented they may be. In fact, a serious discussion of the issues raised in and by the MP shows that the direction taken by generative semantics in the late 1960s contained promises for a long-term rich, coherent, and fruitful research program, called "mediational grammar" in this book. This development, however, was nipped in the bud, in circumstances which have recently invited a great deal of comment that is less flattering to Chomsky and his school than it might have been if the suffering party had observed the rules and principles of proper academic conduct with greater fervor (see, for example, Harris 1993, Murray 1994, Huck and Goldsmith 1995, Seuren 1998:ch. 4). When the MP is dissected and the old issues are mooted again, it becomes clear—on philosophical, methodological, empirical, and interdisciplinary grounds—that the mediational view of language, though subjected to ridicule since the early 1970s, is in every way superior to the random-generator view.

It is ironic to see that since the publication of his 1995 book on the MP, Chomsky has taken more and more to the use of formulations involving the notion that language is the *expression of thought*, a notion that is alien to the random-generator concept of grammar but is central to mediational grammar. It should be noted that his own conception of language and grammar as worked out in his more technical writings leaves no room at all for an account of how language could possibly express thought. All his theory of language and grammar does is provide for a purely algorithmic account of how a potentially infinite array of different sentences can be built up from a finite collection of primitive elements, but how sentences built up in this manner can be seen to *express thoughts* is left totally unexplained. Even so, over recent years, Chomsky has been speaking more and more frequently, especially in his public speeches, about the fact that the primary function of language is to express thought and that the origin of the potential infinity of language lies in the human capacity to form an infinite array of thoughts that are expressible in language, suggesting at the same time—against all reason and all evidence—that his theory of language provides a natural (minimalist) account of that primary function. More is said about this in section 1.5.

1.2 The hard truth about the MP

The MP is based on two overarching ideas, the first being a runner-up to the second, which is the main defining idea of the MP as a whole. The first idea is the proposal that there is one single universal grammatical system for all languages, the differences among them being accounted for by different choices made from the available options built into the machinery. This idea is as old as the late Middle Ages, when a beginning was made to describe the grammars of languages other than Latin. When this was done, the universal mold was the grammar of Latin, which was taken to instantiate universal principles. By the eighteenth century, the French grammarian Nicolas Beauzée had long left Latin grammar behind and expressed, albeit in eighteenth-century terminology, much the same basic idea that is presented in Chomskyan linguistics. One may regard the MP as a late-twentieth-century attempt at casting this idea in modern terms and placing it in the context of modern science.

The second idea, which actually defines the MP, is that the universal machinery should be seen in the perspective of the technical problem of how best to link up propositional thought with sound. The central idea of the MP is to investigate (a) what language is supposed to do given its cognitive and biological environment—that is, what the core function of language is; (b) what sort of machinery would ideally fulfill the core function of language optimally—that is, in the simplest and most economical way—the sort of machinery "a superbly competent engineer might have constructed, given certain design specifications" (Chomsky 1998:15); and (c) to what extent human language, as it has evolved during the past 100,000 years or so, actually resembles the ideal construction as it would have been made by the "superbly competent engineer." To the extent that the answer to (c) is positive, the machinery of grammar is considered "conceptually necessary." (Chomsky anticipates the answer to (c), though with some reservations, by saying that human language is probably near-perfect.)

Needless to say, an enterprise such as the one just sketched is extremely ambitious. Although there is nothing wrong with intellectual ambition, surely the success of any such research program crucially depends on the soundness of the answers to (a), (b), and (c). That is, a sound analysis is needed of the main functions that language must be taken to have in the human environment. Then, it takes an intellect of well-nigh superhuman quality to define the optimal solution to the problem of how to carry out the main function of language, whatever that may turn out to be, in an optimal way. And, finally, it takes a virtually complete and adequate insight into the nature of human language as it is to set off human language against the "ideal" structure devised by our "superbly competent engineer."

Unfortunately, as is set out in detail in the following chapters, the question of the functionality of language in a general sense is still far from settled. Moreover, Chomsky's specific notions in this respect are so deficient in essential respects (see section 5.4) that, in themselves, they suffice to take any meaning out of the entire MP enterprise. His denial of the communicative function of language and, in general, of the social context in which speech utterances have systematic effects, and his exclusive reliance on largely unknown "legibility" conditions imposed by the cognitive and motor-perceptual "interfaces" make for such unclarities, uncertainties, and distortions in the basic conditions to be met by a language system that one is justified in having the gravest doubts regarding the MP right from the start.

Moreover, for an author to identify with a "superbly competent engineer"—that is, with nature at its best—will naturally invite charges of hubris, or worse. This identification is particularly embarrassing as the random-generator solution defended by Chomsky as "conceptually necessary" is just about the opposite of "the best possible solution": it is hard to think up a solution that is worse.

This fact is closely connected with question (c). To answer that question properly, one needs, as a necessary condition, an adequate insight into the structure and the workings of the language system. Unfortunately again, as is shown in considerable detail in the following chapters, Chomsky's ideas about the language system as a whole, though presented over the years as indubitable wisdom, should, in fact, be dismissed as hardly relevant.

All this taken together is amply sufficient to justify regarding the MP as spurious science, which would defy comment and invite an embarrassed silence were it not that it has attracted an inordinate amount of attention.

For the MP to be branded as spurious will at least provoke surprise, but it will more likely be met with disbelief, displeasure, or even outrage, especially among those who follow or sympathize with the Chomskyan view of autonomous syntax as it has been developed since 1970. On the other hand, many linguists outside the sphere of influence of Chomskyan linguistics will be quick to approve since they have always mistrusted Chomskyan linguistics or judged it downright wrong from the start. For the latter, the MP is the product of an overwrought and overambitious concern with certain a priori formal ideas concerning grammar, which are unsupported by adequate data surveys or by sufficient knowledge of the wider semantic, logical, and psychological implications. They discern, moreover, a parochialism perhaps unprecedented in serious science but well known in other areas of cultural life that are less based on solid principles of rationality. This parochial attitude implies that no one outside the group of followers could possibly have anything relevant to contribute or should be mentioned for ideas that are used or have been incorporated into the system or may invite comparison.

The adherents, however, and also those who have heard more or less distant rumors about this new modern linguistic theory, will find it hard to believe that such a widely advertised and widely acclaimed linguistic theory as the MP and its predecessors should fail so dismally under cool scrutiny. This is why a critique of Chomskyan linguistics generally, but especially such a wholesale rejection as is argued for in this book, is certain to meet with considerable resistance. The man Chomsky has risen to the very pinnacles of fame, a status unparalleled in the history of linguistics (due to a large extent also to his political writings). His fame and influence are enormous, not only among professional linguists but also in the wider circles of intellectuals with no more than a marginal interest in the study of language. In these circles especially, there is a widespread belief that Chomskyan linguistics is the only serious form of scientific syntax. A mythology has arisen around the man and the theory.[1]

It is important that the myth be shattered. It has done great damage to linguistics and surrounding disciplines, intellectually and sociologically.

---

1. A (more or less random) example is Johnson-Laird (2003:9): "Theorists understand the principles of grammar, thanks to the work of linguists such as Chomsky (e.g. 1995)." See also note 1 of chapter 3 in this volume. One could cite numerous other authors who put blind faith in Chomsky's linguistics without, apparently, having actually studied his works. Such is the power of myth.

Open, rational discussion of empirical and theoretical issues has been severely impaired, owing to an attitude, displayed by Chomsky and his followers, of having seen the light and therefore being superior to others. In-group quotations abound, while references to "outsiders" appear to be banned. Arguments only count insofar as they do not call into question the dogma of the day. In this sense, Chomsky's *The Minimalist Program* and subsequent publications are indeed a crowning achievement, as they preclude discussion at all points. Possible counterevidence, already unpopular for decades, is now branded a priori as "apparent" and if it were real it would not count anyway, given the "Galilean style" of doing linguistics, which, as Chomsky reads poor Galileo, allows him and his followers (see, for example, Freidin and Vergnaud 2001) to dismiss any counterevidence as irrelevant from the start. For reasons like these, this book is not meant just to be a negative review of the MP, it also aims explicitly at showing that the emperor is not wearing the clothes that so many think he is wearing.

It is a part of every intellectual's basic training to distinguish between status and intellectual value when judging scientific work. All textbooks of good method mention arguments from authority as a specific type of fallacy. Even so, it turns out to be very difficult to separate the two in actual practice. This is easier to do when the work in question represents some fad in art or fashion, or a philosophy of life without academic relevance, or "parascience," which preys on serious work done by others and indulges in vague and often ethically colored musings of an uncontrollable nature. In the case of Chomskyan linguistics, however, it is generally believed that it represents real "hard" science, deserving a central place in the Pantheon of Knowledge. To try and dethrone such an authoritative doctrine will immediately be seen by many as something close to sacrilege, casting doubt on the author rather than on the object of his criticism.

It is to those who are inclined to feel like that that this book is addressed. It appeals to the reader to take some distance from the here and now and make an effort to take an uncluttered and sober view at the arguments presented here, pushing into the background all preconceived ideas about who is great in this world and who is not. If history teaches anything, it is that true and lasting values can only be recognized in the long run, and even then there often are periodic reappraisals. In other words, readers are invited simply to look at the evidence and the matter at hand. If they do that, I am sure that it will make them see Chomskyan linguistics in a different light from that in which the faithful followers tend to see it. An appeal is made, therefore, to readers to apply their powers of discrimination, regardless of status, prestige, or any other consideration that is alien to the matter itself.

The critique presented in this volume is based on a variety of elements—historical, empirical, methodological, and philosophical—but the central theme is one of methodology, concerning the criteria of good, professional science. But what is good, professional science? At the outset of his famous book *The Crayfish* (1880), Thomas Huxley describes science as "simply common sense at its best; that is, rigidly accurate in observation, and merciless to fallacy in logic." Karl Popper, another stalwart, writes in the preface to the first English edition (1959) of his famous *The Logic of Scientific Discovery* that "scientific knowledge . . . is *common sense knowledge writ large.*" Huxley was, of course, a great nineteenth-century biologist, and Popper a great philosopher of the middle of the twentieth century. For authors such as these, science is not only based on and restricted by common sense but also largely timeless: serious scientific results should be eternal, totally objective, and thus unchallengeable, a solid monument that will withstand all erosion by time.

In more recent times, however, a less lapidary view of science has arisen. Younger philosophers of science have stressed that social factors, including the prevailing worldview and the set of values of the day, influence the criteria of good scientific work. They also argue that the predicate "scientific" is no guarantee for absolute, objective truth: science is more a question of evaluation than of hard-and-fast criteria. Paul Feyerabend (1975) even goes so far as to maintain the principle that "anything goes," no matter how arbitrary or nonsensical, provided it is backed up with good public relations, a careful strategy to shoot down your opponents, and a well-oiled machinery for obtaining funds. This is more than a little over the top, however. If the success of a scientific theory depended entirely on such external factors as rhetoric, fundraising, and public relations, then, I think, a great many excellent scientists would not consider science to be worth pursuing.

The sensible course to follow, it seems, is the middle way, avoiding the extremes. True, most science is subject to social value systems and subjective elements of evaluation and appreciation—even, one has to admit, to prejudices. It also has to fit into current sociological conditions, or else it will fail to attract good intellects. Yet it goes too far to deny science all lasting objective value and give rhetoric free play. No matter what limiting factors play a role in the development of science, there always is a core of what we want to consider good work of lasting value, which will always retain validity, though it may be supplemented with work motivated by other perspectives or even supplanted by theories placed in a wider and more general context. Accordingly, scientific methodology clearly has universal features. There always is a difference between shoddy and serious or intelligent work. And the criteria remain, by and large, the same: in the end, people always recognize good work.

We can still feel the excitement of a sharp analysis or intelligent argument of a scientist of ages past. We have no difficulty appreciating Newton's acumen when he presents his argument that the earth must be slightly flattened at the poles or else all water of the oceans would flow to the equator due to centrifugal force. The compensating force of gravity should therefore be greater at the equator, thus maintaining the equilibrium we observe. Nor do we fail to admire Frege's insight when he solves the problems connected with the principle of Substitution Salva Veritate by extrapolating the medieval distinction of extension and intension from predicates to terms and propositions, thus saving Aristotle's theory of truth. Of course, we have all kinds of corrections and observations to make, but no one will deny that Frege produced work that was serious and of lasting value.

I therefore take a moderate view with regard to questions around the "eternal" value of scientific results. While making allowance for a certain amount of relativity, historically and epistemically, I still hold, with the vast majority of scientists, that work that presents itself as in any way scientific or academic should satisfy certain judiciously applied elementary criteria of common rationality: clarity of expression; faithfulness to the relevant facts that are, or can be made, available; acceptance of whatever can be concluded on the basis of these facts; and a mandatory preference for "the best theory"—that is, for the theory that explains more facts with less machinery than rival theories on the market. Such criteria are not hard-and-fast. There is as yet no formal and testable charter whose observance guarantees good science, but there are plenty of principles whose nonobservance guarantees bad science. We may not have at our fingertips all sufficient conditions for good science, but we have plenty of necessary conditions. It is these that will be applied to Chomsky's latest theory, and one should not be surprised to find that it fails to meet them by a long shot.

I will, moreover, though with less stringency, rely on more intuitive criteria of plausibility or persuasion. A good theory typically provokes the sensation that it is too good to be false, whereas the feeling that a proposal is too bad to be true usually bodes ill. It is granted immediately that this principle is intuitive and not testable in a relevant way. Yet it is an undeniable fact that to those who are familiar with the facts and the problems, bad science is dour, boring, and irritating, while good professional science has a special appeal.

1.3 Further misgivings

The main conclusions of this book run counter to a belief expressed by some linguists to the effect that the new MP provides a promising and totally new methodological basis for the study of language, based on the concept of a maximally efficient generalized universal grammatical system for all languages. *The Minimalist Program* has been characterized as "a masterpiece" (Zwart 1998:214) or "a major breakthrough . . . to a new level of abstraction" (Freidin 1997:581), or, more lyrically, as a book that "allows us to participate in one of the most fascinating conceptual adventures of our time . . . a revolution within a revolution" (Piattelli-Palmarini, as cited in Uriagereka 1998:xxi–xxii).

These opinions are not to be dismissed lightly. On the contrary, one must take into serious account the possibility, presented as realistic in *The Minimalist Program*, that what Chomsky proposes is a new and productive way of thinking about language, taking place at a higher level of abstraction, generality, and descriptive economy than has been customary till now, and showing his theory of grammar in a more compelling setting of internal necessity and functionality.

That is, anyway, what the MP claims to achieve. As we have seen, the underlying idea is (a) there really is only one grammatical system for all languages: every language constructs its sentences according to one single universal procedure, which (b) is taken to be the best possible technical answer to the problem of linking up sound with meaning. The fact that languages differ from each other the way they do is attributed to differences in the lexicons of the various languages, where lexical items, apart from being phonologically different, are fitted out with different features, which will make them follow different paths through the universal machinery of grammar. In this view, the universal faculty of language consists partly of the grammatical system to the extent that this is common to all languages.

The question is, of course, if Chomsky's ideas about how such a system can be made to work stand a reasonable chance of being tenable. If they do, there is good hope that they constitute a breakthrough of the type described by Zwart, Freidin, and Piattelli-Palmarini, at least in the social context of present-day generative grammar. If they do not, they are more likely to be just vacuous.

It is worth observing that a breakthrough of the nature described was achieved in linguistics by Zellig Harris around 1950, when he proposed to stop concentrating on the question of how to motivate *individual* tree-structure analyses, which was what the European introspectionists and the American "God's Truth" linguists were doing, just as had been done by Bloomfield himself. Instead, Harris proposed, in conjunction with Rulon Wells (1947), to look at the *overall structure of the grammar* as a whole so as to decide whether a particular tree structure proposal for a given sentence should or should not be considered adequate. At first, this unheard-of step provoked disbelief and puzzlement throughout the field, simply because one was not used to or trained in thinking about language and grammar at this level of generality. In time, however, it became the central foundation of generative grammar. Clearly, if Chomsky's MP is anything of the sort, it should be taken as an invitation to step up one's level of thinking about language to a higher plane of generality and abstraction. Much of the confusion, unclarity, and inconsistency found in this new approach could then be understood as the inevitable uncertain and tentative probing typical of all creative, new thinking.

Yet, if creative, new thinking is to be taken seriously, it must satisfy minimal conditions of originality, cogency, and persuasion. It must also contain the promise of a new perspective or a fresh light on empirical questions that have hitherto remained unsolved or have been solved unsatisfactorily. And, if possible, it should capture the imagination. The story should somehow arrest the attention, showing how things fall into place if certain assumptions are accepted and their consequences pursued. If that happens, an opening is shown into a new realm of thinking, where, conceivably, old unsolved questions could be settled on a rational basis and in a more explanatory light.

Again, these measures and conditions are to some extent subjective. No rational principle can force anyone to be captivated, intrigued, or arrested by anything. Nevertheless, one is fully justified, on rational grounds, to apply accepted and well-motivated standards of clarity, cohesion, and persuasion to any new proposal, no matter how innovative or creative. Mere musings or half-mystic pipe dreams won't do, and unsubstantiated appeals to "deep" but ill-understood principles or properties are not acceptable either. There must be a prospect of clear and tangible advantages.

So the question is: are there sufficient rational grounds for considering at least the possibility that Chomsky's new MP constitutes the kind of breakthrough into a new realm of linguistic thinking that he suggests it is and that some of his followers take it to be? This question is the topic of this book and, as has been made clear, the answer will be negative. This conclusion is based, among many other considerations, also on the fact that the minimalist perspective as presented by Chomsky contains no promise of a new light on old questions that have remained unsolved or whose solution has been unsatisfactory. The "fable," introduced in Chomsky (1998) and reverted to in Chomsky (2002), of a superbly competent engineer receiving the commission to design an ideal language faculty according to a given set of design specifications lacks cohesion and hence persuasion, since it is admitted at the same time that the set of design specifications is not given but largely unknown, which makes the engineer's task ill defined and thus impossible to carry out. It is simply not known what an "ideal" language faculty would or should amount to, which makes it incoherent to use this concept as a standard by which to measure a theory of language or the language faculty.

The difference with Harris's breakthrough around 1950 is striking. There the central question was: what motivates individual tree structure assignments? Harris's answer was that one should look at the totality of proposed tree structures for all sentences of a language, and then see what *system* of structure assignment was the simplest and most economical. This was not only truly original, it was also a real program, not a theory, in that all of the work still had to be done. No complete grammar was available, assigning tree structures to all sentences of a language. And when this task was actually undertaken, it soon transpired that the only principled way of doing so was to construct an algorithmically organized grammar. Then, as such grammars were being designed, further insights broke through, proving Harris's happy hand in choosing this perspective.

None of this is found in Chomsky's MP. First, despite assurances that this "is a *program*, not a theory" and that "there are minimalist questions, but no specific minimalist answers" (1998:16), the publications at hand are full of answers that are said to follow from minimalist principles and assumptions (even though that is not actually the case). Unlike Harris's earlier program, the minimalist principles and assumptions are accompanied by a large amount of grammatical machinery said to follow from them. The fact that the grammatical machinery does not follow from the minimalist principles and assumptions calls into question not only the grammatical machinery itself but also the MP as a whole. Then, empirical questions that were unsolved still are, and the program contains no promise of convincing solutions that will enhance insight. Not that no promises are made. *The Minimalist Program* is full of promises, but there is no collateral. In the end, one is left with a story that is partly an incoherent fantasy (see, for example, section 2.2.3 in this book) and partly a repetition of old principles and methods.

Some may wish to defend Chomsky by saying that he is merely the thinker, the one who comes up with the "deep" insights, leaving the more precise formulations and the empirical shoring up to others. Yet creative, new thinking should at least be able to stand on its own feet, and any shoring up by others should be motivated by the inherent value of the work supported. This, one fears, is not the case here. Good empirical work, such as that by Mark Baker (1988), is at odds with Chomskyan theory on many counts. And as for popularizing books, such as Radford (1997) or Uriagereka (1998), although they bring some clarity in that they present a machinery distilled (and in the case of Radford heavily watered down) from Chomsky (1995) and earlier works, the empirical support they provide is as poor as Chomsky's. As in Chomsky's works, examples are selected haphazardly, suggesting support for the MP but hardly providing any, due to lack of systematic data collecting. Moreover, the methodological foundations of the MP are simply taken for granted, even if, as in Uriagereka, they are presented in the artistic garb of an extended quasi-Platonic dialogue.[2] Although one appreciates that such works streamline and popularize the ideas of the MP, they are nevertheless merely derivative and provide no independent support for it.

In the MP, *conceptual necessity* is presented as a central criterion, but it is unclear what substance can be given to this notion. This is of central importance since the core theses concerning the overall architecture of language and grammatical structure are motivated as being "within the domain of virtual conceptual necessity" (Chomsky 1995:169). Yet the notion itself is left without any further analysis. (In Chomsky's publica-

2. For a fierce and fatal critique of both Uriagereka (1998) and the minimalist program on which it is based, see Levine (2002).

tions after 1995 there is a sharp decrease of talk about conceptual necessity and a corresponding increase of unsubstantial and largely inaccu-
rate appeals to great scientists of the past, in particular Galileo, Descartes,
Newton, and Darwin.)

A related question concerns Chomsky's position with regard to the
modularity of grammar, in the strictly realist sense of modularity as a
known concept in psychology (see section 3.2). A cognitive *module* is
defined in general terms as a "subsystem having a well-defined set of
inputs, a well-defined set of outputs, and a well-defined relation between
inputs and outputs" (Arbib 1987:334). Modules in this sense are not open
to introspection or awareness and are to some extent autonomous in that
they are defined by specific computational principles. A specific form
of modularity is described in Fodor (1983). At a few places in *The
Minimalist Program* and elsewhere, Chomsky speaks of the language
faculty as being "biologically isolated," in a way that makes one suspect
that he is referring to modularity, but that notion is left without any further explanation. One reads (Chomsky 2000:117):

> The performance systems can be selectively impaired, perhaps severely
> so, while the cognitive system remains intact, and further dissociations
> have been discovered, revealing the kind of modular structure expected
> in any complex biological system. Note that "modularity" here is not
> understood in the sense of Jerry Fodor's interesting work, which keeps to
> input and output systems; the cognitive system of the language faculty is
> accessed by such systems, but is distinct from them.

What "modular structure" is meant to be if it is not Fodorian is left unexplained, however.

In section 3.2, it is argued that what Chomsky presents as "biological
isolation" is only doubtfully identifiable with either the Arbibian or the
Fodorian notion of modularity, mainly owing to the unclarity of the notion of "interface" employed. It is argued in section 3.2 that an interface,
or "gate," should be taken to involve the passing on of an independently
produced output to a subsequent system, which may be modular or non-
modular, and internal or external to the organism, and that an interface
should be assumed at least at those places where the speaker or listener
has the possibility of conscious output monitoring.

When the language machinery is in production mode, then, given this
notion of interface, an interface or gate must be assumed at the output
end of whatever machinery produces thought, where the thought output

passes into the lexicon; then again at the output end of the lexicon, where the lexical selection made is passed into the grammar module; then again at the output end of the grammar module, where the output is screened and passed on to the phonetic-orthographic machinery; and finally at the output end of that, where the product is released as sound or writing. The comprehension mode appears to be largely modeled on the production mode, in that the listener registers the choices made by the speaker, which suggests that comprehension is to a large extent a process of reconstruction-by-hypothesis, constrained by input data. If this is correct, parsing must be noncompositional (see section 3.2 for further comment).

This naturally raises the question of how to explain Chomsky's ambiguous attitude regarding modularity. In section 3.2, the answer is said to lie in Chomsky's long-standing preference for a *random-generator model* of language. The class of random-generator models presents the syntax as an unguided sentence generator, randomly selecting items from the lexicon and "merging" these into proper syntactic structures. The grammatical computation is taken to deliver representations of sentences at two levels: the level of phonetic representation at the interface with the motor-perceptual system, and the level of semantic representation at the interface with the cognitive system. These two levels of representation are then characterized as "instructions" to the "external" systems of vocalization or perception on the one hand and semantic interpretation on the other.

The problem with regard to the modularity concept is that if such a random-generator grammar is taken to be a module in the accepted sense, then the postulated grammar *must* be taken in a realist sense—that is, as a representation of what is assumed to actually take place in the speaker's brain. This then would mean that speakers *must* be assumed to have a random sentence generator somewhere in the brain, a conclusion that even Chomsky is reluctant to draw. Ever since the introduction of the extended standard theory (EST) in the early 1970s, Chomsky has advocated a random-generator model, in various guises. His MP continues that tradition, which, as we have seen, does not sit well with the concept of modularity.

This raises the further issue, discussed earlier in some depth by Rudolf Botha (1989), of Chomsky's equivocal attitude of *realism* with regard to the machineries and concepts introduced in his theories. The issue of whether, how, and to what extent Chomsky's approach is to be characterized as realist or instrumentalist or anything in between is discussed in section 3.3. It is argued that since this random-generator model has no satisfactory answer to the question, discussed in section 6.1.2, "what drives the random generator?" it stands little chance of representing correctly the actual system of causal relations involved in the production and comprehension of sentences, and will thus defeat any serious realist claim of the MP. On the other hand, if the claims made or projected in the MP are to be interpreted in an instrumentalist vein, they must be considered "perverse" in the technical sense that the presentation deviates unnecessarily from the system and direction of causal relations that may be taken to be present in the real object of investigation—the language faculty and its instantiations in the grammars of specific languages.

The real state of affairs is represented much more naturally in terms of a *mediational model*, which sees a language as a device that mediates between thought and vocalization. The top-down part of the system (production mode) reflects, in essence, the generative semantics model of grammar of the early 1970s. It receives a semantic input from the system of thought, selects lexical items or ready-made phrases that correspond well enough to the content to be expressed, casts these in an appropriate syntactic format, and feeds the product into the grammar, which transforms it into a surface structure. This is then fed into the phonological component that passes on instructions for proper vocalization. The bottom-up or parsing part (comprehension mode) receives sound and reconstructs the original thought, probably by means of a system of reconstruction-by-hypothesis (see section 3.2), relying on external cues drawn from context and available world knowledge. In the mediational model the causal relations thus go primarily from thought to vocalization (production mode), and only secondarily from vocalization to thought (comprehension mode). This issue is discussed in various sections, and it is concluded that the mediational model fits the modularity concept well and is more consistently interpretable in a realist sense, besides being motivated by better empirical support than the random-generator model.

A final central aspect of the discussion concerns the notion of *optimal language design* or of a *perfect language*, described as follows (Chomsky 1995:1):

> To the extent that the answer to question (2) is positive, language is something like a "perfect system," meeting external constraints as well as can be done, in one of the reasonable ways. The Minimalist Program for linguistic theory seeks to explore these possibilities.

Question (2) is formulated as: "To what extent is the language faculty determined by the general conditions that the human language faculty should be expected to satisfy, without special structure that lies beyond them?"

There is a series of problems here. The first is that there is no well-motivated base line or null hypothesis defining the notion of "optimal design" in such a way that a "perfect" language faculty would not deviate from it at all. This is so because the "external" systems with which language interacts and in which it is embedded are themselves already geared to language by evolutionary adaptation, despite Chomsky's claim that "the bones of the middle ear don't change because of language" (2002:108): they, as well as the inner ear, have changed during evolution, to ensure optimal discrimination for the normal frequency range of speech sounds. Likewise for the well-known descended larynx (Lieberman 1984), which has increased the range of speech sounds to be produced. Moreover, the brain itself has undergone evolutionary changes in tandem with the emergence of language, if the cranial endocasts of early hominids are anything to go by (see also Levelt 1999:84–85). An optimal design would thus have to encompass not only the language faculty but also the external systems, as well as the biological carrier, the brain, and since these are, in turn, organically linked up with a multitude of other human functions, it would have to encompass more or less the entirety of human existence. In principle, an optimal design for language would have to strike the best possible balance between a language system per se and possible adaptations in those parts of the organism that are somehow connected with it. Certainly, there is no practical use for any such criterion. (For further comment, see sections 3.5.2 and 5.4.)

Moreover, a minimalist language as suggested in the MP could probably do with just one level of linguistic representation, which would have an interface with cognition on the one hand and with a motor-perceptual system on the other, each interface being blind to the features that are reserved for the other. For Chomsky, however, it is "conceptually necessary" that there should be two levels of representation, each geared to the demands of one of the two interfaces mentioned. The nature of this form of conceptual necessity is not clear.

Then, if the scope of the optimal design is narrowed to the environment as it actually is, there is the problem that "the general conditions that the human language faculty should be expected to satisfy" are not known. Available knowledge of these minimalist conditions is still primitive and fragmentary, as Chomsky concedes (1995:222–223):

We do not know enough about the "external" systems at the interface to draw firm conclusions about conditions they impose. . . . The problems are nevertheless empirical, and we can hope to resolve them by learning more about the language faculty and the systems with which it interacts. We proceed in the only possible way: by making tentative assumptions about the external systems and proceeding from there.

It is indeed so that science is to a large extent a bootstrapping or feedback operation where real or possible results are used to extend or improve existing hypotheses. But Chomsky goes further and proposes that the theory should be constrained by the methodological principle that the object of inquiry is *preferably* to be described as being "determined by the general conditions that the human language faculty should be expected to satisfy, without special structure that lies beyond them" (1998:2021):

We also try to show that no structural relations are invoked other than those forced by legibility conditions or induced in some natural way by the computation itself.

This is said even though these "general conditions" are not or insufficiently known, and even though it is possible—and, in fact, arguably the case—that language often resorts to strategies that are distinctly antifunctional when considered in the light of the criteria set out in *The Minimalist Program*.

Chapter 5 elaborates this point further. It is largely devoted to demonstrating that such an argument leads to a methodological tangle, which Chomsky is unable to undo. Without independent evidence, it is circular to say that it is to be expected that "language is very well designed, perhaps close to 'perfect' in satisfying external conditions" (Chomsky 1998:16). And in the light of what little evidence is available, the answer to the question "how perfect is language?" can only be heavily qualified in that some features appear superbly functional, while others give the impression of being grossly counterproductive, and others again look neutral in this respect. In fact, it is repeatedly found that, on the one hand, language contains all kinds of features and properties that turn out to be functional in unexpected ways once they have been discovered. On the other hand, however, other features and properties are also frequently observed that appear to have no special functionality value or even appear antifunctional. (In section 5.6 an example is given, taken from Mauritian Creole, of the way functional and antifunctional rule applications interact and appear to have established a sort of bargaining equilibrium.) It follows that it is, in principle, impossible to determine the extent to which language satisfies the general conditions imposed by the external systems, since there is no way of deciding for any feature that looks functional whether it is so in the best possible way.

One is, moreover, caught by surprise when, on the one hand, one reads that the MP wants to determine the extent to which the language faculty can be called "perfect," while, on the other hand, the view is defended that each specific language is defined by the values selected on a set of parameters. For it is hardly thinkable that each value selected will result in an equal degree of functionality. Apparently, this question has worried Chomskyans. In Chomsky (2002:130) one reads: "we might consider a variety of minimalist theses of varying strength. One, which has come up in seminars in Siena, is that every possible language meets minimalist standards." Yet there is no word on how that prima facie impossible deal could be struck.

1.4 Presentation and terminology

Reading Chomsky has never been an easy matter, but since *The Minimalist Program* it has become harder than ever before. One reason is that the four chapters that make up the book were written at some distance in time, with the result that they reflect different positions with regard to some of the central issues in the book. Chapter 4 of the book, in fact, dismisses most of what is said in the first three chapters, giving what is presented as the final statement of the minimalist program. This is readily acknowledged at the end of the introduction and should be no reason for special concern (although one has reason to be disappointed when questions raised in the earlier chapters are left without an answer in the final chapter 4).

A more serious ground for getting confused while reading Chomsky lies in the fact that some formulations give the impression that one has understood his position on the matter at hand, while other statements then give one to understand, or so it seems, that the opposite view is taken or that one has, apparently, misunderstood what was said before. In general, Chomsky's formulations on issues of central importance tend to be surrounded by hedges, couched in ambiguous and often evasive wordings, and supported by appeals to unspecified results and investigations or by admonitions that only "proper understanding" (1995:168) will lead to the desired insight, whereas other people's discussions suffer from "serious confusion" (1998:7). This is a recurrent feature of the text, which inevitably leads to frustration and sometimes even irritation.

An example is Chomsky's ambiguous stance on the realist-instrumentalist issue. His various statements on this issue make it, if not impossible, extremely hard to understand what he actually wishes to claim. On the one hand, there is the opening paragraph of chapter 3, which professes an unambiguously realist position in terms of the natural world and the human brain, and theories dealing with these objects (Chomsky 1995:167):

> Language and its use have been studied from varied points of view. One approach, assumed here, takes language to be part of the natural world. The human brain provides an array of capacities that enter into the use and understanding of language (the *language faculty*); these seem to be in good part specialized for that function and a common human endowment over a very wide range of circumstances and conditions. One component of the language faculty is a generative procedure (an *I-language*, henceforth *language*) that generates *structural descriptions* (SDs), each a complex of properties, including those commonly called "semantic" and "phonetic." These SDs are the *expressions* of the language. The theory of a particular language is its *grammar*. The theory of languages and the expressions they generate is *Universal Grammar* (UG); UG is a theory of the initial state S_0 of the relevant component of the language faculty. We can distinguish the language from a conceptual system and a system of pragmatic competence. Evidence has been accumulating that these interacting systems can be selectively impaired and developmentally dissociated . . . , and their properties are quite different.

On the other hand, there is the statement in note 3 to chapter 4 (Chomsky 1995:380):

> Recall that the ordering of operations is abstract, expressing postulated properties of the language faculty of the brain, with no temporal interpretation implied. In this respect, the terms *output* and *input* have a metaphorical flavor, though they may reflect substantive properties, if the derivational approach is correct.

This invites one to "recall" something that has not been stated before and is in direct contradiction to the otherwise mainly realist position taken in *The Minimalist Program*.

Similar real or apparent contradictions are easily found. Thus one is naturally startled when reading that well-formedness and grammaticality "remain without characterization" and "played virtually no role in early work on generative grammar" (1995:213), having first blissfully been working through arguments whose conclusions were based on observations of grammaticality. Likewise one is puzzled when reading that "there are minimalist questions but no specifically minimalist answers. The answers are whatever is found by carrying out the program" (1998:16). For why are the answers found by carrying out the program not minimalist answers? Or again, one frequently comes across passages where it is said that the matter at hand should be decided on empirical grounds (see section 4.4), but nowhere is there any attempt to do so. On the contrary, evidence that is taken to be both available and serious is explicitly "swept under the rug" (1995:220). More examples could easily be provided.

Or consider Chomsky's statements on the "usability" of language. On the opening page of *The Minimalist Program*, the question is raised to what extent the faculty of language (FoL) is determined by the specific conditions imposed by the phonetic and semantic performance systems, and throughout the book there is the suggestion that the FoL satisfies these conditions rather well. However, on p. 18 of the same book this question is answered negatively: "In general, it is not the case that language is readily usable or 'designed for use.' The subparts that are used are usable, trivially; biological considerations lead us to expect no more than that." This point is repeated on p. 29: "Language appears to have the expected properties; as noted, it is a familiar fact that large parts of language are 'unusable,' and the usable parts appear to form a chaotic and 'unprincipled' segment of the full language." One naturally wonders how many linguists will find this alleged fact familiar. I am not one of them. Yet in Chomsky (2002:148) one finds: "The fundamental question that language has to meet is that it can be used, that the person who has it can use it." But on p. 168 of Chomsky (1995) the question itself is considered to be meaningless: "There is no clear sense to the idea that language is 'designed for use' or 'well-adapted to its functions.'" However, despite the meaninglessness of the question, it is said to be part of the MP to "show that no structural relations are involved other than those forced by the legibility conditions or induced in some natural way by the computation itself" (1998:20–21), and a definitely positive answer is anticipated: "The answer to the question might be that language is very well designed, perhaps close to 'perfect' in satisfying external conditions" (1998:16). At this point, Chomsky's reader will hardly have a clear idea of what his author *really* has to say about this subject. Chomsky (2000) contains a whole chapter called "Explaining Language Use" (pp. 19–45), but it has nothing to say on language use, only on individual languages not being public objects but located in each individual speaker's brain. In Chomsky (2002:77) one reads, "language use is largely to oneself: 'inner speech' for adults, monologue for children," which appears to reduce language to a system primarily intended for the pathological condition of compulsive mumbling. In short, a survey of the ways in which the notion "language use" occurs in Chomsky's writings reveals a bewildering variety, in which the present writer, for one, has been unable to detect any coherence.

This, together with Chomsky's total neglect of the speech act factor in language and language use and his apparent difficulty in coming to terms with the notion of a specific language as a public object, makes one suspect that the well-known reification of *social reality*, which may not have individual existence but nevertheless has a strong form of reality profitably studied in the social sciences, appears to escape Chomsky's power of comprehension. (See sections 3.5.7 and 5.4 for further comment.)

A further cause of the difficulty one has in understanding and interpreting Chomsky's texts as they have been produced over the years lies in his habit of constantly changing his terminology. This is a curious habit, since standard terminology is rich enough to cater to almost any needs Chomsky might have. And when, occasionally, he needs a new term for a new concept (as we all do from time to time), he does not stay with a term once introduced but apparently finds it necessary to change that, too, all the time, without there being any tangible reason for that to be done. The result is that one has to get used to a new set of terms each time a new theoretical proposal is made. The result is also that those who faithfully follow the latest terminology thereby make it known that they are acquainted with the latest developments, a circumstance that may have played a role in the introduction of the constantly occurring terminological renewals.

Finally, there has been a growing tendency, over the years, to treat technical issues in what is rather too cavalier a fashion (see also Pullum 1989, 1996). In this sense, Chomsky (1995) really is a crowning achievement. The more technical passages in the book are unnecessarily hard to read, as notions are haphazardly defined, while tree structures that might illustrate them are few and far between. And when tree structures are presented, they are always fragmentary and the node labelings change almost from tree to tree. Even for those who have considerable experience in reading technical texts, the perusal of many technical passages in *The Minimalist Program* amounts to a cruel and unusual form of punishment, not because they are difficult but because they are sloppy.

1.5 Mysterious paradigm mixing

A related, and rather more important, puzzlement arises when one reads Hauser, Chomsky, and Fitch (2002). On p. 1571 the question of the architecture of grammar is briefly discussed:

> The internal architecture of FLN [= "narrow faculty of language", i.e., grammar] so conceived, is a topic of much current research and debate. Without prejudging the issues, we will, for concreteness, adopt a particular conception of this architecture. We assume, putting aside the precise mechanisms, that a key component of FLN is a computational system (narrow syntax) that generates internal representations and maps them into the sensory-motor interface by the phonological system, and into the conceptual-intentional interface by the (formal) semantic system. . . . All approaches agree that a core property of FLN is recursion, attributed to narrow syntax in the conception just outlined. FLN takes a finite set of elements and yields a potentially infinite array of discrete expressions.

This account reflects the old view, with a random recursive sentence generator whose products are fed into the two "interfaces." In these terms, there is no account of how thoughts are expressed or "externalized." The random-generator view only accounts for the "potentially infinite array of discrete expressions" found in the languages of the world, and clearly not for the way thoughts are expressed by means of them.

Then, however, something bordering on the mediational view is suddenly presented on p. 1578 of the very same article:

> The computational system [i.e., syntax] must (i) construct an infinite array of internal expressions from the finite resources of the conceptual-intentional system, and (ii) provide the means to externalize and interpret them at the sensory-motor end.

Now there is no longer any question of mapping the syntactically generated structures "into the conceptual-intentional interface by the (formal) semantic system" but rather of "construct[ing] an infinite array of internal expressions from the finite resources of the conceptual-intentional system" and feeding those expressions into the sensory-motor interface. But they also still have to be fed into the conceptual-intentional interface, which means that the expressions in question are taken to be *lexically* driven by cognition but *structurally* driven by the grammar. Though this is odd in itself, it does mean a certain approximation to the paradigm of mediational grammar. All that is needed to have a *fully* mediational architecture is the admission that the construction of the "infinite array" already takes place inside the "conceptual-intentional system," so that thought is no longer regarded as a set of "finite resources" but as the real place where a potentially infinite array of products is generated, to be expressed through language.

This step is actually taken in Chomsky (1998:1):

> There is no serious reason today to challenge the Cartesian view that the *ability to use linguistic signs to express freely-formed thoughts* marks "the true distinction between man and animal" or machine, whether by "machine" we mean the automata that captured the imagination of the 17th and 18th century, or those that are providing a stimulus to thought and imagination today. [italics mine]

And again, more emphatically, in Chomsky (2002:45):

> Galileo may have been the first to recognize clearly the significance of the core property of human language, and one of its most distinctive properties: the use of finite means to express an unlimited array of thoughts.

And again on p. 76: "Language is not properly regarded as a system of communication. It is a system for expressing thought, something quite different." Moreover (pp. 121–122), "We are asking about thought without language, in traditional terms, a concept often rejected, though it seems to me reasonably clear that something of the kind must exist."

Quite apart from the question of whether natural language is primarily designed for communication (an issue that is not relevant right here; but see sections 3.5.7 and 5.4), one sees that the "resources of the conceptual-intentional system"—that is, of thought—are taken to be infinite, not finite, as in the earlier quote. This identifies Chomsky's position with that of mediational grammar and thus, in principle, with erstwhile generative semantics. No explanation is given for this creeping transition from a random-generator to a mediational paradigm.

The reader is justifiably nonplussed. Given the high-profile character of the issue and its acrimonious history (see, for example, Newmeyer

1980, McCawley 1980, Harris 1993, Murray 1994, Huck and Goldsmith 1995, Pullum 1996, Seuren 1998), one is surprised at seeing Chomsky mix paradigms in this fashion. It is noteworthy that locutions of this type, presenting *language as a system for the expression of thought*, are absent from the more technical Chomsky (1995) and from Chomsky (2000), which is a collection of essays written and presentations made between 1992 and 2000. Yet an early harbinger of the recent rash of such expressions is found in Chomsky's Managua lectures, where he is commenting on the property of "discrete infinity" found in human language and also, notably, in the human capacity for arithmetic (1988:170):[3]

> Without this capacity it might have been possible to think thoughts of a certain restricted character, but with the capacity in place, the same conceptual apparatus would be freed for the construction of new thoughts and operations such as inference involving them, and it would be possible to express and interchange these thoughts.

By contrast, talk about language *expressing* thoughts appears to be actually avoided where it is naturally expected (Chomsky 1998:16):

> Suppose we make up a "Just So Story," . . . with design determined by natural law rather than bricolage through selection. Suppose that there was an ancient primate with the whole human mental architecture in place, but no language faculty. The creature shared our modes of perceptual organization, our beliefs and desires, our hopes and fears, insofar as these are not formed and *mediated* by language. Perhaps it had a "language of thought" in the sense of Jerry Fodor and others, but no way to form *linguistic expressions associated with the thoughts* that this LINGUA MENTIS makes available. [italics mine]

3. Chomsky's notion of a "property of discrete infinity" as one of the properties of a brain/mind resulting from evolution (Chomsky 1988:70 and elsewhere) is strange in itself. This "property" would be manifest in human language and also in the human capacity for unbounded arithmetical operations, all describable by means of recursive algorithms. But surely, there are all kinds of recursively defined structures in biological nature. One thinks of bees building honeycombs, spiders spinning webs, and numerous other examples, including those instances where Fibonacci sequences occur in nature (see section 3.3), all involving recursive structures that are unbounded in principle but always bounded in practice, just like sentences of natural languages. What Chomsky means is, again, unclear. It is, therefore, highly doubtful that there is such a thing as a "property of discrete infinity" in the human or any other mind or brain. It would seem to make more sense to speak of algorithmically defined recursive processes, which lack an upper bound other than what is automatically imposed by the processing capacity of the machinery involved. Mathematical necessity does the rest.

Interestingly, the term "mediated" is used to denote the function of language as a *mediator* between thought and sound.[4]

It is difficult to make sense of all this. One thing is clear: in none of its successive varieties does the Chomskyan random-generator concept of grammar contain or imply anything like an account of the notion "expression of thought through language." On the contrary, it invites the utterly unintuitive notion "production of thought through language." The language faculty as described by Chomsky does account, in principle, for the "discrete infinity" of human language through its assumption of a recursive random sentence generator. But the notion "expression of thought through language" is totally alien to Chomskyan conceptions of grammar or language. Yet, apparently, Chomsky feels free to attribute to his random-generator theory of grammar powers it clearly lacks. Such powers, moreover, were properly attributed to the grammar model proposed and defended by generative semanticists between 1965 and 1975 (and since then by me), but fiercely attacked by Chomsky and the Chomskyans at the time (and ignored later).[5]

Since the question of the architecture of a grammar is substantive and not a question of minor notational variation or of "extending" the theory, as is confirmed by Chomsky himself ("the internal architecture of FLN

---

4. Chomsky's groundless identification of random-generator algorithmic systems with the human capacity for expressing thoughts goes back to his *Cartesian Linguistics* (1966), where he seeks out Lancelot and Arnauld's Port Royal Grammar of 1660 and von Humboldt's famous *Introduction* of 1836 as his spiritual ancestors. Throughout the book, but especially on pages 29–30, he falsely identifies their view of language expressing an infinity of thoughts with his random-generator notion of generative grammar. Note that *Cartesian Linguistics* was written in a period when Chomsky still felt sympathy for the newly emerging generative semantics movement.

5. The confusion seems to have caught on, as one sees, for example, in Pinker and Bloom (1990:771):

> Pesetsky and Block, by focusing on what linguists find "worth studying," state that the complex features of grammar play no role in allowing people to communicate, to express an infinite number of meanings using a finite number of lexical items, and so on. Wasn't it Chomsky who characterized a grammar as defining a mapping between sounds and meanings, and who said that a speaker can "make use of an intricate structure of specific rules and guiding principles to convey his thoughts and feelings to others, arousing in them novel ideas and subtle perceptions and judgments"?

The answer is, of course, that it wasn't Chomsky at all who came up with this notion but the generative semanticists, whose ideas Chomsky appears to appropriate in his public performances when that suits him.

so conceived, is a topic of much current research and debate"; see earlier), one is entitled to an open statement, to arguments, and to attributions. Since, moreover, the issue has given rise to large amounts of mostly highly polemical publications and has profoundly affected the lives of many linguists over the past thirty or so years, questions of professional ethics and of intellectual property rights are inevitably raised. The matter is taken up, from time to time, in the following chapters.

1.6 Empirical issues

Empirical support is an old sore of Chomskyan linguistics, due in part to the surprising paucity of reliable data used in the theory and in part to the abundance of counterevidence.

As regards the paucity of evidence actually used, it must be pointed out that not a single coherent data complex has been sorted out with anything approaching observational accuracy, either in *The Minimalist Program* or in any of the preceding or subsequent publications. There is, for example, no adequate data survey on Subject Raising in English and other languages, or on the *there* construction and its counterparts in other languages, or on WH-constructions in questions and the related category of relative clauses, to mention a few examples, although these are among the most discussed topics in the MP. Other central elements in the syntax of languages, such as the overall treatment of complement clauses, an analysis of the syntactic behavior of modalities, negation, or sentential and VP-adverbs, to mention just a few, are hardly touched on. Moreover, by far most of the material is drawn from English, with some few poor and secondary additions from a small handful of other languages. Clearly, when an ambitious research program such as the MP, which would encompass all the human languages of the past, present, and future, turns out to rest on such flimsy evidence, it is difficult to consider it serious work.

The more so when one notices that counterevidence is not treated with the respect it deserves (see in particular section 4.4). In the past, a variety of strategies have been developed to escape from falsification by contrary data, which were said either not to be sufficiently idealized, or not to belong to "core grammar," or to be substandard or dialectal (as if that would matter), or which were simply ignored. Recently, a new strategy has been added: leaning on a false analogy with Galileo's heliocentric theory of the solar system, it is now said that, just as Galileo (who still lacked knowledge of the force of gravity) had to ignore certain kinds of unexplained facts to uphold his theory, in the same manner Chomsky, practicing a "Galilean style" of doing linguistics (Chomsky 2002, Freidin and Vergnaud 2001), is free to ignore any kind of contrary or refractory evidence to uphold his theory (see section 3.6 for further comment). One wonders what would become of science if everyone took similar liberties. In fact, the very nature of data or empirical evidence in the theoretical study of grammar is obfuscated. It has been customary in linguistics for the past forty or so years to take the empirical evidence to consist of native speakers' judgments of good pronunciation, grammatical well-formedness, admissible interpretation, and proper lexical selection. In *The Minimalist Program* the new term "deviant" is introduced to replace the traditional term "ungrammatical," which now recedes into a vague limbo. It is then said that "the concepts 'well-formed' and 'grammatical' remain without characterization or known empirical justification; they played virtually no role in early work on generative grammar except in informal exposition, or since" (1995:213). This obviously raises the question of what Chomsky means: does he mean that what he *now* calls "ungrammatical" has played no role, or what was *then* called "ungrammatical" and now "deviant"? The latter is obviously false (in fact, throughout *The Minimalist Program* the criterion of ungrammaticality or un-well-formedness is freely used, though under the new name of "deviance"). But the former is startlingly misleading, first because it is not known what the term "(un)grammatical" should be taken to mean in Chomsky's new terminology, and second because the question of the role of that form of "(un)grammaticality," whatever it may be, in early work on generative grammar is of no concern to anybody. Chomsky certainly knows how to confuse his readers. (See 4.4 for further comment.)

Then, as is amply documented in section 4.4, there are frequent claims or suggestions of empirical results already achieved or still under way in "promising work," without them ever being identifed. What is actually presented is a collection of sketchy grammatical analyses that hark back to what was presented in earlier work but are now reviewed in the light of the minimalist conception, in that they are looked at from the point of view of the possibility of further streamlining in terms of one universal grammar. A typical statement to this effect is the following (Chomsky 1995:187):

> The empirical justification for this [old] approach, with its departures from conceptual necessity, is substantial. Nevertheless, we may ask whether

the evidence will bear the weight, or whether it is possible to move toward a minimalist program.

What one finds, however, is that no serious attempt is made at answering the question of "whether the evidence will bear the weight" of any decision to deviate from what is seen as "conceptually necessary." The evidence that is taken into account is always fragmentary and never based on a serious survey of the relevant data, even in cases where that is perfectly feasible.

It should be noted, in addition, that posing the question of "whether the evidence will bear the weight" is nothing but an application of the old Ockhamist principle that one may multiply theoretical assumptions, and thus deviate from otherwise useful generalizations, only if forced by the facts. What one wants to find out is, therefore: to what extent does the MP express, or does it lead to grammars that express, useful possible generalizations, and to what extent and why does it force itself to deviate from them on account of available data or facts?

But before we can go into issues of this nature, we must first have a look at the kind of machinery the MP is supposed to be. This is done in the following chapter.

2

The Mechanism of the
MP under Scrutiny

2.1 Some "guiding ideas"

What does the MP actually look like? It is useful to distinguish the actual grammatical machinery from what Chomsky himself calls "the guiding ideas" of the MP (1995:219)—that is, its wider conceptual, philosophical, and methodological embedding. The latter, as has been said, is discussed in later chapters of this book. Yet one should have at least a global idea of the guiding ideas before investigating the actual machinery of the grammar.

First, the theory envisaged in the MP is presented as the best approximation, given the empirical facts of language and given the nature of speech sounds and of the cognitive processes that confer meaning, to what may be considered *conceptually necessary* with regard to any system associating meanings with sounds. Human language, moreover, is seen as a *close to perfect product of evolutionary processes of natural selection*, something a superbly competent engineer would have created had he been given a free hand, given the external constraints imposed by sound and meaning. The MP is thus taken to reflect the genius inherent in the human language faculty.

In Chomsky (1995, 1998) human language is considered exceptional from the point of view of evolution. It differs from other faculties, which tend to suffer from evolutionary hazards, not least because the answers they embody to the demands imposed by the struggle for survival are necessarily prejudiced by the fact that the starting position is always one that resulted from different demands in different struggles. Species and their faculties never start from scratch but patch up existing structures, adapting them to new functions—a process called *exaptation*. For Chomsky, however, the human language faculty is largely exempt from this common and practically inescapable corollary of natural selection. It is presented as a superb technical achievement in its own right. How this exceptional position of human language is to be explained is not made clear. In section 3.4 we shall see that the most probable interpretation of Chomsky's vague and noncommittal suggestions in this regard, in the context of the MP, would seem to imply that, in fact, his views tend toward an instantaneous origin of language, leaving the many questions raised by such a position unanswered. This position is modified in later publications, in particular in Hauser, Chomsky, and Fitch (2002), where a more exaptational hypothesis is proposed, again, however, without any relevant factual support.

Apart from the evolutionary aspects of language, any particular language is considered to be an instantiation of the species-specific innate grammatical ("cognitive") system of the faculty of language (FoL), with values set for parameters expressing universal principles. (The use of the term *cognitive* for what is normally called *grammatical* is introduced in the first pages of Chomsky 1995.) This ancient idea (see 3.1) is instantiated in the following way. The FoL specifies that each language consists of a lexicon containing lexical items defined by values for semantic, grammatical, and phonological features. The grammatical features are partly categorial (indicating the grammatical category) and partly "morphological" (mainly specifying case, gender, number, person, and tense—that is, flectional morphology). The *grammar*, or "human language computational system" (C_{HL}), is invariable for all languages and deals with the lexical items according to the values of their categorial and morphological features (the phonological features are dealt with in a separate language-specific phonology). The FoL is taken to be constructed in such a way that all parameters allowing for variation among different languages are located in the lexicon, either in the meaning descriptions of the lexical items, or in the phonological features, or, significantly for the theory of grammar, in the grammatical features ("morphology") of the language in question.

Then, the FoL is embedded in an architecture that gives it two points of access, or two interfaces, with "external performance systems": (a) an articulatory-perceptual (A-P) interface with a motor-perceptual system, and (b) a conceptual-intentional (C-I) interface with a "language use" or conceptual system. Within the terms of such an FoL, a language is a generative system that constructs pairs (phonetic form-logical form), or (PF-LF), also called (π,λ), of representations that are interpreted as instructions to the external motor-perceptual and conceptual-intentional performance systems, respectively. Thus, PF is interpreted or "read" at the A-P interface, and LF at the C-I interface.

Both the motor-perceptual and the conceptual-intentional performance systems impose "legibility conditions" on their input, which the PF and LF representations, respectively, must satisfy. The PF and LF representations must, therefore, consist exclusively of "legitimate objects" that can receive an interpretation at the appropriate level. If a generated representation consists entirely of such objects, it is said to satisfy the condition of "legibility" or "full interpretation" (FI). A linguistic expression of a language, or sentence, is at least a pair (PF-LF) meeting this condition.

As has been said, the *grammar*, or "human language computational system" (C_{HL}), is taken to be common to all languages, and computes sets of derivations, some of which will result in sentences of a language. In computing the derivations, C_{HL} follows its universal principles, applying them to the grammatical features of the lexical items selected. In rough outline (I will be more specific in a moment), a computation starts with a selection N of lexical items from the lexicon in an operation called Numeration. The items chosen are gradually put together into a structure Σ by the operation Merge. A computation of a structure Σ consists, first, of an "overt" computation, at the end of which there is an operation Spell-Out (SO), after which Σ goes two separate ways: a phonological computation leading to the A-P interface, and a "covert" semantic one leading to the C-I interface.

A derivation is said to "converge at one of its interface levels" if it yields a representation satisfying the legibility conditions imposed by FI at this level—that is, if it consists entirely of objects that can be interpreted or "read" at this level. A derivation is said to "converge" *tout court* if it converges at both the A-P and the C-I interface levels. Otherwise, it is said to "crash."

2.2 A closer inspection of the "computational system"

2.2.1 Select and Merge

The actual grammatical machinery proposed, or C_{HL}, thus consists of the computation leading from N, the particular choice made from a pre-existing language-specific lexicon, to PF and LF (or π and λ, respectively). N is a set of pairs <I,i>, where "I" is a lexical item (i.e., a package of fully specified semantic, grammatical, and phonological features), and "i" is a natural number > 0 (index) indicating the number of times I is to be used in the derivation. A successful derivation D should exhaust N: at the end of D, N should be depleted.

A derivation D is taken to consist of successive stages of tree construction and tree modification. Bits of trees are constructed by means of the operations Select and Merge. The operation Select picks out a pair <I,i> from N, "prints" an instance of I as a syntactic object O in the stage Σ of the derivation D, reducing the index i by one. When $i = 0$, the pair <I,i> is removed from N. After n applications of Select, Σ consists of the set $\{O_1, \ldots, O_n\}$. Since, at the end of D, Σ must consist of just one O, some operation must combine different Os into one O. This is done by Merge, which takes two Os (simple or complex) and unites them, in some order, as constituents of a subtree under a new constituent label. Thus, if α and β are (labels of) syntactic objects affected by Merge, they are combined into one constituent under a label γ. No argument is offered for the implicit assumption (1995:243 and elsewhere) that branchings resulting from Merge should be binary.

The operations Select and Merge are said to be "conceptually necessary"—hence "costless" in terms of the economy metric invoked for selecting the optimal derivation from a set of alternatives (see section 2.2.1). However, as Paul Postal pointed out (personal communication), all these two operations do is define a set of tree structures with a putatively fixed terminal vocabulary, which is precisely what is done by means of standard axiomatic definitions of trees and lists of terminals. But in fact, the lexicons of natural languages are open-ended. For example, almost anything between quotes can count as a new word, such as *'lait'* in *The French word for milk is 'lait'* (Postal 2004:187). In the Select-and-Merge setup, sentences containing such ad hoc words could never be generated, as such words are not in the English lexicon. The entire Select-and-Merge system thus seems ill-conceived.

In chapter 3 (p. 172) of Chomsky (1995), the resulting structures are taken to follow "some version of X-bar theory," which is "therefore fundamental." In chapter 4 (p. 244), it is argued that the version of X-bar theory to be used in the MP should identify γ as being identical to either α or β: when α and β are united into one constituent C, C should be labeled either α or β. This is so, because, it is said, "the simplest assumption" would be that γ—the variable for the labeling of C—is either (a) the intersection, or (b) the union of (the features of) α and β, or (c) one or the other of α, β (1995:244). Options (a) and (b) are rejected out of hand as they may lead to a null or an inconsistent result, and option (c) is chosen. This means that under Merge α and β form a constituent of the form $_\alpha[\alpha,\beta]$ or $_\beta[\alpha,\beta]$ (the order of α and βin $[\alpha,\beta]$ being irrelevant). The O chosen to name the new constituent is said to *project* and to be the *head* of the new constituent. The O not chosen is the *specifier* (or *adjunct* or *complement*). While this is naturally seen as a specific application of X-bar theory, Chomsky prefers to say that "standard X-bar theory is thus largely eliminated in favor of bare essentials" (1995:246). Later (1998:20–21; see section 6.2.1 in this volume) X-bar theory is said to disappear altogether in the MP.

The projecting version of Merge is, again, presented as somehow "conceptually necessary" since option (c) is the only viable one of the three that are mentioned (compare Uriagereka 1998:176–178). But there is no mention of the fourth option (d), with γ being neither α nor β, in which case γ contains one or more features not present in either α or β. And this is an option grammar cannot do without.

One should bear in mind that in all four cases we have a *mathematical function*—either a function α from β to γ, or a function β from α to γ (in terms of constituency trees; in dependency trees the function notation is different). Functions are the central mathematical tool for carrying out compositional computations through tree structures. They have a high degree of conceptual necessity in view of the semantic problem of computing complex meanings from simple ones. From this angle, option (d) is at least as good as (c)—in fact, it is indispensable, since it is common in language for two or more elements to combine into a new constituent whose category differs from those of its constituents. A propositional structure, for example, consists of a predicate and one or more terms, none of which has to be a propositional structure itself, and it is not hard to argue that this is a conceptual necessity (see sections 3.5.1 and 6.2.1 on the propositional principle). A participle may consist of a verbal stem and an affix, neither being members of the category "participle," and so on. The new category *may* be identical to one of its constituents, but it doesn't have to be. The conclusion is that the MP notion of "projection" is poorly supported and far from conceptually necessary.

2.2.2 Move

A third operation is Move. Move applies within one syntactic object O, and only if O is the result of several applications of Merge and, possibly, Move. It involves the transportation of a bundle of features, usually a whole lexical item or phrase, from one position in the tree to another, leaving behind a trace t. The movement is obligatory and unidirectional. The obligatory character is expressed by the condition of *Last Resort*, which says that the movement, though it may be carried out at any moment in the derivation, has to take place and can take place only when driven by the relevant features. Unidirectionality means that movement is possible only from a lower to a higher position in the tree that constitutes O. That is, only raising is allowed (always leaving behind a trace t), never lowering. Thus, if the tree is right-branching, the raising movement is from right to left. The element raised is somehow attached to its *target*, which has to be a head of a higher construction. There appear to be various modes of attachment, whose inconclusive and cryptic descriptions take up many pages in *The Minimalist Program* (for some greater clarity, see Uriagereka 1998:257–263). However, since our critique of the system transcends such details and concerns higher levels of generality, it seems unnecessary to engage in the demanding exercise of sorting out all the possibilities that are investigated and their consequences for the limited amount of data that are taken into account.

What is relatively clear is that Move is induced by (flectional) morphological features (case, gender, number, person, tense, modality), which have to be "checked." Every suitable syntactic object will at some stage of its derivation have a higher structure consisting of functional categories, mainly complementizer, tense, and, it seems toward the end of *The Minimalist Program*, a, perhaps causative, "light" verb v allowing for an expression of the subject function. The feature values of the heads of the functional categories will then have to be matched with those of the corresponding phrases with lexical heads. This matching constitutes the required "checking." However, since the checking can only take place within the "minimal syntactic domain" of a functional head H, whereas the lexical phrases whose features are to be checked (matched) will be outside (below) the minimal syntactic domain of H, the lexical category must be raised to a position within the minimal syntactic domain of H. If the features match, the derivation may proceed; otherwise, it will crash. Successfully matched morphological features that have no semantic impact (such as case features) are deleted, or rather made "invisible at the interface" (p. 229).[1] Semantically relevant features are kept (or remain visible) till LF.

At the CI-end of the derivation, in LF, all elements in the higher functional structure should be filled with semantically relevant semantic and grammatical ("morphological") features. But this does not necessarily mean that the phonological manifestations of the corresponding lexical items (words) must also be in the position assigned to their semantic and grammatical features. In other words, the position of a word or phrase in the phonetically realized sentence need not correspond with its position in LF. This is because at the stage where Spell-Out (SO) applies, all phonological features are siphoned off from the rest and enter a separate phonological component leading to the A-P interface where they can be "read" and converted into sound (or writing). However, SO does not prevent nonphonological features to be raised by Move. The only difference is that raising after SO is covert—that is, without any perceptible result.

Given the extreme opacity of the text of chapter 4 in *The Minimalist Program*, it is hard to make out what the actual structures are meant to look like. A good guess is made in Johnson and Lappin (1997:282) for the LF of the sentence *John saw Mary*, which would be something like figure 2.1 (in a simplified notation not involving a specification of the features and their values). The subscripts indicate the chains linking the actual items with their traces. The movement of *Mary$_4$* from the position of t_4 to the position in the domain of T' is taken to be covert in English, so that in the overt sentence (one is not supposed to say "surface structure") *Mary* occurs in the position of t_4.

There is a considerable amount of leapfrogging going on, as one sees from figure 2.1. The movements are both restricted and enhanced by the *Minimal Link Condition* (MLC), which restricts raising to the shortest

---

1. Chomsky's notion of "visibility" to the "reading" devices at the interfaces is somewhat odd, if one is to take seriously the suggestion that CHL, while "looking" at some chain, may at the same time "see" other chains as well "out of the corner of its eye" (1995:265). What this could mean in formal or computational terms is left unclear.

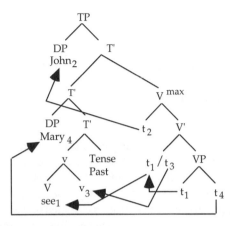

FigURE 2.1. Projected structures implied in *The Minimalist Program*, chapter 4

distance and thus prevents the passing by of any intermediate possible targets. Separate leaps are required for each shortest distance. That there should be such a heavy traffic of constituents, even for such a simple sentence as *John saw Mary*, is not in itself a point of criticism. Surface simplicity often conceals an intricate underlying system. It becomes a criticism, however, when the movements are not or insufficiently motivated, and that does seem to be the case here.

One should realize that figure 2.1, or something not too different from it, is presented as the logical form (LF) of the sentence *John saw Mary* and therefore as the structure to be "read" at the C-I interface. (In more ordinary language one would say that figure 2.1 is the linguistic object open to semantic interpretation.) The problem is, however, that LF is never properly defined, from neither a semantic nor a syntactic point of view. It is said to be fully determined by "external" criteria of semantic interpretation. Yet no such criterion is ever mentioned. All that is found in the way of a formal specification is that LF may contain arguments in argument (A-)position, adjuncts in A-bar position, lexical elements in zero-bar position, predicates (position unspecified), and operator-variable constructions, the operator in A-bar and the variable in A-position; the source of each chain of traces indicates the semantically proper position of the element concerned (1995:153–154). (Yet on p. 155 it is suggested that existential *there* should be considered "an LF affix," a kind of element not mentioned before.)

It is clear that the MP will generate LF-structures which, in general, display all elements that are to be interpreted in the "functional" section—that is, in the upper part of the tree—which is then followed by a tail of traces indicating their semantically proper position. But then why have the elements in question moved at all from their original position? Why does Merge not put them straight away in their proper position? The answer will presumably be that the higher part of the LF tree contains the functional elements of case, gender, number, person, tense, modality, and probably also quantifiers, and that the predicate and argument terms must be united with them for proper interpretation. Yet semanticists will object that this is not so for tense, modalities, and quantifiers. Elementary knowledge of modern Predicate Calculus tells one that tense and modality are operators over propositions, while quantifiers are operators over (pairs of) propositional functions. Gender, number, and person, moreover, do not belong in the functional upper part of the LF tree at all but are inherent features of argument terms. The fact that they may "spread" to predicate morphology is accounted for much better by feature transfer than by the contrived process of feature checking and raising.

In the MP there is hardly any comment on the status of the formal language of Predicate Calculus (LPC), devised by Russell and Whitehead a century ago, although semanticists and philosophers of language largely agree that LPC, extended with a lexicon and a few additional expressive devices, is by far the most effective and well-founded language available for the systematic representation of meanings, and thus a serious a priori candidate for any claim to psychological reality. The result is a dilettante and offhand treatment of central semantic notions such as operator scope. The syntax and semantics of such primary scope-bearing elements as negation and the quantifiers is badly neglected. Furthermore, no indication is given of what the semantic interpretation envisaged might be taken to consist in, though there are hints that standard model-theoretic methods of semantic interpretation are not looked upon favorably.

In short, the notion of LF is left without any empirical or formal criteria and without anything approaching a definition. This means, for one thing, that the computation from N to LF is subject to clear criteria only insofar as it is determined by phenomena recoverable from the overt phonological form of the sentences concerned, which in itself should suffice to consider the MP with the greatest possible suspicion. Even more seriously, we must now conclude that the movements postulated in the MP are left without motivation, since, on the one hand, the structures generated by Merge lack sufficient support and, on the other, the targets of the movements are determined by what has to be considered a vacuous notion of "logical form." The system of movements, features, and principles thereby becomes something like a game that can perhaps be played when all the rules have been made explicit, but that will be unlikely to have any relevance for an adequate understanding of what goes on in natural language. The chances are that the relation of the MP to natural language is like that of the game of Monopoly to the real estate market.

But we must press on. Unless inhibited by special stipulation, all operations in C_{HL} are applicable at any stage in the derivation D. This is called the requirement of *uniformity* (1995:229). It means that selections can be made from N and that movements are allowed even after SO, during the covert phase of D on its way to LF. To ensure that no undue selection is made after SO, it is stipulated that only lexical items without any phonological features (such as certain covert complementizers) can be introduced by Select and Merge after SO. Moreover, to prevent any undue overt raising by Move, the principle "Procrastinate" is introduced. This principle says that raising should be postponed for as long as possible, in any case till after SO, if that is permitted. The permission is made dependent, in principle at least (we skip details that are irrelevant in this context), on a distinction between *strong* and *weak* grammatical features. Strong grammatical features want to be checked before SO and carry the phonological features with them while they are raised. Weak grammatical features will wait till after SO, inhibited as they are by Procrastinate. For them, the question of whether to bring along the phonological features does not arise, since the phonological features have already been siphoned off into the phonological component and are on their way to PF. Languages differ as to the assignment of strength to grammatical features. The principle of Procrastinate, combined with the stipulation that no phonologically endowed items must be selected after SO, effectively ensures that LF will not contain any phonological features.

It should be mentioned, in this context, that the desired effect of herding all phonological material into the phonological component and thus keeping the covert part of D free from phonological blemishes is achieved more simply by defining SO as a station of D—as a proper level of representation, at which N must have been depleted (all its items must have been used up), and all phonological features must be isolated and directed toward the A-P interface. Nothing seems to be gained by allowing selections from N after SO. However, Chomsky seems to set great store by the avoidance of levels of representation beyond N, PF, and LF, any further levels being considered conceptually unnecessary. This question will be pursued in a moment (but see also the discussion in section 5.5). In a general sense, the operation Move is seen as an unwanted concession forced on the theory by the facts of language. Natural language suffers from what is called the "displacement property" (also sometimes "dislocation property"), which causes elements in sentences to be moved around, apparently without that being "conceptually necessary."

A perfect language should, therefore, be able to do without Move, since there appears to be no intrinsic reason why elements should move. That they must be taken to do so results from the obvious fact, recognized by all professional linguists, that the surface form of sentences is, generally speaking, unfit for direct semantic interpretation. In the generative framework, this means that a transformational procedure is required relating surface structures with corresponding semantic representations formulated in terms of a properly regimented language of semantic representation that should be either universal or at least much less language-specific than the surface sentences of individual languages.

Since the period of generative semantics, which lasted from about 1965 to 1975, it has been generally accepted, in most formal theories of grammar, that this mapping procedure should be considered the central part of the grammar of the language in question. This notion of grammar deviates from an earlier notion, developed in the context of American structuralism, where a grammar was taken to be merely the set of rules that define well-formed structures built up of morphemes. The more restrictive generative semantics notion adds the requirement that well-formedness be defined, in principle, in terms of a mapping procedure between semantic representations and surface structures, with structural "surface filters" playing only a minor role, if any. The MP has now implicitly adopted this generative semantic notion of grammar, though it applies it in a random-generator way, which not only goes against the spirit of generative semantics and of most other schools of grammar, whether formal or traditional, but is also internally incoherent, as appears from the analyses presented in chapter 7. Moreover, since the Chomskyan notion of semantic representation is both formally and semantically undefined, it must remain unclear what the relation between surface forms and semantic representations must be taken to look like, even though the formal disparity between the two levels of representation is recognized.

It must, furthermore, be observed that, even in the perspective of the MP, the discrepancies between surface form and semantic form must be taken to involve much more than just "displacement" (raising) (see in particular chapter 8 in this volume). First, there are the many forms of deletion—not only the obvious ones involving the subject of embedded nonfinite clauses (handled by PRO in the MP and its predecessors), but also deletions involved in various forms of conjunction reduction, comparative constructions, and contextually determined forms of ellipsis, quite apart from idiosyncratic lexically determined deletions, as in the German *Dann bin ich hinein* <*gegangen*> (then I <went> in). Moreover, many languages have grammatically defined forms of copying, or spread, examples of which are given in section 8.2. To reduce grammar to "displacement" or "dislocation," embodied in a supposedly universal rule Move, as is done in the MP, is therefore unduly restrictive in view of many well-known and widespread facts of grammar. What these facts show is that the transformational machinery relating surface forms to semantic representations makes use of all the mathematically possible devices of a transformational system. The grammar will, therefore, have to belong to a mathematically unrestricted form of rewrite procedures, its restrictions coming from other than mathematical sources.

But quite apart from that, there is also the point that, in terms of the MP, it is not only the operation Move that has to be considered a breach of "conceptual necessity." The operation Spell-Out is likewise dispensable in a minimalist setup. For it is easily conceivable (in the otherwise repellent terms of a random-generator language system) that a language L should be defined merely by the operations Select and Merge, these two jointly constituting the grammar of L. Carried through to the end, these operations would exhaust N and result in one single syntactic object, which might conceivably be "legible" to both the C-I and the A-P interface, the former reading only the semantic features, the latter only the phonological ones. The features that are semantically or phonologically irrelevant would then not be needed in the grammar (see section 5.5 for further comment).

2.2.3 Reference sets

A further point concerns the notion of "reference sets." There is no guarantee that a numeration N will lead to a successful end, nor is it guaranteed that there will be no more than just one successful derivation yielding full interpretation at both ends. Yet to limit the set of possible derivations and to impose some order, Chomsky proposes that each N be associated with a "reference set" of possible derivations from N, the idea being that the most economical derivation from N to LF (PF appears to be considered less relevant in this respect) should win the race and reach the interface(s). No exclusivity is implied, however. As there is no statement to the contrary, the possibility is left open for more than one admissible derivation to be assigned equal ranking on the scale set by the economy metric. If two derivations achieve the highest ranking, they will both be considered "optimal" and will both generate grammatical sentences of the language. In general, more economical derivations are taken to "block" less economical ones (1995:227).

To evaluate different admissible derivations from the same N for derivational economy, it is necessary not only to assign "cost" values to (overt and covert) operations but also to compute all possible derivations from N, including those that will crash. The cost values are not properly specified, however. All that is said is that Select and Merge should be considered "costless" as they are necessary for any procedure that constructs tree structures from numerations (1995:226). It is, moreover, conceded that "selection of an optimal derivation in the reference set determined from the numeration N poses problems of computational complexity too vast to be realistic" (1995:227).

It is suggested (1995:228) that "global" properties of derivations should be applied to reduce computational complexity. A global property would enable the derivation in question to "see through" itself and determine the right moment for Move to apply in the case at hand.[2] How this should be implemented is left unclear. It is said that "we expect to find some ready algorithm to reduce computational complexity" and that "we are still a long way from a comprehensive theory of economy, a topic that is now being explored for the first time within a context of inquiry that is able to place explanatory adequacy on the agenda" (1995:228). However, given the doubtful status of the notions concerned, it is highly

---

2. Johnson and Lappin (1997:283) correctly point out that "global economy conditions bear an obvious resemblance to the transderivational constraints proposed by Generative Semanticists." They observe, moreover: "Surprisingly, Chomsky does not refer to the connection between the derivational constraints of the MP and those of Generative Semantics, nor does he cite his own arguments of twenty-five years ago (Chomsky 1971 [= Chomsky 1972]) against the Generative Semantics model." See also Pullum (1996).

unlikely that they contribute "for the first time" to a "context of inquiry that is able to place explanatory adequacy on the agenda."

Johnson and Lappin (1997) discuss the problems raised by Chomsky's notion of a reference set for each numeration. They show that, to the extent that this notion can be given a precise content, it is computationally intractable, and they conclude that it should be dispensed with altogether, as it can be replaced, without loss of empirical coverage, by local constraints on Move—a point further elaborated in their later work (1999). They also observe that the notion of reference set as suggested by Chomsky is acutely problematic in the context of his view of language as a near-perfect product of evolution. They observe, with good reason, that "the economy metric of the MP renders it computationally far less efficient than grammars that do not employ global derivational conditions of this kind" (1997:329).

They might have added that one wonders about the fate of those sentences that would be the product of less economical derivations than others, given the same N, and are blocked by the economy metric. One of two things. Either such sentences are grammatical but are unhappily blocked by the economy metric, which would make the grammar empirically inadequate, or they are ungrammatical, in which case this mysterious metric will have taken over the function of the grammar. This being so, it seems unnecessary to spend any further time on the issue.

2.2.4 Numeration and the random-generator position

There is some uncertainty about the procedure by which numeration produces N. It is implied (Chomsky 1995:225) that the selection N made from the lexicon by the operation Numeration of C_{HL} is arbitrary or random. This is, in itself, odd and counterproductive, since a collection of random selections from the lexicon, with a random index associated with each item taken, will, in the vast majority of cases, lead to what Chomsky calls a "crashing" derivation. Yet no limits or guidelines are set for the composition of N, despite Chomsky's insistence on economy principles as a valuation measure for derivations. On p. 294, however, at the end of an inconclusive section on question sentences (clauses) with the question word either raised to initial position or remaining in situ, the following "economy principle" is introduced: "α enters the numeration only if it has an effect on output." This implies that "output conditions enter into determination of the numeration itself; they affect the operation that constructs the numeration from the lexicon" (1995:294).

Regardless of the rationale for any such principle, it would seem that a machinery that would have to check different outputs from the same N on some criterion of equivalence or identity (left unexplained in the MP) and would then have to revert to N to eliminate any items that have apparently played no role (the only way in which this "economy principle" can be taken to work) would cry out for drastic redrafting. In Chomsky's view, as we have seen, the economy of C_{HL} derivations is itself a factor in guiding, or selecting, the optimal derivation of a sentence, the economy measure invoked being based on his "reference sets." Johnson and Lappin observe that if, as Chomsky says, output conditions enter into the determination of the numeration itself, "this renders the individuation of numerations dependent upon the derivations obtained from them, which is flatly circular, given that derivations are, in turn, partially determined by the numerations from which they start" (1997:302). This may not be entirely correct, since a feedback procedure would cut the circularity (although Chomsky's formulation "α enters the numeration only if it has an effect on output" does invite a charge of circularity). Yet the machinery would immediately become so unwieldy that any mention of "economy" with regard to such a system would be wildly out of proportion.

The point at issue is far from peripheral. It is central to the entire concept underlying the MP, touching as it does on the issue of random generation, as well as on the question of a possible realist interpretation of the MP. A radical but straightforward solution to the cluster of problems and questions associated with the operation Numeration making arbitrary selections from the lexicon would consist in abandoning the idea altogether and letting derivations start not with an incoherent or arbitrary set of lexical items but with either a cognition-driven selection of lexical items, as is implied in Hauser, Chomsky, and Fitch (2002:1578), or with whole propositions cast into the format of some regimented formal language, to be transformed subsequently into possibly elliptical surface sentences, as is implied or proposed in Chomsky (2002:45, 66). This, however, would make the system mediational and take away its random-generator character.

One would have thought that, given the painful recent history of the discussions around this topic, Chomsky would hardly be open to suggestions of a mediational nature. Yet, as we saw in section 1.5, and are seeing here again, this appears not to be the case. Consider first the proposal implied in Hauser, Chomsky, and Fitch (2002:1578)—the second quote given in section 1.5. According to that proposal, a minimalist grammar should be regarded not as a random generator but as a purely "abstract" description of what happens to lexical items chosen by a speaker who is in the process of expressing his or her thoughts. N would thus no longer be a random selection but would be restricted by the underlying thought process. The grammar would then merely be a formal machine carrying out the instructions that come with the lexical items involved. Although this would remove the problems presented above to some extent, it would still not be a coherent proposal, because one will immediately ask why the lexical items involved in the expression of a thought should be fed into the grammar, while the thought itself should not be but should be the result of the conceptual interpretation of what the grammar does with the items in question. In such a system, a numeration such as

{<Girl,1>,<Boy,1>,<Love,1>,<Many,1>,<All,1>}

would come out as either *Many girls love all boys* or *Many boys love all girls*, or *All girls love many boys* or *All boys love many girls*, all of which express clearly different thoughts. If, alternatively, it is proposed that not just the lexical items but the whole thought involved should be fed into the grammar, following the suggestion made in Chomsky (2002:45, 66) and elsewhere, then this would involve a radical change, in fact a paradigm change, in the grammatical system, which would then become a variant of mediational grammar.

There is a fatal flaw underlying Chomsky's reasoning regarding lexical selection. The flaw stands out most clearly in the following passage (Chomsky 1995:227):

> Within the framework just outlined [i.e., of Select and Merge], there is also no meaningful question as to why one numeration is formed rather than another – or rather than none, so that we have silence. That would be like asking that a theory of some formal operation on integers—say, addition—explain why some integers are added rather than others, or none. Or that a theory of the mechanisms of vision or motor coordination explain why someone chooses to look at a sunset or reach for a banana. The problem of choice of action is real, and largely mysterious, but does not arise within the narrow study of mechanisms.

While one will fully agree with Chomsky that it is not part of a theory of grammar to specify what a speaker will say (that being typically a question—and, indeed, largely a mysterious one—of psychology and pragmatics), and while one will likewise agree that a theory of grammar should stay within the narrow limits of a study of mechanisms, it does not follow at all that a theory of grammar should therefore assume an arbitrary numeration of lexical elements as a starting point, with all the consequences thereof. If one wishes to stay within the narrower limits of a study of mechanisms involving users or subjects, and avoid a study of users' whims, the least one should do is specify what the mechanism is supposed to operate on and what it is supposed to do given any input. Otherwise there simply is no study of the mechanism involved.

Consider the classical algorithms of arithmetic—for example, multiplication. The algorithm will start by taking a pair of rational numbers as input and then specify the algorithmic function that results in their product. It will not start with a "numeration" of digits and fractional points to be combined into rational numbers by operations corresponding to Select and Merge. The theory of vision, also mentioned by Chomsky as an example, is not a very good parallel, since vision corresponds to the parsing rather than to the generation of sentences. Even so, it will start by assuming arrays of real or imagined sense data within the range of visual perception and will have to explain how these are interpreted as three-dimensional meaningful phenomena placed in, or moving in, a "scene" (Barwise 1981, Marr 1982, Arbib 1989:242–247, Van der Does and Van Lambalgen 2000). A better parallel would be a theory of the mechanics involved in the painting or drawing of meaningful (representational) scenes, if that were a realistic project. But no matter how realistic, or how illusory, such a theory might be, it would not describe the start of a generative process resulting in a painting or drawing as an arbitrary "numeration" of whatever materials might be used (for the visual-perceptual interface) or of whatever meaningful features might occur (for the conceptual-intentional interface). Such a "theory" would not describe the "mechanism" underlying the human capacity for painting or drawing in any sense. At best, it might serve as a blueprint for an artificial machine randomly generating pictorial representations from a heap of materials used in painting or drawing and a list of pictorially meaningful elements. A theory meant to describe the human "mechanism" of painting or drawing would take as input a mental representation of the scene to be painted or drawn (in terms of some reasonably adequate "language of pictorial meanings"), and then specify in general terms how such a mental representation is best taken to be converted into a corresponding interpretable disposition of materials on a canvas, panel, or sheet of paper.

In short, theories of the mechanics involved in human activities leading to perceptible products signifying mental structures or processes have no choice but to begin by specifying, in some adequate system of representation, the mental structures or processes involved and will then specify the principles and processes that lead to the perceptible output. This has nothing to do with the question of why or how humans choose to express this or that mental content, nor with the question of what enables human subjects to come up with mental contents of the kind envisaged. But it has everything to do with whatever mechanism may be supposed to underlie the capacity of expressing any aribitrary mental contents involved.

In the case of human language, this means that a description of the mechanism underlying the human capacity for uttering meaningful sentences had better consider structures representing thoughts, conceived as combinations of speech act elements and propositions as input to the mechanism, while taking it as its specific task to analyze and describe the principles and processes that will successfully transform these thought structures into proper, well-formed perceptible (surface) forms. Analogously, of course, any proper theory of the mechanism involved in the reduction of spoken signals to their semantic counterparts will take the spoken signals as input and describe their reduction to corresponding semantic representations.

This point is so obvious that it hardly needs to be belabored. It underlies all work in grammar from its inception in Aristotelian and Alexandrian times up to the advent of American structuralism. But even in structuralist and early transformational grammar, behaviorist as it may have been, it was always tacitly assumed that sentences express meanings in the way described, though it was felt that a systematic study of such "mental" processes could not be regarded as strictly scientific. Only when the notion of "autonomous grammar" appeared, around 1970, did the traditional and natural notion of a grammar as a mapping procedure specifying surface forms for semantic content (and vice versa) begin to be challenged, leading to a random-generator view of language, of which the MP may be considered the crowning achievement.

A random-generator theory of language, such as the MP and its predecessors from 1970 on, aims at an algorithmic characterization of the sentences of a language with zero input, assigning the structures that are generated a phonological and a semantic interpretation. As is explained in detail in section 6.1.1, the origins of this view of language lie in (a) the structuralist-behaviorist tradition that dominated American linguistics during much of the twentieth century and (b) the modern mathematical theory of algorithms, developed at roughly the same time, which showed that formal languages can be defined by algorithmic means. The formal mathematical languages considered were mostly of a relatively simple phrase-structure type requiring nothing more than a *primitive* algorithm based on a given finite alphabet or vocabulary, and hardly ever of the more complex transformational type requiring *derived* algorithms, which take as input structures already generated by one or more primitive algorithms. (This is perhaps surprising, since the classic arithmetical algorithms—addition, subtraction, multiplication, and division—which formed the basis of the modern theory of algorithms, are all derived and not primitive. Their primitive antecedent simply generates number notations from digits and the fractional point and is hardly to be considered part of arithmetic.)

The random-generator view of language, as developed in the context of autonomous grammar after 1970, is, on the one hand, a continuation of the structuralist-behaviorist tradition in the more modern context of cognitive science, and as such an alien element in this context. On the other hand, it manifests a stubborn adherence to the view that a grammar must ultimately be defined in terms of a primitive algorithm, having recourse to a vocabulary given in advance. As has been explained, this is not necessary at all, since the input to a derived algorithm may come from different sources (in this case cognition in a general sense) and may thus not be part of the algorithmically structured theory. This, as we have argued, is actually the case with the theory of grammar as a "narrow study of mechanisms"—the mechanisms, that is, which are involved in the production of well-formed sentences.

The assumption of a primitive algorithm for the theory of grammar is not just unnecessary, it is also undesirable since the input to the mechanism of grammar consists of structures produced well outside grammar, in cognition, even though the semantic representations in question do, of course, obey certain (simple) well-formedness constraints. These may be caught in terms of a primitive algorithm, but one should realize that thát algorithm cannot possibly be taken to be part of the cognitive machinery involved in the production and understanding of sentence tokens, and can, therefore, not play a part in "the narrow study of mechanisms."

This is the most fundamental reason why the MP, though posing as a realist theory of language and grammar, cannot possibly be interpreted in a realist sense and can only be seen as an instance of formalist instrumentalist theorizing, uncalled for in present-day linguistics, which is basically realist and is, from a methodological point of view, much more congenial to the very realist discipline of psychology than to the purely formalist discipline of logic. (Formal semantics, though largely based on logical notions and techniques, is rapidly turning away from a purely formalist methodology and is increasingly presenting itself as a modeling of really occurring mental processes.)

In this wider context it is easy to see why the concept of an operation Numeration is alien to a proper theory of grammar. A grammar must take as its input a representation of full sentence meanings, with the speech act and propositional components properly specified in a regimented language of semantic representations. Generative semantics proposed to do precisely that, and till the present day no convincing arguments have been presented showing why that proposal should be rejected. The arguments presented in Chomsky (1972), largely to do with phenomena that, according to Chomsky, require semantic interpretation directly from the surface structure and not from the semantic structure, lack conviction, as is shown in chapter 7.

2.3 Conclusion

This review of the actual MP machinery envisaged for the computation—that is, generation—of well-formed and meaningful sentences of a natural language has shown not only that whatever little transpires with any clarity is heavily underspecified and badly lacking in empirical support, but also that the entire design, sketchy as it still may be, is based on faulty preliminary analyses. Therefore, if any such machinery is at all implementable, which is doubtful, it is bound to be counterproductive to the extreme. An engineer delivering such a product, far from being "superbly competent," would be subject to dismissal on account of utter incompetence. In the following chapter, we pass on to broader issues regarding the overall architecture of the language faculty and its place in the wider context of the ecology of the human mind and the world in which it lives.

3

The Language Faculty

In this chapter two things are done. First, Chomsky's overall characterization of the language faculty is considered. Then, in section 3.5, this is
contrasted with a different conception of what the language faculty
amounts to and what the points of view are from which it can be studied
most fruitfully.

As regards Chomsky's own view of the faculty of language (FoL), there
is a problem, since his interest in the ecological embedding of the FoL is
not only recent but also limited to its possible effects on syntax, his C_{HL}
or "human language computational system." Syntax has always been
Chomsky's prime concern, and this has not changed. Minimalism is an
attempt to show on "external" grounds of functionality the inherent necessity of a specific, pre-existing syntactic system, which hitherto had to
stand on its own empirical feet. It is, therefore, not an impartial study of
the FoL. The nature of the syntax or C_{HL} is not left open till it is filled in
by external requirements of functionality. On the contrary, most of the
syntax is already in place and minimalism is brought in to provide a justification post hoc in terms of functional requirements. This attempt at
functionalist reduction of syntax to communicative necessities has been
signally unsuccessful (see chapter 5), but what is relevant here is that the
resulting perspective on the FoL inevitably lacks the balance and the
broadness one expects to find in analyses that are less driven by results
already anticipated. This feature radically vitiates the minimalist attempt
throughout.

There is also the fact that Chomsky has never paid much attention to the semantic or the social aspects of language. His comments on meaning and logic are derivative, generally uninteresting, and often uninformed. What he has to say with regard to semantics does not enrich his view of the FoL. And his pronouncements with respect to the social aspects of language—that is, the communicative function of language, sociolinguistic and dialectal variation, and language as a reified public object—show either a deep-seated aversion or an inability to come to terms with such aspects. His views in this respect are accordingly uninteresting and irrelevant (see in particular sections 5.4 and 5.7 for further comment). His recent conversion to functionalism has thus hardly led to a broadened view of the FoL.

The main "guiding ideas" underlying the MP were set out in section 2.1. Among them are some ideas concerning the FoL—in particular, its position in the wider context of human cognition and human ecology, including the evolutionary aspects. It is these ideas that are subjected to a closer scrutiny in this chapter.

First examined is the notion that goes under the title of "Principles and Parameters" and find that this notion is not only relevant and useful but also quite traditional and not at all unique to the Chomskyan view of language. Nevertheless, despite the avowed concern with universal parameters and their possible values, no serious investigation into these matters has been carried through in any of Chomsky's many writings, including the MP.

Then discussed is the notion of modularity as a central feature of the FoL. We find that there is hardly any mention of the modularity of the language faculty in the MP, which is remarkable since it is this notion that distinguishes modern concepts of universal grammar from more traditional ones. Chomsky's apparent unwillingness to regard modularity of any kind as a serious restriction on the FoL is seen to have far-reaching consequences, in particular with regard to his random-generator position and his unclear and ambiguous realism.

Next considered are Chomsky's views on the evolutionary nature of human language; his position on this score is likewise speculative, noncommittal, and bordering on the inconsistent. The many questions that are inevitably raised in this respect are left unanswered in his writings.

Section 3.5 is taken up with a sketch of what the FoL may be taken to be like in terms of mediational grammar. Needless to say, this sketch is very different from Chomsky's ideas as presented in the MP. Its function is, first, to highlight some essential gaps in Chomsky's view of the language faculty and, second, to show that there is a strong and perfectly viable alternative.

3.1 Principles and Parameters: a historical note

Let us now consider the notion, defended in Chomsky (1995) and elsewhere, that all human languages are subject to universal principles (parameters) that allow for different choices (values).

Before we look at the actual notion, however, a historical note is in order. According to Chomsky, this idea originated with his Principles and Parameters (P&P) approach presented in the early 1980s, and in large sections of the linguistic and wider intellectual community it is actually believed that this is so.[1] According to Chomsky (1995:5–6):

> The P&P model . . . constituted a radical break from the rich tradition of thousands of years of linguistic inquiry, far more so than early generative grammar, which could be seen as a revival of traditional concerns and approaches to them. . . . The P&P approach held that languages have no rules in anything like the familiar sense, and no theoretically significant grammatical constructions except as taxonomic artifacts. *There are universal principles and a finite array of options as to how they apply* (*parameters*), but no language-particular rules and no grammatical constructions of the traditional sort within or across languages. [italics mine]

It must be observed, first, that what are referred to as "rules in the familiar sense" or "theoretically significant grammatical constructions of the traditional sort" are not at all part of "the rich tradition of thousands of years of linguistic inquiry." What is meant by "rules in the familiar sense" depends on the tradition one stands in. For some linguists, the familiar notion of rule of grammar goes back to the late nineteenth cen-

---

1. One example is Gould (1997:60), who, clearly with the best intentions, attributes the idea of universal grammar to Chomsky: "Noam Chomsky's linguistic theories represent the paradigm for modern concepts of proper integration between nature and nurture—principles of universal grammar as inborn learning rules, with peculiarities of any particular language as a product of cultural circumstance and place of upbringing." See also note 1 of chapter 1.

tury and is the product of a tradition in the theory and practice of grammar writing that dates from the late seventeenth century. In his *Grammaire Françoise sur un plan nouveau* of 1714, the French grammarian Claude Buffier writes (11):

> A true and just design of grammar thus can only be one which, accepting a language as established by usage, without wishing to change or modify anything in it, provides only reflections called "rules," to which can be reduced the manners of speaking customary in this language. It is this collection of reflections that is called "grammar." [my translation]

The notion of a grammatical rule as a "customary manner of speaking" was subsequently refined and formalized to a considerable degree by later grammarians, crystallizing into what may be called a "familiar" notion by perhaps the 1880s. For other linguists, the familiar notion of rule of grammar is that presented in Chomsky (1964b), a much more recent publication.

The notion "grammatical construction of the traditional sort" is likewise recent. Traditional linguists will trace this notion again to the nineteenth century, whereas in modern theoretical linguistics it is coextensive with that of a class of tree structures and is taken from Bloomfield (1933), although its origins lie in ideas presented by Wilhelm Wundt in and after 1880 (see Seuren 1998:219–227). In any case, the (apparent) rejection of these notions in Chomsky's P&P approach can hardly be said to be of the historical importance he attributes to it.

Moreover, the idea that "there are universal principles and a finite array of options as to how they apply" is literally found in Beauzée (1767,1:xvi–xviii):

> Constantly following this method I found everywhere the same views, the same general principles, the same universality in the laws common to Language. I saw that the differences of specific languages, the idioms, are nothing but different aspects of general principles or different applications of common fundamental laws, that these differences are limited, based on reason, reducible to fixed points, that therefore all the peoples of the earth, despite the differences of their tongues, speak, in a sense, the same Language, without anomalies or exceptions, and that, finally, one can reduce to a relatively small number *the necessary elements of Language*, and the teaching of all languages, to a simple, brief, uniform and easy method. [my translation]

The similarity with Chomsky's notion of universal grammar and of the language faculty is obvious.

Beauzée's notion of universal grammar, however, is not the oldest we have. Among the many surprising ideas put forward by medieval philosophers, there is one, widespread in medieval philosophy, that all human languages follow one single pattern, dictated by the general categories of thinking which were thought to be either largely congruent with the world (realism) or autonomous from it (nominalism) (see Seuren 1998:29–34 and the references cited there). Since, in the medieval philosophers' geographically and historically limited perspective, Latin was the only language really worth considering (Greek was practically unknown until the end of the fifteenth century and the new popular vernaculars were, for a long time, not considered real languages), it was the grammar of Latin that served as the model for universal grammar. Later grammatical descriptions of the new European languages therefore strongly conformed to Latin grammar and forced Latin grammatical categories on the languages under description. Twentieth-century structuralism, as we know, reacted strongly against what was considered the improper imposition of Latin grammar on all the languages of the world, each language being considered unique and autonomous. Yet, in hindsight, many linguists now feel inclined to say that the structuralist reaction was overdone in that all languages are bound by an innate linguistic charter. And Latin is as good, or as bad, an instantiation of the universal charter for grammars as any other language (such as English).

But there is a clear difference between modern and traditional views of universal grammar as they were current in the Middle Ages or expressed by Beauzée in the preceding quotation, and that difference does not lie in the notion of universally fixed parameters that receive a value or "setting" for each specific language or language variety. That much has been traditional lore for a long time. The real difference lies in the *modular concept* of linguistic competence as sketched in section 3.3. In the traditional conception of universal grammar, the parameters or general principles were considered to be of a general cognitive, "rational" or "logical" nature: the structural properties of universal grammar were taken to be exclusively derivable from the structure of thought, which was taken to follow closely the ontological categories of being. It is, again, Beauzée who states this clearly (1767,1:ix–x):

Grammar, which takes as its object the expression of thought by means of spoken or written speech, thus allows for two sorts of principles. Some are of an immutable and universal validity. Being connected with the very nature of thought they follow its analysis and thus result from it. The others have only hypothetical validity and depend on fortuitous, arbitrary, and variable conventions, which have given rise to the different languages. The former constitute universal grammar, the latter are the object of the grammars of specific languages. [my translation]

In contrast, the standard modern view, which has been molded in part by Chomsky but also by authors like Ross (1986 [1967]), Peters and Ritchie (1973), Postal (1972, 1974), and McCawley (1973) and has, on the whole, proved empirically highly fruitful and stimulating, holds that the parameters of the FoL are of a specific structural nature, inaccessible to introspection or conscious control, and to do with restrictions on or specific modes of grammatical structures or transformations. Beauzée's "hypothetical" principles are thus no longer considered "fortuitous" or "arbitrary" but constrained by the principles of universal grammar, lodged in the faculty of language. The structural properties of general cognition, or rational or logical thought, are now only considered to pose overall limiting conditions within which the special restrictions that the FoL imposes on specific grammars are supposed to be operative. In this modern view the FoL is divorced from general intelligence or cognition and produces grammars that are modular in the modern sense.

It is only in this respect that Chomsky's Principles and Parameters approach differs from the "rich tradition of thousands of years of linguistic inquiry." Given obvious differences in historical context, Chomsky's notion of universal grammar or the language faculty is not a break with, but part of, a continuous tradition that is at least six centuries old.

Historical backgrounds are a constant source of difficulty and confusion in Chomsky's writings. On the one hand, one sees repeated claims of "radical breaks" with recent, mostly structuralist, traditions, even though in effect, Chomsky's work represents a direct continuation of the traditions concerned. On the other hand, the more distant past has been requisitioned, as in Chomsky (1966), with the aim of forging more ancient pedigrees. Although this tendency is much less manifest in Chomsky (1995), where just one, largely vacuous, reference is made to Aristotle (on p. 2) for the unsurprising notion that language links up form and meaning, it has flared up again in the most recent publications, in particular Chomsky (2000, 2002) and Hauser, Chomsky, and Fitch (2002), where prominent figures in the history of science, such as Galileo, Newton, Darwin, and many others, are constantly appealed to with the aim of establishing methodological legitimacy by comparison and association, though not by analysis and argument.

3.2 Modularity and the random-generator position

Since it is the concept of modularity that distinguishes traditional from modern views of universal grammar, it is important to have a closer look at that notion. This modular conception of linguistic competence in any specific language implies, first, that the module in question is a rapid, automatic, domain-specific input-output machine: it receives an input and is made in such a way as to produce an output. For that reason it has at least two *interfaces* with other sections of either the cerebral machinery or with organism-external systems—one with the section providing the input (unless the module is a spontaneous generator), and one with the section or system receiving the output, and possibly also with auxiliary supply units.

A module is, moreover, *domain-specific*. In the case of language it has the specific task of transforming thoughts into recipes for pronunciation, writing, or gesturing. It is also *automatic*, *fast*, and *isolated* from external factors: once it has been set into motion it cannot be stopped or interfered with and will produce the appropriate output at a surprising speed. It is *inaccessible* to any form of introspection or awareness: no amount of self-searching will reveal its inner workings. The interfaces, on the other hand, may be open to awareness and allow for a certain amount of control or monitoring. In fact, when there is the possibility of conscious monitoring, an interface must be assumed, though not conversely. Finally, a module is taken to be implemented as *neurological hardware*, though, in the case of the language module, the precise nature of this condition is still largely unclear. (Fodor's 1983 claim that it has a specific location in the brain is open to much debate.)

There is (was) a concept of "module" in Chomskyan theory (1995:27), but this is unrelated to the Fodorian concept of the same name or any variant thereof. Chomsky's notion of modularity implies that a grammar consists of "modules" (binding theory, θ-theory, case theory, government theory, morphology, etc.), each "module" having its own restrictions on rules and structures, apart from restrictions that are common to all such modules. But this concept of module, still considered acceptable in (1995:27), then turns out to be less desirable in the minimalist program and is, in fact, dropped (Chomsky 1995:229; N stands for Numeration, λ for logical form, π for phonetic form):

> The simplest assumptions are (1) that there is no further interaction between these computations [from N to π and λ] and (2) that computational procedures are uniform throughout: any operation can apply at any point. We adopt (1), and assume (2) for the computation from N to λ, though not for the computation from N to π; the latter modifies structures (including the internal structure of lexical entries) by processes very different from those that take place in the N → l computation. Investigation of output conditions should suffice to establish these asymmetries, which I will simply take for granted here.

The implication is that the succession of proposals regarding alleged universal restrictions on grammatical structures and rule systems made by Chomskyan linguists during the past few decades with the aim of solving "the logical problem of language acquisition" or "Plato's problem" should now culminate in a much more economical system that encompasses them all and is based on "conceptual necessity." Apart from the fact that such a reduction cannot be merely invoked but must also be shown, this issue is only terminologically related to the question of modularity.

The issue that concerns us now is the fact that modularity is definitely underplayed in the MP. All one finds is a casual statement, in which modularity is assigned to the language faculty, rather than to its fleshed-out manifestation in the form of specific grammars (Chomsky 1995:221):

> Suppose that [the minimalist] approach proves to be more or less correct. What could we then conclude about the specificity of the language faculty (modularity)? Not much. The language faculty might be unique among cognitive systems, or even in the organic world, in that it satisfies minimalist assumptions. Furthermore, the morphological parameters could be unique in character, and the computational system C_{HL} biologically isolated.

And again: "Human language appears to be biologically isolated in its essential properties" (1998:1). What this means is not made clear, but if it is an implicit reference to modularity, the MP suffers from one more contradiction.

According to Chomsky, the FoL is embedded in an architecture that has two interfaces with external performance systems: an articulatory-perceptual (A-I) and a conceptual-intentional (C-I) interface. A closer analysis, however, of the notion of interface (left undefined by Chomsky) in terms of modularity shows that this position is open to qualification. Since the computational system or systems of language are modular and therefore in principle automatic and inaccessible to introspection, it makes sense to assume that at least those places where there is the possibility of active conscious control or monitoring of output constitute interfaces between separate systems. The points at which speakers can exert control over or can monitor their linguistic utterances—that is, with the machinery in production mode—appear to be the following:

1. The output end of the thought-producing machinery, where the thought output passes into the lexicon, taking into account contextual and situational conditions;

2. The output end of the lexicon, where the lexical selection made is monitored for adequacy with regard to the thought input and passed into the grammar module;

3. The output end of the grammar module, where the surface structure output is screened for adequacy with regard to the combined thought and lexical input and passed on to the phonetic-orthographic machinery;

4. The output end of the phonetic-orthographic machinery, where the speaker monitors decisions made on the manner of pronunciation or writing and passes the product on to the organism-external systems of the physical world.

Competent listeners and readers register the choices made at these four levels and are able to bring them into consciousness—to make them cognitively explicit even to the point of being able to report on them. Since there appear to be no junctures at which listeners screen the input signal for proper reception (though delayed phonetic-lexical processing does occasionally occur), grammatical structure or lexical identification, one is inclined to conclude that comprehension is to a large extent a process of reconstruction-by-hypothesis, of course crucially constrained and guided by the phonetic input but also assisted by all kinds of clues drawn from the context of utterance, from available world knowledge and from overall knowledge of the language and its typical uses.

That being so, one may feel justified in concluding that the language machinery is equipped with at least four interfaces or gates, located at the appropriate positions and geared to the production mode. We therefore assume that there are, for any language, at least four interfaces involving separate functions of the brain:

1. The *thought interface*, passing on thought output to the lexicon;
2. The *lexical interface*, passing on lexical output to the grammar;
3. The *grammatical interface*, passing on grammatical output to the physical realization systems of speaking or writing;
4. The *perceptual interface*, passing on phonetic or written output to the outside environment through the medium of sound or material receiving written symbols, respectively.

One will wonder why modularity is so dramatically underemphasized in the MP, where it is presumably referred to as the property of being "biologically isolated," without any further consequences being attached to it. It would seem that Chomsky's reluctance to adopt the notion of modularity with all its consequences derives from his desire to uphold his old random-generator notion of autonomous syntax, first presented around 1970 in the context of what was then called the "extended standard theory" or EST. Although it never became quite clear at the time what exactly the issue was, the practical upshot was that, in EST, syntax was considered a free-generation machine for sentences, whose products are open to, on the one hand, phonetic and, on the other, semantic interpretation. The opposite party, formed by the generative semanticists, defended what we call the "mediational position" and maintained that syntax is for the most part a transformation device between semantic analyses originating in cognition and surface structures that are fed into the phonetics. While EST allowed transformations to change meaning, generative semantics did not.

Clearly, if modularity is accepted and lexical choice is treated (as it should be) as open to conscious decision, the random-generator notion of syntax as a random sentence-generating machine must be given up. The random-generator position, which implies that syntax is "autonomous" in the sense just sketched, is not defended explicitly in Chomsky (1995) but taken for granted. It now becomes clear that this is still, or again, a position that has to be argued for, and, as will be shown below, no compelling arguments in favor of that position appear to be at hand.

Although the questions have faded a little over time, they have never been resolved on the basis of accepted forms of academic argument (see Huck and Goldsmith 1995). By ignoring the modularity concept, despite its obvious significance, Chomsky appears to circumvent the issue of random generation as a realist stance. Yet it is there, and it has to be faced, even though it has rested for a number of years.

3.3 Chomsky's ambiguous realism

One may, of course, abandon realism, give up the modularity view, rule psychological considerations out of court, and reduce the description and analysis of language to a mere formal exercise as if it were a mathematical game.

When one takes this instrumentalist course, one is less constrained and has a larger margin of liberty to rearrange the description in ways that may seem more elegant from a descriptive or from a mathematical point of view, or more amenable to a machine implementation, or what not. But one must give up any functionalist aspirations.

Just to avoid confusion, let us summarize what exactly is involved. The standard realist position implies (a) that there is a fund of basic *observational data* considered to have ontological reality of some kind, (b) that a *causal question* is asked as regards the coming about of certain aspects of the data, (c) that an *underlying reality* is postulated embodying the causal origin of the observed data, and (d) that a *formal theory* is devised, preferably ultimately in a deductive or algorithmic format, that will serve as a hypothesis answering the causal question in the sense that designated theoretical terms are taken to refer to elements in the underlying reality under some consistent formula of interpretation. The formal theory is said to *explain* the observed data. A realist theory aims at *describing and specifying the workings of the hidden underlying reality* that is the object of the theory under some formula of interpretation.

Realism is gradable. The strongest form of realism applies to theories that specify the postulated underlying reality in pure hardware terms down to the most basic form of specification of physical matter. This form of realism is relatively rare. Weaker forms are satisfied with more global physical specifications, precise enough to serve the purposes of a restricted field of inquiry. The weakest form of realism is *non-hardware realism*, which is characterized by a formula of interpretation that leaves the question of hardware implementation of the theory largely open, or anyway does not commit itself to any constraining force the hardware nature of the assumed underlying reality may have on the theory. Non-hardware realism is normally motivated by a failure to gain empirical access to the underlying physical reality assumed to be there. But as soon as some form of empirical access to the postulated physical reality is provided, non-hardware realists will strengthen the formula of interpretation in the direction of a stronger, more specific commitment to hardware specifications. The instrumentalist position is less committing. It comes in a few varieties, all of which typically aim merely at specifying properties that the object of investigation must somehow satisfy, but without any intention of describing or specifying the workings of any assumed underlying reality or of presenting causal relations between any such reality and the observed phenomena. On the whole, this position is inspired by the kind of scientific positivism that dominated the sciences during the earlier parts of the twentieth century and dictated that any search for non-observables should be considered unscientific.

One variety, let us call it *moderate instrumentalism*, does accept the hidden, underlying reality behind a fund of basic data but rejects any causal question or any causal explanation and merely tries to capture observed regularities in terms of an algorithmically organized system or formal theory, without any causality or reality claim regarding the theoretical terms employed in the theory. In a more extreme form, however, instrumentalism denies the existence or relevance of any possible underlying reality altogether and merely aims at a mathematical characterization of a body of observed and potentially observable data. Let us call this *mathematical instrumentalism*. It is typically found in modern theoretical physics, where, in general, no ontological status is claimed for anything possibly corresponding to the elementary particles and forces or for anything else possibly causing the observed phenomena. It was likewise represented in certain forms of behaviorist psychology during the first half of the twentieth century, where the reality or existence of anything corresponding to what is commonly referred to by the term *mind* was denied.

It is widely accepted that a realist theory, if proved right or crucially confirmed by evidence for the postulated underlying reality, has greater explanatory value than an instrumentalist theory that is crucially confirmed by correct predictions. The reason for this preference seems to lie in the fact that the more realist a theory is, the more means are available for its possible falsification on grounds of incompatibility with the kind of reality that is posited for the theory at hand. Thus, physiology could falsify a particular theory of grammar T, provided T had a formula of interpretation that involves hardware physiological objects and processes. Needless to say, no existing theory of grammar has yet attained that status of hardware realism.

The question is: what is Chomsky's position in this regard? Botha (1989:159–164) has shown that the answer to this question is far from simple in that Chomsky's views as expressed over the years show a considerable amount of oscillation and ambiguity. But what is Chomsky's position now? Has he sided with realism and, if so, under what formula of interpretation? Or has he sided with instrumentalism and, if so, with which variety? Or does the ambiguity still continue? The question is relevant for an adequate assessment of his actual claims, especially because any kind of functionalism in linguistics is incompatible with instrumentalism.

The opening text of chapter 3 in *The Minimalist Program* suggests a realist stance in a general sense, though the formula of interpretation is left vague (Chomsky 1995:167):

> Language and its use have been studied from varied points of view. One approach, assumed here, takes language to be part of the natural world. The human brain provides an array of capacities that enter into the use and understanding of language (the *language faculty*); these seem to be in good part specialized for that function and a common human endowment over a very wide range of circumstances and conditions. One component of the language faculty is a generative procedure (an *I-language*, henceforth *language*) that generates *structural descriptions* (SDs), each a complex of properties, including those commonly called "semantic" and "phonetic." These SDs are the *expressions* of the language. The theory of a particular language is its *grammar*. The theory of languages and the expressions they generate is *Universal Grammar* (UG); UG is a theory of the initial state S_0 of the relevant component of the language faculty. We can distinguish the language from a conceptual system and a system of pragmatic competence. Evidence has been accumulating that these interacting systems can be selectively impaired and developmentally dissociated. . . , and their properties are quite different.

Yet, as so often with Chomsky, his position is far from straightforward. Jürgen Lenerz, one of the reviewers of *The Minimalist Program*, was quick to see this (1998:110):

> This (derivationally conceived) computation takes place as a logical structure outside time and space (cp. p. 380, note 3). The question remains to what extent one can speak here of a description of the biologically given human language faculty, which can only be a concrete system bound in time and space. The abbreviation C_{HL} ("computational system of human language"), occasionally used by Chomsky, is therefore at least problematic, as long as the unclarity persists regarding the connection between

the logico-deductive descriptive system and the concrete biological-mental system.

> One also wonders what could possibly justify the imposition on a logical system outside time and space of both economy criteria and the specific criteria derived from the performance systems A-P and C-I that are external to the computation system, which, in the end, only mediates between them. [my translation]

Let us look at the passage to which the note 3 referred to by Lenerz is attached (Chomsky 1995:223):

> A related question is whether C_{HL} is derivational or representational: does it involve successive operations leading to (π,λ) [phonetic form-logical form] (if it converges), or does it operate in one of any number of other ways—say, selecting two such representations and then computing to determine whether they are properly paired, selecting one and deriving the other, and so on?

Note that this is unambiguously a realist question, as it is a question about the *actual* structure of the human language computational system. At this point in the text the note 3 referred to by Lenerz is added (Chomsky 1995:380):

> Recall that the ordering of operations is abstract, expressing postulated properties of the language faculty of the brain, with no temporal interpretation implied. In this respect, the terms *output* and *input* have a metaphorical flavor, though they may reflect substantive properties, if the derivational approach is correct.

Can one blame Lenerz, or anyone for that matter, for being genuinely puzzled? What does it mean to say that "the ordering of operations is abstract with no temporal interpretation implied" in the context of the clearly realist question "whether C_{HL} is derivational or representational," involving "successive operations"? What is meant by the statement that "the terms *output* and *input* have a metaphorical flavor"? What is the commitment that comes with the intimation that "they may reflect substantive properties, if the derivational approach is correct"? This note 3 is clearly an echo of Chomsky's earlier equivocations carefully set out in Botha (1989).

It looks as if the confusion still persists. Further down on the same page Chomsky writes: "My own judgment is that a derivational approach is nonetheless correct, and the particular version of a minimalist program I am considering assigns it even greater prominence" (1995:223). This seems to betray an inclination toward realism again. The term *correct* invites a realist interpretation (or else it can only mean "computationally correct," which is not at issue here). And so does the implication that the derivational approach is assigned "even greater prominence" by the minimalist rule system. But then one reads (Chomsky 1998:6–7):

> The initial and attained state [i.e., the FoL and full linguistic competence in a specific language, respectively] are states of the brain primarily, but described abstractly, not in terms of cells but in terms of properties that the brain mechanisms must somehow satisfy.

Here one has a feeling that one is back in the (moderate) instrumentalist court.

One wonders if Chomsky might not be under the misapprehension that if a scientific description is not given in terms of hardware ("cells"), in which case it is, of course, realist, it must be "abstract" and hence express "postulated properties with no temporal interpretation implied," or "outside time and space," in the words of Lenerz. But there is no such dilemma, as the actual situation is more complex than that.

It is true that a description in terms of hardware is necessarily a realist description. But realist descriptions can be, and usually are, further removed from hardware reality in virtue of less committing formulas of interpretation. A geographical map is a fully realist description, or else it is unreliable. But in most cases it abstracts from geographical hardware as it also abstracts from elements that are not represented on the map, for whatever reason. Moreover, it may contain elements, such as coordinates, that are not intended to be interpreted realistically but merely serve purposes of efficient use and reference.

Such realist descriptions are distinct from instrumentalist specifications or computations like many mathematical models in theoretical physics, economics, or climatology, whose realist interpretation is less important than their predictive power. Often nature turns out to have properties that are definable in terms of mathematical functions. It has been found, for example, that many phyllotactic arrangements in nature, such as that of petals on a sunflower, are describable as an algorithmic function producing a sequence of Fibonacci numbers (the series of numbers, starting with 1,1, such that each subsequent number is the sum of the two preceding ones: 1,1,2,3,5,8,13,21, etc.). This startling fact makes for all kinds of reliable predictions in biological nature. But the mere arithmetical function just given will not do in any realist theory aiming at explaining how Fibonacci series come about in nature, simply because it is totally unrealistic to attribute to the living organisms at issue (plants) a faculty enabling them to carry out the necessary computation. Unless a *mechanism* is postulated that generates Fibonacci numbers as an epiphenomenal by-product, the theory stays within an instrumentalist frame, where the arrangements are "described abstractly, not in terms of cells but in terms of properties that the mechanisms must somehow satisfy," to use Chomsky's words from the preceding quote.

Now imagine a genetically determined growth process proceeding in cycles, whereby each element in cycle C_n reproduces itself twice, once in cycle C_{n+1} and once in cycle C_{n+2}, as illustrated in figure 3.1, where the inner circle represents C_0. The cardinalities of the successive cyclic sets of elements will then be the Fibonacci numbers. Postulating such a system amounts to a causal, hence realist, hypothesis, but in a nonhardware fashion. It is this form of non-hardware realism that provides the optimal interpretation for modern theories of grammar, as long as no closer approximation to the actual underlying biological reality can be achieved.

Interestingly, Fibonacci himself, in his *Liber Abaci* of 1202, presented his number sequence as the answer to the problem of how many rabbit pairs

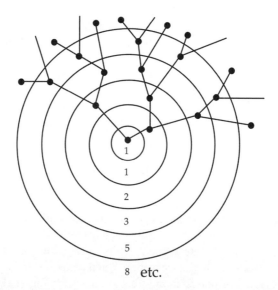

FIGURE 3.1. A non-hardware realist system generating the Fibonacci numbers

P are produced from a single *P* in one year if each *P* begets a new one every month, starting from the second month after birth (*Encyclopedia Britannica* [1984] 13:350). This likewise is an instantiation of a model for generating the Fibonacci numbers but in a different way from the one just described. Which of the two, if either, is implemented by nature? All things being equal, there is no way of knowing until molecular biologists have spoken. The hardware is a separate empirical issue, yet closely related in that it restricts possible realist theories and may falsify them. One notices the striking methodological parallel with theories of grammar.

That Chomsky does indeed fail to see the distinction between hardware and non-hardware realist descriptions emerges from Chomsky (2002:72–73):

> These very recent debates about chemistry, and their suspected outcome, should be instructive for the brain and cognitive sciences. They suggest that *it is a mistake to think of computer models of the mind that are divorced from biology—that is, in principle unaffected by anything that might be discovered in the biological sciences* [italics mine]—or Platonistic or other non-biological conceptions of language, also insulated from important evidence, to their detriment, or to hold that the relation of the mental to the physical is not reducibility but the weaker notion of *supervenience*: any change in mental events or states entails a "physical change," though not conversely, and there is nothing more specific to say.

Chomsky seems to equate the notion "divorced from biology" with "unaffected by anything that might be discovered in the biological sciences." But this equation does not hold: one may very well have, and often it is all one can have, a description that is realist in aim and intention but not (yet) expressible in hardware terms. Such a theory subjects itself to possible falsification by more detailed hardware data. That is precisely the methodological advantage of realism over instrumentalism: realism has a larger array of means of falsification than instrumentalism has.

Meanwhile, the false dilemma between hardware and instrumentalist descriptions opens the way to relegating all kinds of theories presented in the past to a limbo of "abstract formalisms" which can then be jettisoned without loss of substantive claims. One wonders if this is what is done in the following passage (Chomsky 1998:21):

> A core assumption of the work within the Principles-and-Parameters framework, and its fairly impressive achievements, is that everything I have just proposed [i.e., that one can do without phrasal units, X-bar

theory, binding theory, and "a variety of other relations and interactions"]
is false—that language is highly "imperfect" in these respects, as might
well be expected. So it is no small task to show that such apparatus is
eliminable as unwanted descriptive technology; or even better, that descriptive and explanatory force are extended if such "excess baggage" is
shed. Nevertheless, I think that work of the past few years suggests that
these conclusions, which seemed out of the question a few years ago, are
at least plausible, quite possibly correct.

Yet at the time, the theorics at issue were presented as substantive claims
about the language faculty, meant to explain the language acquisition
problem. Some clarification is, therefore, in order.

Our concern here is the notion of "unwanted descriptive technology."
This notion makes good sense if it is taken to cover any formalism that is
unnecessarily complex or unnecessarily deviates from what is perceived
as the real nature of the object of inquiry or the causal forces at work in
it. Let us say that any such formalism is *perverse* in a technical methodological sense. A "perverse" formalism stands little chance of a successful realist interpretation.

It is to be observed, in this context, that sometimes the scientist is not
sure whether a law or hypothetical structure is to be interpreted in a realist or an instrumentalist spirit. In such cases the realist interpretation is
preferred as having greater explanatory force, and the scientist will look
for clues that might support a realist view. A grammarian, for example,
will be happy when it is found that a particular grammatical operation,
considered to have some explanatory force as it stands, crucially corresponds to some specific activity in the brain. In the absence of such confirmation, the scientist, if realist and not an old-style positivist, will have
to hedge the theory by leaving the question of the precise hardware interpretation open or underspecified.

But no serious scientist will present a theory or description in terms
that deviate unnecessarily from what is already known about the object
of inquiry. A scientist will always try to avoid perverse formalisms in
the sense defined above and will prefer formalisms that stand the best
chance of an eventual realist interpretation. For example, although it is
technically possible to reformulate all mathematical equations describing the movements of the planets in the solar system in geocentric terms,
making it look as if the sun and the other planets revolve around the earth,
such a description is "perverse" in that it presents the facts in a perspec-

tive that is both confusing and misleading with regard to the causal properties of the objects and phenomena described.[2]

Perhaps this is what underlies Chomsky's statement: "My own judgment is that a derivational approach is nonetheless correct, and the particular version of a minimalist program I am considering assigns it even greater prominence" (1995:223). If so, the term *correct* must be read as "non-perverse" or "standing the best chance of an eventual realist interpretation," implying that the hypothetically posited derivations of the MP do indeed somehow correspond to actual computations in the mind of competent speakers. But then note 3, expressing as it does an instrumentalist reservation, must be considered at least inappropriate. (In fact, given the poor state of our knowledge of the possible hardware implementation of specific grammatical formalisms, the grammarian's preference for a rule-based (derivational) or a constraint-based (representational) description depends largely on the extent to which the computational facilities afforded by either method serve the grammarian's purpose.)

Let us assume for the moment that, at least in *The Minimalist Program*, Chomsky holds a position of reasonable doubt between instrumentalism and possible realism, as this might seem the most favorable interpretation of his statements in that publication on the realist-instrumentalist issue. If that is so, however, the question inevitably arises of whether the MP will bear the weight, light though it may be, of that not very committing position. To find an answer to that question, we must look again at the issue of random generation or syntactic autonomy.

The question is whether Chomsky's presentation of a random sentence-generating machine is or is not perverse in the sense described earlier. Recall that in the random-generator minimalist perspective, the internalized grammar of a competent speaker is presented as a machine, possibly an "abstract machine," randomly selecting items from the lexicon to construct a sentence structure, which is then fed into a system that delivers a double output in the form of a phonetic and a semantic representation, both representations being cast as "instructions" to external performance systems—

---

2. With regard to this particular example one might say that such a "perverse" geocentric description may be justified as an account of the phenomenological way humans perceive the movements of the planets and the sun. The description would then amount to a mathematical account of certain aspects of perception. No such justification, however, can be adduced to defend the random-generator position as expressed in the MP.

a motor command system for the phonetic representation and a cognitive system for the semantic.

It is clear that if the thesis of random generation is upheld in a realist vein of any color, it is absurd, since a random-generator description unnecessarily goes against obvious causal relations. But this means that if it is upheld in a moderate instrumentalist spirit, which accepts an underlying reality but rejects any form of causal explanation, it is perverse in the sense indicated, since there is an alternative mode of presentation, in terms of a mediational position, whose chances of a successful realist interpretation are much better. On a moderate instrumentalist interpretation, therefore, the random-generator setup is equally unmotivated and unwarranted. What remains is a mathematical instrumentalist interpretation, of the kind usually found in computational linguistics. But this form of extreme instrumentalism is explicitly and (this time) unambiguously ruled out by Chomsky and has been so from about 1960.

This takes us back to the modularity issue discussed earlier. At the end of section 3.2, it was concluded that if the modularity view, which requires some form of realism, is accepted, the random-generator position, with its random lexical selection, must be given up. Now we see that the random-generator position is untenable—in fact, absurd—on *any* realist interpretation and that, moreover, a flight into instrumentalism does not help. For even if a less committing, moderate instrumentalist position is taken, the random-generator view vanishes on grounds of being both without substance and unnecessarily contrived. The random-generator view thus finds itself caught between absurdity and perversity, which means that the position of reasonable doubt is, after all, not so reasonable.

In his more recent publications, in particular Chomsky (2000, 2002) and Hauser, Chomsky, and Fitch (2002), Chomsky goes for hardware realism in a big way, insisting on as direct a link with biology as he can imagine and constantly calling in historical celebrities like Newton, Darwin, Einstein, Kepler, Descartes, Turing, and, above all, Galileo, as witnesses for the soundness of his hardware realism, despite its internal inconsistencies and lack of factual support. He even claims Galileo's authority (2002:45) to bolster his random-generator view. Unfortunately, however, as we have seen (section 1.5), Galileo does not support Chomsky's random-generator view at all. Galileo's preference is a mediational view of language, as is made clear by the very wording of the quote in question. (Nor is it likely that Galileo, or any of the other celebrities, would have agreed with Chomsky's way of sweeping relevant facts under the rug. But that is a topic for section 4.4.)

3.4 Instantaneous language evolution

Chomsky's comments about the biological plausibility of his type of minimalist grammar further commit him to a realist position with regard to the mechanisms postulated in the FoL. This is an interesting aspect, whose main outlines can be sketched as follows.

As part of his MP, Chomsky repeatedly asks "how well language is designed" while at the same time taking it for granted that "language is very well designed, perhaps close to 'perfect' in satisfying external conditions." Let us pursue this somewhat startling story in his own words (Chomsky 1998:15–17):

> We are now asking how well language is designed. How closely does language resemble what a superbly competent engineer might have constructed, given certain design specifications. . . . I suggested that the answer to the question might turn out to be that language is very well designed, perhaps close to "perfect" in satisfying external conditions. If there is any truth to this conclusion, it is rather surprising, for several reasons. First, languages have often been assumed to be such complex and defective objects as to be hardly worth studying from a stern theoretical perspective. They require reform or regimentation, or replacement by something quite different, if they are to serve some purpose other than the confused and intricate affairs of daily life. That is the leading idea that inspired traditional attempts to devise a universal perfect language, or on theological assumptions, to recover the original Adamic language; and something similar has been taken for granted in much modern work from Frege to the present. Second, *one might not expect to find such design properties in biological systems, which evolve over long periods through incremental changes under complicated and accidental circumstances, making the best of difficult and murky contingencies.* [italics mine] . . .
>
> Evolution is an opportunist, an inventor that takes whatever materials are at hand and tinkers with them, introducing slight changes so that they might work a bit better than before. . . .
>
> Human language lies well beyond the limits of serious understanding of evolutionary processes, though there are suggestive speculations. Let us add another. Suppose we make up a "Just So Story," . . . with design determined by natural law rather than bricolage through selection. Sup-

pose that there was an ancient primate with the whole human mental architecture in place, but no language faculty. The creature shared our modes
of perceptual organization, our beliefs and desires, our hopes and fears,
insofar as these are not formed and mediated by language. Perhaps it had
a "language of thought" in the sense of Jerry Fodor and others, but no
way to form linguistic expressions associated with the thoughts that this
LINGUA MENTIS makes available.

Suppose a mutation took place in the genetic instructions for the brain,
which was then reorganized in accord with the laws of physics and chemistry to install a faculty of language. Suppose the new system was, furthermore, beautifully designed, a near-perfect solution to the conditions
imposed by the general architecture of the mind-brain in which it is inserted, another illustration of how natural laws work out in wondrous ways;
or if one prefers, an illustration of how the evolutionary tinkerer could
satisfy complex design conditions with very simple tools.

To be clear, these are fables. Their only redeeming value is that they
may not be more implausible than others, and might even turn out to have
some elements of validity. The imagery serves its function if it helps us
pose a problem that could turn out to be meaningful and even significant:
basically, the problem that motivates the minimalist program, which explores the intuition that the outcome of the fable might be accurate in
interesting ways.

But what is the "outcome of the fable"? Presumably, the hypothetical
fact that "a mutation took place in the genetic instructions for the brain,
which was then reorganized in accord with the laws of physics and chemistry to install a faculty of language." But any such "mutation" bringing
about the existence of the, or a, language faculty in the human organism
would be instantaneous, and thus not the result of the long-term oppor-
tunist tinkering ascribed to evolution. In fact, Chomsky appears to invite
his reader to conclude that the FoL is not a biological system after all,
though it is not made clear what it could be if not a biological system
(Chomsky 1998:20):

> Let us turn to the question of optimality of language design: How good a
> solution is language to the general conditions imposed by the architec-
> ture of the mind/brain? This question too might be premature, but . . . it
> might have no answer at all: as I mentioned, there is no good reason to
> expect that biological systems will be well-designed in anything like this
> sense.

Where are we now? What does Chomsky actually want to say? His own
answer is as follows (Chomsky 1998:18):

Plainly, the faculty of language was not instantaneously inserted into a mind/brain with the rest of architecture fully intact. But we are now asking how well it is designed on that counterfactual assumption. How much does the abstraction distort a vastly more complex reality?

The patient reader, however, will now ask: if all we want to find out is how well the faculty of language is designed, what do we need the counterfactual assumption for, with its fabulous engineer or its miraculous intervention in nature? The reader might well feel that his or her patience is better spent on a careful analysis of (a) the function of language in communication, (b) the conditions imposed not only by the biological but also by the external physical and sociological environment in which language is used, and (c) the means afforded by language or, in other words, the nature and structure of the language faculty as it is, without any counterfactual assumptions.

Only when we have some reasonable idea of the extent to which the faculty of language is well designed can the question of the manner of its biological evolution be sensibly broached. If the faculty of language turns out to produce practical results that are not so terribly functional, an evolutionary bricolage solution may come in sight. If, on the contrary, language turns out to be extremely cleverly designed and optimally functional in the sense that no improvements seem possible, then the problem of language evolution may become comparable to the question of the evolution of those biological organs that likewise appear optimally functional, such as the vertebrate eye. All this provided, of course, that biologists come up with the expertise required for linking up entities in the cognitive language domain with biological entities. Since, however, we are still light years removed from a situation where all the answers have been found and all the conditions are fulfilled, posing questions relating to the biological aspects of language evolution must be taken to be a largely vacuous exercise, even though that is precisely what tribes of psychologists, linguists, and biologists seem to be doing at the moment, and even though their speculations are attracting an inordinate amount of popular scientific interest (see Botha 2003 for a dispassionate analysis of this curious situation). The thinking up of counterfactual assumptions appears to be simply part of this development, which is more trendy and fashionable than substantial. One should not have to waste time on it.

But let us try our patience just a little more. Let us see whether the counterfactual assumption of instantaneous language evolution might be useful as a mere thought experiment. Suppose it is found that language is, after all, not so very perfect, a result that would be independent of any counterfactual assumption of instantaneous genesis. In that case there is no point in positing an assumption of instantaneous genesis. For bricolage-type theories do a much better job in explaining non-perfect results.

Now suppose it turns out, as is anticipated by Chomsky, that language is near-perfect, likewise a result that needs no counterfactual assumption of instantaneous genesis. Given that result, what could such a counterfactual assumption add to our understanding? The answer has to be disappointing again. Suppose the hypothetical instantaneous language genesis took place through *one single mutation*, as counterfactually assumed by Chomsky. Since there is hardly a chance, and certainly no guarantee, that one single mutation would result in anything more "perfect" than a sequence of mutations would result in, the counterfactual assumption seems to do nothing on that hypothesis. Alternatively, one might think of a *set of simultaneous mutations* jointly resulting in precisely the anticipated near-perfect result. This might seem more reasonable, because it is known that the emergence of language went in tandem with adaptations of the external systems of auditory perception, motor command, and thought formation, even if Chomsky has repeatedly denied that such adaptations took place or belittled their importance (see section 1.3). Yet such a complex event is not only improbable on an apocalyptic scale, but any such assumption is nonexplanatory as well. For the chance that a set of *simultaneous* mutations jointly results in a near-perfect system is even smaller than the chance of a set of *subsequent* mutations having the same effect: when mutations are subsequent, the result of an earlier mutation may have a constraining or selective effect on a later one. In fact, that is precisely the rationale behind adaptive-selective explanations of the functionality of organs or organisms found in nature. In the case of a simultaneous conjunction of mutations, however, that factor is simply lost.

Nothing much, therefore, seems to be gained by any counterfactual assumption of instantaneous language evolution, not even as a thought experiment. The only way, it seems, that such a counterfactual assumption can make sense is in the context of creationist approaches to the genesis of language. The faculty of language would then not be the result of evolution but would have been implanted by a divine power setting off the human species from the rest of the animal kingdom. Such an external intervention in the natural process of evolution by a superior being would indeed "explain" the near-perfection of language given any theory whatsoever of natural evolution: language would simply not be part of it. Although such views cannot be ascribed to Chomsky, who has repeatedly denied being a creationist, one must at the same time concede that at times his own formulations evoke creationist associations. One reads, for example (Chomsky 1998:1):

> There is no serious reason today to challenge the Cartesian view that the ability to use linguistic signs to express freely-formed thoughts marks "the true distinction between man and animal" or machine, whether by "machine" we mean the automata that captured the imagination of the 17th and 18th century, or those that are providing a stimulus to thought and imagination today.

This, together with the suggestion of an instantaneous origin of language, and seen in conjunction with the curious terminology signaled in note 4 in this chapter, is apt to raise creationist suspicions. Chomsky, in any case, does not seem to feel that what is specifically *human* about the human species might perhaps be the result of an evolutionary process following the well-known lines of homo erectus, homo habilis, homo sapiens, and homo sapiens sapiens. Nor does he seem to feel that a being without language but in full possession of the cognitive, moral, and emotional faculties of modern man could be properly called "human."

The truth is that we do not know to what extent human language satisfies functional needs, for a double reason. First, too little is known about language in general and specific languages in particular; second, we have only a very partial view of the needs to be satisfied in human communication. From time to time one stumbles upon phenomena that seem strange or unexpected at first, but then turn out to be superbly functional with regard to a specific aspect of communication, even if one had no idea of that particular aspect to begin with, as in the case of the energy-saving devices discussed in section 3.5.9. But one also hits on phenomena whose functionality simply remains unclear for the time being or that strike one as being positively harmful to the functionalities of communication.

In sum, to the extent that we think we have a view of language, language appears to be just the kind of phenomenon one would expect in nature—surprisingly functional on the one hand, but with possible imperfections on the other—leaving us with a multitude of unanswered questions. The MP has added nothing to that insight.

3.5 An alternative view of the language faculty

In this section an attempt is made to specify what one may reasonably take to be the main outlines of the language faculty, given the best available insights today, incomplete and possibly incorrect though they no doubt are.

3.5.1 The human race without language

While trying to give an idea of what the FoL amounts to, we take a historical and implicitly evolutionary perspective that will make us investigate what must have happened between the days that the human species was still without language and the present time, the coming about of the FoL. That is, we shall try to take stock of what must have happened in the meantime that allows humans to use a language for the purpose of linguistic interaction, regardless of how or when the changes may have taken place.[3] The point of this exercise is that in trying to specify what human language is or does, we will find that even well-trained professional linguists have no more than a fragmentary and often theoretically biased overall view of their object of investigation. The contours of language are still largely out of sight, and any general description of the functions of language and of the general strategies built into language to fulfill those functions must necessarily be partial and incomplete. This applies to Chomsky's attempt at characterizing the FoL in terms of what he calls the "guiding ideas of the Minimalist Program" (1995:219), but also and with equal force to the attempt presented here.

It is widely accepted that about 150,000 years ago the human race was not in possession of what we now call human language (though forms of protolanguage cannot be excluded), but that its intellectual powers were already fairly well developed. Let us take that to be correct, and assume

---

3. The questions of *how* and *when* the FoL has become part of the genetic endowment of the human species are the object of a "neo-Darwinian" debate that has been going on for some time (e.g., Piattelli-Palmarini 1989, Pinker and Bloom 1990, Uriagereka 1998:1–87, Hauser, Chomsky, and Fitch 2002). Unfortunately, this debate suffers from an excess of highfalutin but speculative generalizations without empirical bite, as well as from a lack of mutual expertise on the part of the linguists, biologists, psychologists, and philosophers who participate in it. Mostly, however, it is flawed by the fact that the logically prior question of *what* has become part of the human genetic endowment has not been answered yet. See Botha (1997a, 1997b, 1998a, 1998b, 1999, 2003) for ample comment.

that primeval man was capable of postulating causal relations, on the basis of implicit inductive "theories" formed about the environment. These theories were no doubt often quite wild and uncontrolled, and full of magic in the sense that unnatural causes were assumed to explain natural phenomena, but they were theories.

We also take it that primeval man was good at forming propositional thoughts. This means that he had the capacity to construct mental representations in which a certain property is assigned to some entity or entities, and to project such representations in the past, the present, or the future. In addition, he had some, though perhaps not always correct, idea, not only of what would follow causally if he implemented a plan but also of what was, had been, or would be the case when any of his propositional thoughts were true. That is, in addition to his (still somewhat erratic) notion of causality, he had some idea of truth and entailment.

Finally, we assume, he had a sense of social responsibility. He knew that he had a position in his clan and his village, that he was responsible for carrying out certain tasks, and that there would be sanctions if he were to be found guilty of misbehavior, negligence, or deceit. But, as we have said, he had no language.

These assumptions are, one may take it, shared by Chomsky, at least if one is to attach significance to what he presents as a "fable" (Chomsky 1998:17), quoted earlier but repeated here:[4]

> Suppose that there was an ancient primate with the whole human mental architecture in place, but no language faculty. The creature shared our modes of perceptual organization, our beliefs and desires, our hopes and fears, insofar as these are not formed and mediated by language. Perhaps it had a "language of thought" in the sense of Jerry Fodor and others, but no way to form linguistic expressions associated with the thoughts that his LINGUA MENTIS makes available.

Exactly how much significance is to be attached to this fable is not made explicit. All we have is the text that immediately follows the passage just quoted (Chomsky 1998:17):

> Suppose a mutation took place in the genetic instructions for the brain, which was then reorganized in accord with the laws of physics and

---

4. One notes the terminology: Chomsky prefers to speak of a "primate" or "creature" and uses the pronominal form *it* to refer to the primeval human conjured up in his "fable." The biological-evolutionary aspect of this "fable" is commented on in section 3.4.

chemistry to install a faculty of language. Suppose the new system was, furthermore, beautifully designed, a near-perfect solution to the conditions imposed by the general architecture of the mind-brain in which it is inserted, another illustration of how natural laws work out in wondrous ways; or if one prefers, an illustration of how the evolutionary tinkerer could satisfy complex design conditions with very simple tools.

To be clear, these are fables. Their only redeeming value is that they may not be more implausible than others, and might even turn out to have some elements of validity. The imagery serves its function if it helps us pose a problem that could turn out to be meaningful and even significant: basically, the problem that motivates the minimalist program, which explores the intuition that the outcome of the fable might be accurate in interesting ways.

Yet, despite the evasive manner in which this fable is presented, there seems to be enough common ground to proceed on the assumption that it makes sense to imagine a primeval human being with most of the cognitive powers and the motor-perceptual machinery in place but without language. (Significantly, imagining the opposite—a being in full possession of language but without either the cognitive or the motor-perceptual equipment required for its use—does not seem to make any sense at all.) This is sufficient for it to be agreed that the attempt to sketch the outlines of the FoL by setting off primeval man without language against modern man with language may be helpful in gaining a sharper idea of what the FoL must amount to. We shall see in the following discussion that in some cases the way the FoL took shape appears to have some degree of functional rationale, whereas in other cases either the possible functionality of the development is lost on us or the development appears to be counterfunctional.

3.5.2 Peripheral features: sound, speech, audition

When one tries to specify what human language is or does, a few features stand out immediately. First, sound—rather than visual stimuli— has clearly been selected as the primary medium for the transmission of propositional thoughts. Prima facie this makes considerable sense. For visual communication requires light, and light is available only half the time, while sound propagates well under almost any conditions and can be reinforced by the echo of woods or mountains. Moreover, sound spreads in three dimensions and reaches even the unattentive ear, while images require an uninterrupted rectilinear path from the object seen to the perceiving optical organ, the eye, which has to focus before it allows one to see. But sound also has its drawbacks. Not only is sound heard also when it is not supposed to be, but, more important, it vanishes without a trace, whereas visible objects usually have greater permanency. Writing systems were thus developed in certain cultures in the recent past (the first writing systems came about a mere five thousand years ago) to give some permanency to speech (or to communicate without sound). Moreover, gestural or sign languages have either grown up or been designed for special purposes—for example, to enable deaf people to communicate by means of a language. But, clearly, the primary medium is sound.

In connection with this, one notes that some parts of the human anatomy have changed. The glottis has descended a little, leaving a larger resonance cavity in the vocal tract and allowing for clearer distinctions among vowels (Lieberman 1984, Miller 1991:74). Also, the auditory organ has changed somewhat: the inner ear, in particular, has become maximally sensitive to sounds within a restricted range of amplitude and frequency, so that it has optimal discrimination power for precisely the sounds produced by the articulatory organs for the purpose of speech.[5]

3.5.3 Internal organization: double articulation

Apart from these more or less peripheral changes, a great many things appear to have happened internally, in the brain. These one may try to single out and characterize, even if the physiological details or the evolutionary processes involved are largely opaque. It is here that one finds the central features of the human language faculty, or FoL. We surmise that the FoL is best taken to be a machinery that is self-contained or isolated to a considerable extent, fleshed out as a lexicon-cum-grammar set of modules when a specific language is acquired. The FoL machinery, moreover, has been grafted onto existing cognitive and motor-perceptual systems, though obviously not without a notable amount of adaptation on the part of the latter.

Since the first task of the (fleshed out) FoL is to enable humans to transduce propositional thoughts into perceptible form and vice versa, and

---

5. There is some uncertainty as to the degree to which the motor and the perceptual systems are separate systems or coincide. See Miller (1991:81–82) for some comment.

since the number of possible propositional thoughts is unlimited (denumerably infinite), the FoL must provide the means to supply an infinite number of formally different strings of symbols. Nature's way of making the FoL discharge that task is of a stunning simplicity and functionality.

The FoL first makes the language-using subjects build up a small repertory of perhaps between ten and eighty individual speech sound types (phonemes), which can be realized in the vocal tract and identified by the auditory system. Combinations of phonemes are then used to mark the concepts that capture the properties assigned to entities in propositional thoughts, and hence to label the predicates (lexical items) that form the lexicon of the language in question. The lexical items can then again be combined into larger units called sentences.

This two-tiered system of combination—first of phonemes into lexical items, and then of lexical items into sentences—is traditionally called the *double articulation* of human language. Clearly, since there is no theoretically imposed upper limit to the length of either lexical items or sentences, the number of possible combinations afforded by this system is mathematically unlimited (denumerably infinite), which is precisely what is required. In practical terms, of course, there are limits to the length of a lexical item or a sentence, but the number of lexical items and the number of sentences allowed for within such practical limits turn out to be amply sufficient for the expression of any thought a human speaker might want to express, owing also to the possibility of capturing a great deal of semantic content in specific lexical items by means of often complex satisfaction conditions, and owing to energy-saving devices such as those discussed here in section 3.5.9.

3.5.4 A specific language is a mediating device

In essence, the FoL appears to be an extension added to already available cognitive faculties, enabling a linkup with mechanisms that produce and perceive sounds. But the FoL itself is not sufficient to produce or interpret speech. It is not possible to use the faculty of language in the way one uses air to breathe or water to drink. Unlike air or water, language cannot be used as such: it has to be instantiated ("fleshed out") first as a particular language. In each speech act some particular language is used, a specimen of the species "natural human language." The FoL is not ready for use but is, rather, a brain structure that needs to be triggered and stimulated in order to grow into a machinery that actually carries over purely cognitive and barely graspable propositional thoughts into a shape that allows for direct vocalization, and hence perception and comprehension by fellow humans. Since children born into a language community acquire the language of the environment infallibly within a few years of their birth and according to a largely preset acquisition program, regardless of race, intelligence, or other parameters, it would seem that the FoL has somehow become part of the genetic endowment of the human species.

The FoL has all the characteristics of a genetic endowment containing a blueprint for a mediating device that forms a link between already available cognitive capacities on the one hand and a pair of peripheral machineries on the other—a motor command system for outgoing signals and a perceptual machinery for incoming signals. A fully developed mediating device makes it possible to represent certain cognitive processes in a form that is perceptible and comprehensible to other persons. In principle, the FoL specifies a possible procedure for the mapping of thought structures onto perceptual-motor specifications and vice versa. Although both the cognitive faculties and the peripheral apparatus required for an FoL can function without an FoL, it is obvious that they will be much more effective with one.

What is called the *grammar* of a specific language is a central part of this mediating device. Seen from the production point of view, a thought structure is cast first into a "deep" linguistic mold called *semantic analysis* (SA), built up from elements taken from the lexicon. An SA is already a linguistic (tree) structure, but, unlike surface structures, it is semantically regular and computable (which means that it is built up according to the principles underlying the language of modern Predicate Calculus). At this point the grammar comes into action. The grammar *transforms* the SA tree structure into a surface tree structure according to a universally and typologically restricted rule system. The grammar is thus, in a technical sense, a *transformational grammar*: it transforms tree structures into tree structures. The output of the grammar is a tree structure whose branch-terminal items are provided with a recipe for acoustic realization, including a specification for an envelope intonational contour.

The FoL thus appears to be implementable in an infinite variety of ways in the shape of sociologically shared systems called *languages*, each language allowing for internal variations organized in *dialects* that usually function in relation to the overarching language.

3.5.5 Competence is a biologically restricted module

3.5.5.1 At least four interfaces for output monitoring.

We assume that competence in a particular language, once it has developed according to the language acquisition program set by the FoL, is concentrated in a grammar module in something like the sense of Fodor (1983). What is implied by this notion of modularity has been set out earlier, especially in section 3.2. It was argued there that an analysis of the points at which a speaker/hearer has conscious access to the machinery of language leads to the conclusion that the human language faculty, when crystallized into a specific language, consists of two modules—lexicon and grammar— each equipped with an output gate for conscious monitoring, and that there are at least two further output gates: one connecting thought with the lexicon, and one connecting sound or writing with the corresponding organism-external physical world. As has been said, this gives at least four interfaces, or gates, the possibility of further internal interfaces being left open:

1. The *thought interface*, passing on thought output to the lexicon;
2. The *lexical interface*, passing on structured lexical output to the grammar;
3. The *grammatical interface*, passing on grammatical output to the physical realization systems of speaking or writing;
4. The *perceptual interface*, passing on phonetic or written output to the outside environment through the medium of sound or material receiving written symbols, respectively.

The cognitive output consists of the proposition to be expressed (in its context) in combination with the social commitment taken on by the speaker (see section 3.5.7). The lexical output consists in the lexical items selected. The grammatical output consists in the surface form of the sentence generated: the grammar module simply "prints out" the SA-input as a corresponding surface structure. The phonetic or symbolic output contains a sound or writing recipe for pronunciation or writing.

Close analysis (see Levelt 1989:470, 1999, Cutler and Clifton 1999:152–155) reveals that these four interfaces are probably the only places in the procedures of sentence production (and comprehension if that is a process of reconstruction-by-hypothesis) where the speaker can exert control or make a choice, or where the listener registers conscious information. (This also means that feedback lines to earlier inputs must be built into the machinery, as is emphasized by the authors cited.) Obviously, a speaker is, in principle, in control of the semantic content expressed (complete with the speech act commitment mentioned in section 3.5.7), which is duly registered by the listener. Moreover, given the overall semantic content to be expressed, lexical choice is likewise open to some variation, where choices often have emotional, interpersonal, or social values registered by the attentive listener. Then, speakers may be assumed to have a possibly conscious idea of the sentence that they are about to produce. And last, speakers have some control over the way a sentence is to be pronounced, in that there is a choice of possible pronunciations usually signaling, again, emotional, interpersonal, or social attitudes, which are then duly picked up by listeners—and analogously for the writing process. That the use of language appears to be open to possible awareness and introspection at at least these four gates or interfaces, whereas all the rest of the processing takes place "underground" (with further possible interfaces, to be determined in terms of specific theories), is a further indication of the modular character of the lexical and transformation devices that define each human language.[6]

3.5.5.2 Production versus comprehension.   It is often thought that, in the case of linguistic competence, there are two closely interrelated modules: one for the production of outgoing linguistic messages and one for the comprehension of incoming messages. Yet the relation between the two alleged (sub)modules is still largely unclear (Levelt 1999:113). Most work in theoretical grammar has concentrated on top-down generation, which naturally translates into the production aspect, while most work in semantics and in computational linguistics has taken an interpretative point of view. In psycholinguistics, those who work on comprehension

---

6. This account agrees in main outlines with what is proposed in Jackendoff (2002:196–205) as a model for the "logical direction of language production" but not as a model for linguistic competence. It is not entirely clear to me what, in Jackendoff's view, a model of competence should do, over and above the processing model that he endorses. If a competence model merely specifies, in an "abstract" way, what structures are legitimate at the phonological, syntactic, and semantic levels, then the question arises if that particular task is not already achieved, by definition, by an explicit processing model. If, on the other hand, his competence model is meant to have psychological reality, all sorts of problems arise, in particular the problem of linking up structures at the three levels as belonging together as the expression of one given thought (the linking problem). Simply dropping that notion of competence seems the most rational way out. That, however, would turn Jackendoff's analysis into a mediational theory—a development that would be most welcome.

and those who work on production form largely distinct communities, a state of affairs that some feel calls for correction.

Despite the prevailing uncertainty, however, there are reasons for assuming that the comprehension or "parsing" process of utterances, to the extent that it amounts to a reconstruction of the underlying SA-structure, is essentially an input-constrained process of reconstruction-by-hypothesis, or analysis-by-synthesis, involving frequent tacit appeals to general knowledge in ways that are unclear and certainly beyond present limits of algorithmic (modular) modeling.

It seems to me that there are at least three good reasons for thinking that this is probably the case. First, an analysis of the points of conscious access and control (monitoring) during the processes of production and comprehension indicates a top-down rather than a bottom-up flow. This is implicit in the fact that (self-)monitoring as a known psycholinguistic process is *output* monitoring, not *input* monitoring. The monitoring always retraces the top-down path, which would indicate that the grammar module is set in production mode.

Second, the fact that multiple possible scope and other relational analyses for logical and prepositional operators and argument terms are normally resolved immediately, without any apparent loss of time, suggests that an early identification of key lexical items (Cutler and Clifton 1999:124, 142), with the corresponding concepts, makes the listener jump to a reconstruction of the most likely relevant scope and predicate-argument relations in the underlying thought structure, given available background and contextual knowledge, and, of course, given certain syntactic or morphological clues. The early availability of the key lexical items occurring in an utterance entering the system for comprehension, together with a plausible initial semantic structure in which they have found a place, automatically sets into motion the grammar module, which cannot help delivering ("printing") a surface-structure output.

Third, adequate real-life comprehension of uttered sentences often takes place despite defective input or despite insufficient knowledge of the language in question on the part of the listener. Such forms of comprehension make it unlikely that comprehension is an automatic algorithmic procedure. The notion of reconstruction-by-hypothesis seems much more appropriate. Normal speech comprehension is like lipreading, only better supported, and hence more strongly constrained, by sensory data.

Townsend and Bever (2001:160–172) present in essence the same view: utterance comprehension is, in principle, a process of reconstruction-by-hypothesis, or, as they call it, analysis-by-synthesis. This view harks back to old theories of motor-driven phoneme perception, developed in the Haskins Laboratory during the 1960s, and extends them to early recognition of lexical items and, hence, to automatic grammatical generation. The setting up of the cognitive configuration in which the concepts corresponding to the lexical items occur is taken to be guided in part by structural morphosyntactic clues and, in large part, also by knowledge of plausible scenarios.

These authors, however, present their analysis-by-synthesis theory of utterance comprehension as "entirely consistent with the minimalist syntactic model" of Chomsky (1995), which, in their view, comes out as "a rather compelling model" (Townsend and Bever 2001:178–179). The rationale underlying this position is that they consider the numeration N, which is the starting point of a minimalist syntactic derivation, to be naturally provided by the comprehension system as soon as the lexical items have been individuated. Yet this is a little too quick, for the minimalist model still utterly fails as a production model, although that is precisely the prerequisite for an analysis-by-synthesis model of comprehension. In the setup proposed by Townsend and Bever, the "synthesis" is driven lexically by the lexical items found but configurationally—or cognitively— by scenario knowledge, a state of affairs which is totally at odds with minimalism but in full agreement with mediationalism.

All this makes it doubtful whether the concept of modularity applies to the parsing process at all. Given these uncertainties, we shall, provisionally, speak of the grammar module as of one undivided whole, which is set in the production mode and thus naturally modeled as a production algorithm.[7]

---

7. Kempson, Meyer-Viol, and Gabbay defend the opposite view. They start their book by saying (2001:1):

> Knowing a language means being able to segment sounds in that language into units, recover information from those units, and use this information to work out what someone communicating in that language has intended to convey. This statement about what it means to know a language might seem such common sense as to be banal.

Here, the concept of knowledge of (competence in) a language is reduced to the comprehension mode, the production mode being left out completely. This is as one-sided

3.5.5.3 Animal communication. The fact that some animal species have developed genetically fixed systems of communication, whereas other species have not, is a further illustration of the biologically fixed modularity of signaling systems. Many species of animals, such as cats, dogs, or horses, are evidently capable of forming propositional thoughts in the sense described (though these are likely to be more restricted and more domain-specific than the ones produced by humans), but they have no adequate language to communicate their thoughts. Other species, on the contrary, such as bees or finches, whose cognitive specializations and degrees and kinds of intelligence differ greatly from each other and from other animal species, do appear to have developed restricted communication systems which, clearly, do not qualify as human languages but certainly satisfy some essential needs and have obvious survival value. Finches even seem to have specific group-restricted "languages" that have to be acquired on the basis of some innate "language" faculty for finches (Catchpole 1994). It thus seems that animals of the latter category have developed modules enabling them to externalize forms of knowledge or information, whereas the species without any form of language happen not to have done so. The evolutionary growth of a device to externalize cognitive products of a certain nature thus does not seem to be a function of highly developed propositionally organized general intelligence. On the contrary, it seems to be largely independent of the type of intelligence found in the higher vertebrates, which leaves us with the question of what in the nature of certain species brings about the growth of such an externalizing device. Is it social structure, possibly in combination with environmental conditions? We do not know.

---

a view as the opposite one in which comprehension is ignored. Curiously, the blunt statement that their view is "such common sense as to be banal" is implicitly denied by the same authors later on in the same book (Kempson et al. 2001:267):

Nothing we have defined bears any relation to the production process. Production has to be characterized as in some way parasitic on the process of parsing. This is arguably not implausible; but at this juncture, we leave the debate to others, merely noting that a re-evaluation of the competence-performance distinction is demanded in view of the asymmetry between the relation between the grammar and parsing on the one hand and the grammar and production on the other.

Apparently, the authors' views on what constitutes "banal common sense" have changed over the intervening 266 pages.

3.5.6 Lexical predicates and L-propositional structure

It also appears that the possession of a language makes speakers cast their thoughts in rather more precise molds. One may surmise that, before the advent of language, thoughts were only vaguely graspable, just as one now feels introspectively that "thought before language," though real, somehow lacks clarity. What without language is seen, so to speak, through a glass darkly, is seen clearly and distinctly once it has been molded into a linguistic form.

This applies with particular force to concepts, the cognitive units corresponding to the properties assigned to entities in the mental act of a proposition. With language, often still quite dim general concepts come out as lexical predicates, which are far richer and more specialized, probably because labeling leads to the demand for more precise distinctions and for a specification of the conditions of use. First, lexical predicates are defined by fairly definite sets of satisfaction conditions that entities of whatever kind must satisfy to deserve them (their semantic definition). For the most part, these satisfaction conditions are not logically or model-theoretically rigid but are subject to psychologically determined forms of prototypicality, depending on the entities to which the predicates in question are applied. Thus, the predicate *flat* has different, but cognitively related, satisfaction conditions when applied to a mountain than when applied to a car tire. This internal semantic flexibility of lexical predicates has been, and still is, the object of a great deal of linguistic and psycholinguistic research. We shall see, moreover, in sections 3.5.9 and 7.3, that the satisfaction conditions of predicates consist in part of *preconditions* that generate presuppositions—that is, conditions for use in context.

Second, lexical predicates are provided with a sound recipe for acoustic transmission (their phonological definition). Third, they carry with them instructions for particular syntactic constructions, usually involving a subject term, often also a direct object, and sometimes even an indirect object or prepositional object term as well (their syntactic definition or argument structure). Fourth, lexical items or predicates are often marked for certain syntactic or morphological features involving rules or idiosyncratic form properties. Fifth, lexical predicates, often in conjunction with their phonological definition and their rule or form properties, are marked for their sociolinguistic and stylistic registers.

Lexical predicates differ considerably from language to language, and from period to period, partly due to different concepts and needs that have arisen in the speech communities in question. Two hundred years ago, for example, French did not have the predicate *alunir* (make a moonlanding). Differences in argument structures are demonstrated in the following example. Comparing English and German, one sees that the prelinguistic thought roughly approximated as (1), though it probably is no more than a mere inarticulate awareness of the corresponding fact, comes out as, respectively, (2a) or (2b). These express the same propositional thought but cast into very different lexical and grammatical forms:

(1)   Legal liability for illicit killing of fellow humans does not disappear over time.

(2)   a. There is no statutory limitation on murder.
        b. Mord verjährt nicht.
           (roughly: 'Murder does not superannuate')

It is as if the selection of the proper predicate, *statutory limitation* or *verjähren*, is made according to some "thesaurus" method, more or less as follows. Having a thought that is to be expressed means that one has an idea of what property one assigns to what entities. To find a proper linguistic predicate for the property to be expressed one goes, so to speak, to one's lexical thesaurus (the mental lexicon) that stocks the lexical predicates of one's language. With the help of a mental "index," one quickly finds the proper department, where the relevant lexical items are stored: color terms, terms for locomotion, terms for mental processes, and so on. Some being more appropriate for this, others for that, specific purpose, one makes what seems the best choice for the purpose at hand. Since different languages have different collections on offer, translation will be hazardous at times.

Selecting the main lexical predicate provides a syntactic argument frame, whose term positions can be filled by actual terms which, in principle, refer to the entity or entities to which one wants to assign the property expressed by the predicate. By this time one has something which may be called an incipient *L-propositional structure*, representing a state of affairs that has arisen in the mind, but no longer in the nameless, indefinable way of prelinguistic thoughts.

However, the L-proposition is far from complete yet; it needs to be fitted out with the proper temporal, modal, quantificational, and other operators or "hedges" to restrict the applicability of the L-proposition the speaker wants to get across. But we shall leave these more technical aspects of sentence formation undiscussed here.

3.5.7 Speech act commitment

Even with the proper temporal, modal, quantificational, and other operators, the L-proposition is not ready yet for transmission by speech. Nature has made it mandatory for every linguistic utterance to contain an indication of the speaker's *personal commitment* with regard to the state of affairs represented in the L-proposition. It is impossible for a speaker to transmit just the image of a state of affairs, as in a drawing or a mime. Speakers have to manifest at the same time, in any of a large array of variations, (a) whether they *guarantee* the truth of the representation (assertion); or (b) their *opinion* or *attitude* with regard to the state of affairs represented (exclamation, suggestion, wish, expression of abhorrence); or (c) whether they *appeal* to the addressee to assert its truth value (yes/no-question), or to specify the value of a variable (WH-question); or (d) whether they wish to ensure that the state of affairs represented is actually implemented (imperative, request).

The point is that every seriously used speech utterance necessarily adds to an interpersonal or social network of obligations, appeals, and position-takings, in virtue of a speech act operator and other elements built into the prospective utterance one way or another. There is no use of language without some form of social commitment, which is structurally built into the linguistic form used. This fact is one of the strongest indications that language is primarily meant not for the mere communication of factual world-related information but for the establishment of social or interpersonal relations with regard to states of affairs represented in L-propositions, as well as for social "grooming" (Levelt 1999:83; see also the end of section 5.4).

It therefore makes sense to regard *linguistic communication as primarily a process whereby a speaker manifests his or her social commitment with regard to the proposition expressed, or whereby a listener registers the commitment taken on by the speaker.* Nonlinguistic communication is a fairly open-ended notion, encompassing virtually any form of outward behavior, intentional or nonintentional, that is in any way informative, including frowning, smiling, sweating, looking away, or playing with hands—in short, "body language." But linguistic communication can be defined rather precisely with the help of the notions of speech act and L-proposition. On each occasion that a serious and felicitous linguistic utterance is made, linguistic communication takes place, which means that a new element of *social* or *interpersonal reality* is created, which, as one knows, may have serious, even legally binding, consequences for the speaker.

The combination of a speech act operator with an L-propositional structure is what we call a *semantic analysis* or SA. An SA is an instrument made available by the language in question for the socially binding expression of a thought.

In all varieties of Chomskyan linguistics that have appeared over the years, the speech act factor has been totally or almost totally neglected. This has had a crippling effect on Chomsky's entire view of language and its functionality in use, in particular as regards the relation between language and communication (see section 5.4 for further comment).

3.5.8 The transformational grammar

Once the lexical choices have been made and the items and operators selected have been cast into an L-propositional structure and the speech act component has been added, we have the SA, a hierarchical tree structure of immediate and remote constituents ending in a string of lexical and functional elements. This structure should allow for vocalization, provided each of the ultimate elements is fitted out with a sound recipe and there is an envelope intonation for the structure as a whole. One might expect that all one had to do now is simply follow the sound recipes and actually pronounce the string of items in the proper order and under the right overall intonational pattern. In fact, on what Chomsky calls "minimalist assumptions," now applied to mediational grammar, one might expect that the SA level of representation alone suffices to serve the purpose at hand, in that it expresses thoughts with the help of lexical items, provided with sound or writing recipes.

But language turns out not to be that simple. Nature has apparently decided that SAs, complete with their speech act and other operators, have to be transformed into "surface structures" before they can be fed into a phonological component. Why this should be so, is not clear. Perhaps it has to do with requirements imposed by the need for rapid acoustic, and therefore largely serial, transmission of multilayered SA-form. Perhaps the relatively "flat" surface structures are easier to handle for the recognition and parsing mechanisms at work in the processing of utterances. But as long as next to nothing is known about the actual functioning of these mechanisms, one can only speculate as to why a device is needed to transform SAs into surface structures.

In any case, the facts are unambiguous. As is shown in section 8.2, languages are replete with copying ("spread") phenomena, negation copying no doubt being the most frequent. Moreover, languages apply all kinds of processes in structurally well-defined ways, as is shown by the various forms of conjunction reduction, of cliticization of weak pronouns and weak adverbials, of extraposing or preposing of major constituents for a variety of reasons, often to do with discourse structure, of rule-governed or idiosyncratic deletions, and so on. Quantifiers, modals, tenses, and other clausal operators usually do not appear in an operator position but are most often incorporated into the matrix-S—that is, the lexical nuclear part of the SA-structure without any higher operators—according to certain principles. This may cause scope ambiguities, as in:

(3)   I didn't eat bread for two weeks.

This sentence is ambiguous between the readings 'it is not the case that for two weeks I ate bread' and 'for two weeks it was not the case that I ate bread': the same predicate-argument structure but with the operators 'not' and 'for two weeks' with different semantic scopes, and hence in different SA-positions. SA-form avoids this ambiguity, as it specifies operator scope.

Since observations of this kind can be multiplied at will, one must conclude that nature, in her wisdom, has made the FoL in such a way that it requires a device to transform SAs into corresponding well-formed surface structures and vice versa, even if the reason why is not obvious, and even if such transformation may create ambiguities. Speakers who have a command of their language take this device, their grammar, implicitly into account when they interpret utterances.

Formally speaking, a grammar is a rule system that defines the format of SA-structures and maps them onto surface structures. The theory of grammar tries to reconstruct these grammatical rule systems in optimally explanatory ways. However, it must be added immediately that real life implementations of grammars are clearly fitted out with a number of auxiliary or accessory pieces enhancing rapid and efficient processing. There are clear indications, for example, that ample use is made of memory-based routines that process chunks of information directly, without rule-governed analysis or synthesis, and that the analyses and syntheses that do take place do so in a stepwise or "cascade" fashion, allowing the mechanism to start processing a new input while the previous input is still being processed (Kempen and Hoenkamp 1987). The existence of such "accessories," however, does not affect the unifying and explanatory role of an adequate description of the underlying rule systems.

3.5.9 Energy-saving devices

Nature has built into the FoL a number of strategies that help speakers cut down on vocalization. A great deal of what one wants to say can be left unsaid, because, somehow, the other party already knows. One strategy consists in an appeal to available *world knowledge*, which seems to be restricted to the lexicon. For example, each language has a set of "possession" predicates (*have, lack, with, without, of*, dative or genitive case, etc.). These are not very well defined as to the precise conditions that entities A and B have to meet for it to be said in truth that "A has B" or "A is with(out) B." Instead of relying on precise satisfaction conditions, they imply an appeal to general world knowledge that speakers are supposed to possess. Consider, for example, the following two sentences:

(4)   a. That hotel room has a shower.

       b. That student has a supervisor.

For (4a) to be true it has to be the case that the room in question has its own private shower in or near it. Sentence (4a) is legally and conversationally false if the room has to share a shower. But having to share a supervisor does not affect the legal or conversational truth of (4b). What, then, is the meaning of the predicate *have*? Does it or does it not require a one-to-one relationship between the referents of the subject and the object term for it to be used truthfully? The answer would seem to be that *have* and other possession predicates are understood as symbolizing a relation of belonging together *in a manner already known* for the classes of objects involved. Failing that condition, the predicate is insufficiently specified, with the result that a sentence containing such a predicate is uninterpretable. Thus, a sentence like (5) makes sense only if it has been specified beforehand what it is for a house to have front tires (and what it is for a tire to be ripe):

(5)   John couldn't sell his house because its front tires were ripe.

This phenomenon is quite general. World knowledge is required, for example, for a proper interpretation of the predicate *round* in, say, *a round face* or *a round table*, or for the predicate *false* in, for example, *a false statement* and *false teeth*. It is functional in that it allows for a great many things to be left unsaid, thus making for a considerable saving of energy. A further energy-saving device is *presupposition*. Sentence meanings usually involve presuppositions. A sentence like (6a) has the presupposition, induced by the predicate *divorced*, that John has been married before. And (6b) informs the listener of more than Ben's absence because of his being drunk. It also says that Ben is a habitual drinker, owing to the presupposition induced by the word *again*:

(6) a John is divorced.
    b. Why didn't Ben turn up? Was he drunk again?

These presuppositions need not be made explicit, since they are recoverable from the sentences in question, which thus contain more propositional information than just the L-propositional content.

The tacit insertion of presuppositional information before the addition of the L-propositional content to the discourse domain is called *accommodation*, or *post hoc insertion*. This process is not only induced by the semantic properties of lexical items and constructions of the presupposition-carrying sentence but is also monitored by available world knowledge. This is particularly clear in the case of those existential presuppositions where the existence of an entity is presupposed in some "possessive" relation. Sentence (5) is a case in point. Although it presupposes that John's house had front tires, this presupposition cannot be inserted post hoc as long as there is no plausible cognitive scenario that explains what front tires do with regard to houses.

We say that an "occasion sentence" *S* (the term is due to Quine 1960) is *well-anchored* in a context C if C satisfies all conditions for full interpretability of *S*. This means, first, that all referring expressions in *S* must have a unique entity representation in the discourse domain at hand: all definite determiners must be associated with a denotation function that is rich enough to select a unique entity representation in the discourse domain. This denotation function cannot be compositional in the accepted sense (i.e., deriving its values from the structure of the sentence and a semantic description of its lexical items alone), but depends on contextual information. Contextual anchoring also requires that presuppositions of sentences can be properly accommodated (inserted post hoc) without being stopped by contextual contradictions or insufficient knowledge backing. (For an elaborate exposé of contextual anchoring, see Seuren 2000 and Seuren et al. 2001.)

It may be so that, as a matter of principle, all contextual and situational information required can be supplied in terms of sentences that need no contextual anchoring, and hence no specific reference relations or "situational keying" (Quine's "eternal sentences"), but that would mean an enormous increase in actual vocalization, and thus in energy and time consumption. Russell's (1905) and Quine's (1960) program of "elimination of particulars" from a logical language by reformulating all occasion sentences as eternal sentences that need no contextual anchoring and no specific reference relations may have been motivated by a desire to avoid logical complications, since no logical account has so far been provided of occasion sentences (but see Seuren et al. 2001), yet it lacks the support of natural language, which makes a very clever use of contextual anchoring devices precisely for the purpose of saving time and energy.

This particular aspect of language—its intrinsic context-dependency with the functional corollary of energy-saving—has been badly neglected in modern theorizing about language. It has been almost totally neglected in Chomsky's linguistic theorizing, and this neglect has severely impaired his notion of what constitutes a well-designed or "perfect" language.[8] It is clear that this has an overall vitiating effect on the entire minimalist program, insofar as it seeks to define the minimal means required by any specific language as well as by the general language faculty to satisfy the purposes for which they were made.

A further device for saving energy is the use of externally anaphoric pronominal expressions, such as the expression *he* in (7):

(7)   There is a man at the door. *He* is drunk.

Given the large amount of literature on the manifold aspects of sentence-external (and sentence-internal) anaphora, this topic will remain undiscussed here. All that needs to be said is, first, that, like presupposition, anaphora has caused severe problems for the Russell-Quine program of reducing all occasion sentences to eternal sentences (one thinks in particular of the famous problem of the "donkey-sentences"), and,

---

8. There is a passing mention of the discourse-dependency of sentences in Chomsky (1972:100), in connection with the notion of presupposition, but there has been no follow-up of this extremely fruitful area of research in any of his later writings. Now it seems to have been completely forgotten.

second, that, again like presupposition, anaphora clearly is another energy-saving device available to human language, providing further evidence for the intrinsic context-dependency of natural language sentences. Then there is the fact that natural language is thoroughly *object-oriented* in the sense common in computer science. Language has a knack of treating as quasi-objects whatever corresponds to a complex thought construct that would require an inordinate amount of vocalization if spelled out fully. Thus one speaks of "the military-industrial complex," "the end of the day," "the temperature," or "John's envy" as if these were real objects with ontological existence, although one knows they are not. This process of *reification* allows speakers to manipulate complex mental constructs with the ease with which one refers to single objects.

It is clear that appeals to world knowledge in the lexicon, the devices of contextual anchoring by means of presupposition and anaphora, and object-orientedness or reification make for huge savings in overt speech energy. The actual pronunciation of a sentence, no matter how easy and rapid it may appear to the superficial observer, requires a considerable amount of processing and thus of time and energy (for the articulatory aspect alone, the chapter "Articulating" in Levelt 1989:413–457 gives some idea of what is involved). Any device, therefore, that saves on this aspect of communication must be highly valued.

3.5.10 Language-specific semantic checklists

The FoL, moreover, allows for devices that do the opposite of energy-saving. Such devices are not universal but are available to specific languages or language groups. This in itself is an interesting point: it seems that the functionality found in human language is expressed mainly in its universal features, whereas the features that strike one as counter-functional are typically language-specific.

Tense is a case in point. In some language groups, represented by, for example, Malay or Chinese, tense is not at all or hardly expressed. It is left to the listener to infer the time of the event or state of affairs described in the L-proposition on grounds of contextual or situational clues. In most other languages, however, tense must be expressed, often with all kinds of subtle distinctions and under language-specific constraints, even if the semantic nuances expressed are easily filled in by an appeal to situational or world knowledge. Aspect is necessarily expressed in the Slavonic languages, but not in the Germanic and Romance languages. In some languages, such as Spanish, a distinction is made, for copulative sentences, between "essential" and "contingent" properties, whereas that distinction need not be expressed in most other languages. Many languages require, one way or another, an indication of the social distance between speaker and listener, whereas other languages do without such a distinction. For many languages it has to be specified whether what is described in the L-proposition is instantaneous or comes about gradually, or (when set in the past) whether it is set in a distant or a recent past, or whether it is hearsay or direct evidence, et cetera, whereas such questions are irrelevant for other languages.

In fact, it looks as if each language has a kind of *checklist* to be completed by a speaker before an SA-structure of a sentence can be planned. These checklists differ considerably from language to language, which again may make translation, and certainly automatic translation, hard to achieve. The "questions" of the checklist have to be answered, on pain of ungrammaticality, even when the answers can be derived from factual, contextual, or situational knowledge. A maximally economical language would automatically scrap all questions whose answers are derivable from external sources, but there does not seem to be any such universal tendency in human languages. On the contrary, next to language-specific economy measures, one also finds many developments that lead to increased complexity. Efficiency is obviously not the sole criterion for socially acceptable communication. (For further comment see sections 5.6 and 5.7.)

3.6 Conclusion

In conclusion one may say that the guiding ideas of Chomsky's MP are far from "conceptually necessary," but are, rather, idiosyncratic for, and biased by, Chomsky's particular way of looking at language. Nor can they be defended on grounds of any "Galilean-style" methodology, the appeal to which is, in reality, nothing but an excuse for disregarding relevant facts and for a series of internal inconsistencies. Bird's-eye views of language differ according to the bird that does the viewing. Chomsky is subject to limits of viewpoint and horizon, just like any other linguist. Much of what he presents as self-evident or conceptually necessary is actually no more than either a personal, subjective evaluation or a reaffirmation of points of view he has defended in the past but was unable to vindicate on empirical grounds.

4

Questions of Method
and Adequacy

This chapter takes a closer look at the general methodological question of the rationality of the choice one makes for or against a particular theory. A method of simple falsification is, though indispensable in principle, not enough. A wider range of criteria must be applied, not all of them formally definable: there is room for overall wisdom of judgment. Section 4.1 discusses the question of confirmation or disconfirmation of a "paradigm," taken in the Kuhnian sense of an overall theoretical framework or architecture, as opposed to the (dis)confirmation of a smaller bit of theory, better called "hypothesis" or "analysis." Chomsky has never answered that question in any satisfactory way, concentrating instead on the question of how *not* to falsify or have to reject his paradigm or his analyses.

Then, in section 4.2, the curious and disquieting fact is discussed that, over the years, Chomsky has consistently made an implicit appeal to something like a higher authority in adjudicating the adequacy of a linguistic analysis, theory, or paradigm. This fact has, to my knowledge, gone undetected in the literature. Yet, as is shown in section 4.2, it is there, for anyone to see. The inevitable result has been that Chomsky himself is now widely, even if implicitly, seen as the higher authority that must be appealed to for a judgment on the adequacy of a theory or theoretical framework—a situation some will find less appropriate.

Section 4.3 discusses the opposition that has existed through the centuries between *ecologism* and *formalism* in the study of language. Ecologism sees language as a product of nature, with all the unexpected quirky properties that products of nature are likely to possess. Formalism looks on language as a formal object, defined by rules and usable as a vehicle for the storage and transfer of information. Ecologism goes naturally with realism, formalism with instrumentalism. It is shown that Chomsky's attitude on this matter is, again, ambiguous.

Section 4.4, finally, discusses Chomsky's ways of dealing with positive and negative evidence.

4.1 What can confirm or disconfirm a paradigm?

4.1.1 Crucial confirmation

It is often said, following Karl Popper, that confirmation of a theory is nice but not crucial. A theory may hold out through any amount of confirming evidence, but that still does not prove it is the right theory. Disconfirming evidence, on the contrary, does have value of proof: it shows that the theory cannot stand as it is. All this is well known and, from a logical point of view, clearly sound. From an epistemological point of view, however, which includes induction as much as it does deduction, matters are not that simple.

Although positive evidence may not have the power of formal proof, it may well have the power of conviction. Not, of course, run-of-the-mill kinds of evidence. But the situation changes qualitatively, though perhaps not logically, when phenomena that are prima facie highly puzzling and do not seem to fit at all into alternative theories, are an immediate and natural consequence of a theory Θ. Now not only does Θ have a clear advantage over the alternative theories that are less successful in this regard, but one also feels that Θ has been crucially, though perhaps not definitively, confirmed. In such cases, Θ is too good to be false. That is what so-called crucial experiments in the natural sciences are often designed for. In general, the more striking the evidence in question, the more alert the scientist should be to its value. This is an intuitive—some might say, a rhetorical—criterion, yet it is not to be dismissed. Let us speak of *crucial positive evidence*.

I am not too good in physics, but the following simple example may be of help. Newton's theory of gravitation as a function of mass is, of course, confirmed by myriads of run-of-the-mill facts all around us day and night. Yet it was based on the assumption of something, a hidden force, which, at the time, was quite mysterious in its own right and made the theory look somewhat suspect, perhaps even circular: a *virtus attractiva* to explain attraction. But then Newton predicted that the earth must be slightly flattened at the poles, because otherwise the centrifugal force caused by the rotation of the earth would push the waters of the oceans up into a disklike structure at the equator, where the rotation speed is at its highest. Since the oceans do not fly off at the equator, there must be a somewhat greater mass at that position, and therefore a somewhat greater force of gravity counteracting the centrifugal force. Had the oceans been made of a heavy gas, rather than of water, the earth would have been more like a disk than a globe. When it was actually established, through careful measurements, that the earth is indeed somewhat flattened at the poles, this constituted crucial positive evidence for Newton's theory of gravitation. It happened again when it was established, through careful measurements, that the high and low tides of the oceans do indeed correspond with the position of the moon with respect to the shores in question, so that the gravitational force exerted by the moon on the oceans could indeed be seen as the causal factor behind the tidal phenomena (something neither Galileo nor Newton could have known, given the geographical and technical limitations of their day). In this sense, Newton's theory became too good to be false.

One would like to see more crucial positive evidence in linguistics. The MP shows no sign of it, but it must be admitted that the same is true for virtually all alternative theories of grammar, whether in theoretical or in computational linguistics. One is usually content with a formalism, introduced on a variety of grounds, and leaves it at that. In the case of the MP there is not so much a formalism as an architecture. But that, too, should be open to confirmation by crucial positive evidence.

Mediational grammar, implemented as Semantic Syntax (Seuren 1996), fares better in this respect. For example, it has a theory of auxiliation, according to which certain weak verbs, such as modals or aspectual verbs, have a tendency, through history, to leave the position of main verb in semantic structure and nestle in a particular position, the position between the two tenses, in the higher, functional, parts of semantic tree structures. In the context of the theory of semantic syntax, this explains the lack of nonfinite forms, not only in the paradigm of the English auxiliary verbs but also in the French aspectual verb *venir de*, translated as 'just have + Past Participle', and quite a few similar phenomena in other languages, including the lack of nonfinite forms in the German modal futuricity verb *werden*, as opposed to the Dutch modal verb of futuricity *zullen*, which has so far not undergone auxiliation and thus has a complete paradigm. This explains why the German sentence (1) is ungrammatical, while its literal Dutch translation (2) is fully grammatical:

(1)   *Ich erwarte, es morgen erhalten zu werden.
        I   expect   it tomorrow receive to will$_{INF}$

(2)   Ik verwacht het morgen te zullen ontvangen.
        I   expect   it tomorrow to will$_{INF}$ receive
       Both: 'I expect that I will receive it tomorrow'.

This in itself is gratifying, since this fact about the German modal futuricity verb *werden* has so far been regarded as an idiosyncrasy in all existing analyses that take this fact into account. Now, however, as shown in greater detail in section 8.1.6, it appears that the very same auxiliation hypothesis for the German modal futuricity verb *werden* also explains some otherwise puzzling, quirky-looking facts of word order in complex German verb clusters, again facts that, to the extent that they have been observed, have remained unexplained in other analyses (see Seuren 1996:271–280, 2003 for extensive discussion).

More such crucial positive evidence, discussed more amply in Seuren (1996:116–128), comes from prepositional adjuncts in English. This is a fairly complex matter, which can only be dealt with here in rough outline. Oversimplifying, we can say that in semantic syntax prepositional phrases are treated, at SA-level, as scope-bearing operators to be lowered during the transformational cycle into the matrix-S. Thus, a sentence like (3) is treated as in (4a–d) (for details see Seuren 1996):

(3)   John lives around the corner.

(4)

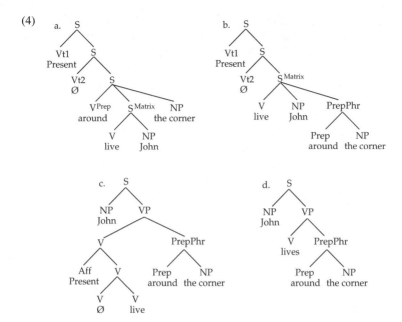

The underlying SA-structure is taken be of the form (4a) (leaving out the speech act operator). During the cycle, the prepositional predicate *around* first attracts the object-NP *the corner* to form the complex predicate *around the corner*, which is subsequently lowered into the matrix-S. Since, in the SA-structure, *around* is below (in the scope of) the tenses, English grammar prescribes that the lowering into the matrix-S has to be to the far right, giving (4b) (with automatic category change to PrepPhr). Then the second tense predicate $_{Vt2}$[Ø] (simultaneous) is lowered onto $_V$[live] of the matrix-S (and deleted postcyclically). At the top cycle, the subject-NP *John* is subject-raised, and the first tense predicate $_{Vt1}$[Present] is again lowered onto $_V$[live]. The resulting end-cyclic ("shallow") structure is (4c). The postcycle, finally, gives the surface structure (4d).

Some prepositional adjuncts, however, require an SA-position above the tenses, as in (5a,b), rendered at SA-level as (6a):

(5)   a. John was happy in Africa.
      b. In Africa John was happy.

Let us call *in Africa* a high prepositional adjunct, or *high PA*, and *around the corner* of (3) a *low PA*. Whether a PA is high or low depends largely on a cognitive decision made by the speaker while formulating the sentence, though for some PAs the position is lexically fixed. High PAs differ syntactically from low PAs in several respects, one of them being that high PAs allow for both far-right and far-left peripheral lowering. Thus, both (5a) and (5b) are grammatical, but *Around the corner John lives* can only be interpreted as something like 'around the corner John comes to life'—that is, as a high PA—and not as an indication of John's address.

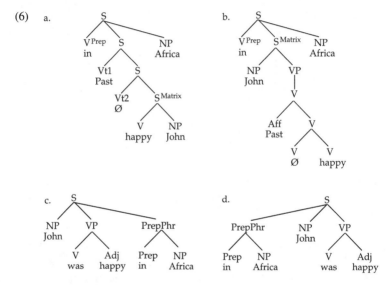

The derivation of (5a) is as in (6a,b,c); that of (5b) as in (6a,b,d). Given the SA-structure (6a), Lowering of the two tense predicates into the matrix-S and Subject Raising of $_{NP}$[John] gives (6b). At this point, the highest cycle must be processed. Since for prepositional predicates in this high position both far-right and far-left peripheral lowering are allowed, the result is either (6c), corresponding to (5a), or (6d), corresponding to (5b).

So far so good. Now consider (7a,b). (7a) is ambiguous between a reading where the leaving took place at six, represented as (8a) leading to the surface structure (8b), and a reading where at six she had already left, represented as (9a) leading to either (9b) or (9c). (7b), in contrast, only has the reading represented as (9a):

(7) a. She had left at six.
     b. At six she had left.

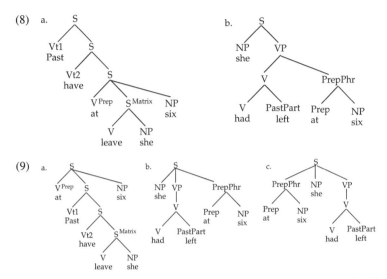

It is an automatic consequence of the processing that low PAs end up in surface structure as VP-constituents, while high PAs end up as high PrepPhrase constituents in surface structure, directly attached to S. We call high surface-structure PrepPhrase constituents, which are directly attached to S, *peripheral constituents*.

Again, this in itself is gratifying, since no other theory, to my knowledge, has been able to account for this semantic difference between (7a) and (7b). But now consider a case mentioned in Jackendoff (2002:85) and taken from Gruber (1965), who presents the following four sentences:

(10) a. Every acorn grew into an oak.
      b. Every oak grew out of an acorn.
      c. An oak grew out of every acorn.
      d. *An acorn grew into every oak.

Jackendoff's comment is: "So far as I know there is no 'natural' solution to this in the literature, one that does not in essence simply stipulate this asymmetry."

This case is a little more complex, given that there is a distinction not only between high and low PAs but also between quantifier scopes.

Semantic syntax automatically accounts for this phenomenon, thereby gaining another piece of crucial positive evidence (see section 7.4 for further comment). The default state of affairs is that the quantifiers (and negation) follow the so-called Scope Ordering Constraint (SOC), which says that higher-scope operators stay to the left of lower-scope operators in surface structure. But there are exceptions. One notable exception is that when a higher-scope operator lands in a peripheral surface-structure constituent, it may violate SOC and thus "cross" a lower-scope operator. An example is the following:

(11) a. I read some poem every day. ∃poem – ∀day / ∀day – ∃poem
     b. Every day I read some poem. ∀day – ∃poem

Here, *every day* is a peripheral constituent, originating as a high PA. Syntactically, therefore, it may occur to the far right, as in (11a) and to the far left, as in (11b). (11b) poses no problem, since it obeys SOC. It only allows for the reading in which *every day* takes scope over *some poem*. It does not allow for the reading in which the scope relations are inverted, since a violation of SOC is allowed only for high PA constituents ending up as peripheral constituents. This explains why (11a) has a reading where *every day* has "crossed" *some poem*: it may do so because *every day* occurs in a high PA, which is a peripheral constituent. It follows that (11a) is ambiguous and (11b) is not.

The corresponding postulated SA-structures are given in (12a) and (12b), following the theory of generalized quantifiers (Barwise and Cooper 1981). (12b) "crashes" when the high PA *(on) y* is lowered to the far left, because in that case the existential quantifier ∃x:poem is not allowed to "cross" the constituent *every day*.

(12)

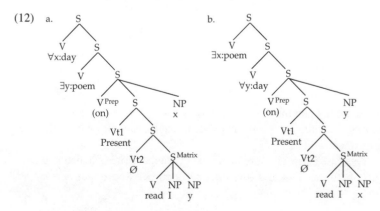

Let us now revert to Gruber's problem, shown in (10a–d), and let us assume that in the expression *grow into NP* the constituent *into NP* is lexically fixed as a low PA (that is, in the idiomatic meaning of 'develop into'), but that in *grow out of NP* the constituent *out of NP* is lexically fixed as a high PA.[1] This gives the four possible SA-structures in (13) and (14) (ruling out the pragmatically deviant structures which imply that one single acorn grew into all oaks or that one single oak grew out of all acorns):

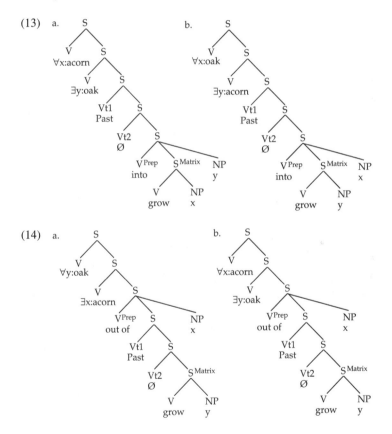

(13)

(14)

---

1. It seems to be generally the case that when a verb and a prepositional phrase show signs of becoming a more or less lexically fixed collocation, the prepositional phrase behaves as a low PA.

The reason (10d) is starred is now clear. It is, strictly speaking, not ungrammatical, as it is the natural expression for the pragmatically deviant reading 'there is at least one acorn such that it grew into every oak'. But it is ungrammatical on the pragmatically normal reading 'for every oak it is the case that there was an acorn such that the acorn grew into the oak'. For on this reading (10d) violates SOC, which it is not allowed to do since *into every oak* is not a peripheral constituent but a VP-constituent, which requires full compliance with SOC. In fact, the pragmatically normal reading just given cannot be expressed in English with the help of the predicate *grow* with the low prepositional adjunct *into NP*, because the higher quantifier must "land" in a constituent that has to be to the right of the landing site of the lower operator, without there being the escape clause of peripheral constituents.

In this respect, (10d) is similar to the case presented in the German sentence (15), which cannot be expressed in equally normal English due to the different treatments of the negation operator in the two languages. English must resort to a different sentence structure for the expression of the same underlying thought.

(15)   Ich habe ein Wort nicht verstanden.
       I   have one word not understood
       'there was one word I did not understand.'

(15) is a normal German sentence, meaning 'there was one word which I did not understand'. The sentence obeys SOC without any problem, because the first (smaller scope) operator to be lowered is the negation *nicht*, which, in German, goes to the far right. The next operator to be lowered is the existential quantifier *ein Wort*, whose corresponding bound variable stands in the normal direct-object position, which is to the left of the previously lowered negation word *nicht*. SOC is thus automatically satisfied. In English, however, the negation *not* lowers onto the verb and thus lands to the left of the direct-object position, which blocks a subsequent crossing by the existential quantifier.

In general, when one looks a little more closely at such facts in different languages, a field of inquiry opens up which has, so far, largely been allowed to lie fallow in most linguistic theories, including Chomskyan grammar. Yet the facts are there, and they want an explanation in terms of grammatical theory. Since it is not clear how alternative theories of grammar could possibly account for such facts, it may be said that they constitute crucial positive evidence for the specific hypothesis concerning the form of semantic analyses and their relation with surface structures put forward in the theory of semantic syntax.

4.1.2 Adequate disconfirmation

Let us now turn to the question of what could possibly disconfirm the random-generator model in its minimalist guise. This question is posed by Adriana Belletti and Luigi Rizzi in their interview with Chomsky published in Chomsky (2002:92–161). The actual question is (Chomsky 2002:124): "AB & LR: What kind of empirical discovery would lead to the rejection of the strong minimalist thesis?" In his reply, Chomsky starts off with some coquetry: "All the phenomena of language appear to refute it, just as the phenomena of the world appeared to refute the Copernican thesis. The question is whether it is a real refutation. At every stage of every science most phenomena seem to refute it."

That may or may not be so, but one still awaits the answer to the question of what a *real* refutation would amount to. What follows is an extended diatribe on the difficulty of designing "the right experiment" (pp. 124–127), focusing on the inconclusive click experiment carried out by Fodor, Bever, and Garrett (1974) to test the psychological reality of constituent boundaries in surface structures. Then (pp. 127–128):

> So, to get back to your question after a long detour. If you want to know what seems to refute the strong minimalist thesis, the answer is just about everything you can think of or pick at random from a corpus of material. That is not particularly interesting because it is the normal situation in the sciences, even the most advanced. Again, this is one of the reasons why people do experiments, which are a crucial part of the "Galilean style": it is the experiments that matter, and the well-designed ones, the ones that fit into a sensible theory.

Again, no answer, not even a hint of what a crucial experiment would amount to. Only, as has become the custom, gratuitous analogies with illustrious figures from the past. Yet Copernicus and Galileo were at least capable of presenting an overall frame of reference that explains large masses of otherwise erratic facts to do with the apparent movements of the planets and other phenomena that could be brought into the picture. True, they lacked an account of gravitation, which left some important gaps in their theories—a point that Cardinal Bellarmine did not fail to drive home in his discussions with Galileo. Yet these gaps did not constitute refuting evidence. They only showed the incompleteness of the otherwise brilliantly successful theory, as the cardinal had to admit. Once the gaps had been filled in by Newton's discovery of gravitation as a function of mass, flat earth theories receded into a limbo of crackpottery. Since Chomsky insists on the analogy between his theory of language and Galileo's theory of the solar system, one is naturally curious to see what linguistic parallels he presents for the masses of "phenomena of the world [that] appeared to refute the Copernican thesis." He resorts to data drawn from a "corpus," though what kind of corpus he has in mind remains undisclosed. Presumably he refers to bare performance data, which are known for being messy (though systematic performance errors may be evidence for or against certain hypotheses about the neurological organization of language). But such performance data do not refute any theory of language, since no theory of language takes these data as the objects of explanation. In fact, it is not too difficult to set up "experiments" that will filter out the messiness and deliver the distilled products that correspond with judgments of "clean" language use. Likewise, Copernicus, Galileo, and their like did not base their theories on observations made on cloudy nights or sunny days, but on clear nights, when the stars and planets shine in full glory, and often with the help of instruments to increase detail and filter out messiness.

So let us ask again: when the equivocations about the nature of the data are removed, is there a linguistic parallel to the biased perspective caused by geocentric observation in the case of the solar system? Perhaps there is. One finds non-professionals and, one has to admit, sometimes also professional linguists formulating their observations and, worse, explanations of semantic phenomena in terms of impressionistic folk psychology, using superficial and largely ad hoc, associative, metaphorical, or otherwise intuitively appealing but insubstantial terminology. They will say, for example, that the French sentence *Il a fait sortir le client* expresses one single event (Achard 1998), whereas its English equivalent *He made the customer leave* expresses two separate events, basing this "judgment" on the close connection between *fait* and *sortir* in the French, and the less close connection between *made* and *leave* in the English sentence. Less introspectively inclined linguists will ask why French does not allow for the expression of two events, as in **Il a fait le client sortir* and why English forbids the expression of one single event as in **He made leave the customer*. They will be skeptical about any such "semantic" or "conceptual" differences and say that these and other related facts of French and English are accounted for by one single, purely syntactic, difference: French has the rule of Predicate Raising (or whatever one prefers to call it), which is absent in English, while English has the rule of Subject-to-Object Raising, which French does not have.

A similar case is discussed in Langacker (1991:412) in relation to datives in causative constructions.[2] An example, one presumes, is the dative *à Albert* (to Albert) in the French causative sentence *Il a fait voir la lettre à Albert* (he made Albert see the letter). Dative, Langacker says, "marks a causee whose role is to some degree agentive, while accusative indicates that its involvement is totally passive," since, in causative constructions, "in contrast to the direct or coercive causation implied by accusative case, dative or instrumental case is usually indicative of indirect or non-coercive causation, where the causee still exercises some measure of volition or initiative"—at least, a footnote adds, when the language "allows an option" because otherwise the distinction between dative and accusative is neutralized. Whether French "allows an option" is unclear, since the dative is restricted to embedded transitive, and the accusative to embedded intransitive, clauses. (I have, so far, not encountered any language with syntactically unrestricted freedom of choice between dative and accusative case for the "causee" in Predicate Raising constructions.) Yet if it does, one wonders about such sentences as *Il a fait subir des tortures à Albert* (he made Albert undergo torture), where poor Albert's volitional role is at least doubtful. Or one wonders why Albert is a "totally passive" causee in, for example, *J'ai laissé manger Albert* (I let Albert eat), but an "agentive" or "volitional" causee in *J'ai laissé manger du pain à Albert* (I let Albert eat bread).

It is reasonable to demand of any linguistic theory that it should restrict inevitably introspective modes of *observation* to reports on (phonological, grammatical, lexical, semantic) acceptability and rule out any *explanation* through the window of introspection and private experience,

2. The case of the dative arising as a result of Predicate Raising in French is actually quite interesting, as the occurrence of the dative appears to be constrained not only by syntactic structure (the subject term of an underlying embedded clause C becomes accusative when C is intransitive and dative when C is transitive), but also by the thematic function of the subject term of C with regard to the main verb of C. For example, when the main verb of C has a causative meaning, the dative is ruled out for its subject term, which now appears as an agent phrase (Langacker's "instrumental") of a passivized clause C. See Seuren (1972; 1996:ch. 4) for extensive comment.

leaving the burden of explanation to formal theories. In this sense, one may perhaps say that linguistic theory has the task of correcting a "biased perspective" of observation and explanation, or quasi explanation, that is too introspective and too much centered on private experiences. But that does not seem to be at all what Chomsky has in mind. Nor is it so that his random-generator theory has a monopoly in correcting that kind of "biased perspective," which is, by and large, rejected and corrected by all serious modern linguistic theories.

Apart from the "biased perspective" question, however, there is, of course, a data problem in linguistics, since all data for linguistic theory are judgmental data, which are to some extent introspective and necessarily fluid because they involve (a) reporting on one's own behavior, a well-known source of error, and (b) membership of a speech community, well-known for its variation and vague boundaries. But that kind of problem is common to practically all the human sciences and hardly provides a parallel with Galileo's situation. It thus seems that Chomsky has left his readers without an answer to the question of what could possibly falsify his random-generator theory of language.

Let us, therefore, try and see what we can do, not only with regard to the random-generator view but also with regard to the mediational model and, for either model, their concrete manifestations in the form of specific theories of grammar.

First and foremost, any scientific theory should be cast in terms that are precise enough for it to be clear what exactly is involved and what exactly is claimed. Failing the necessary degree of precision, a theory must be sent back for further refinement. As has been shown time and again so far and will be shown again in the following chapters, the MP suffers from a severe lack of precision in many respects. If it were not for anything else, it would, therefore, have to be sent back for repair or be rejected if repair is not feasible.

Then, supposing that the precision requirement has been satisfied, one will have to see what considerations of content might possibly lead to its rejection. As a matter of general principle, any scientific theory, whatever its scope, is falsified when it defeats the expectations raised by it. Given this general principle, it seems reasonable to assume a hierarchy of means of falsification. Small, restricted theories, also called hypotheses or analyses, whose theorems are directly applicable to observable data of an agreed kind, are relatively simple in this respect. They are falsified by predictions (theorems) that turn out to be false with regard to the data in question. At this level of scientific activity a simple Popperian situation obtains: counterexamples falsify the theory in the sense that the theory (hypothesis, analysis) has to be either repaired or rejected when repair seems hopeless due to too many empirical holes or when the result of the repair looks too messy to be taken to be correct or true.

A distinction must be made between, on the one hand, straight counterevidence, which consists of facts that are explicitly ruled out by the theory, and, on the other hand, unexplained evidence, which consists of facts that are in principle compatible with the theory but do not, or not yet, follow from it. Unexplained evidence calls for further research; counterevidence calls for repair or, if all else fails, rejection. Thus, owing to the fact that the force of gravity was still unknown at the time, Galileo's theory of the solar system failed to explain the high and low tides in the oceans, or why objects stick to the earth's surface and are not thrown off the earth at the equator by the centrifugal force resulting from the earth's rotation. But this was not counterevidence, only unexplained evidence, which was soon fitted into the overall system, making the system even stronger than it was before.

But small theories are part of wider, overarching theories. A formal setup encompassing a number of smaller theories is often called an *architecture* or, in a less formal sense, a *paradigm*. In general, the wider the theory (architecture, paradigm), the less vulnerable it is to falsification by single counterexamples. It takes batteries of counterexamples, systematically and massively showing the overall weakness or untenability of the overarching theory to demolish or weaken it. The fatal blow usually comes from an alternative architecture or paradigm that has fewer empirical holes and has other advantages such as greater overall simplicity or greater generality—that is, a better integration with other theories dealing with the same underlying reality (in cases of a realist orientation of the theory).

A typical example of an overarching paradigm is Darwinian evolution theory, which, as is well known, is not really falsifiable by counterexamples, since any possible counterexample can be rebutted by an appeal to historical circumstances that are forever lost to verification. Likewise for theories of language change. As we know, the "laws" of historical sound change are not really laws in the scientific sense but are overall regularities induced primarily by sociological processes and admitting of exceptions. In principle, these exceptions will have been due to historical idiosyncrasies of a sociological or demographic nature, but, on the whole, these are not recoverable and have thus been lost to history. Even so, the validity of these paradigms is not seriously doubted, as their overall explanatory force is greater than can be offered by any other thinkable paradigm, and also because we have a fairly clear idea of the causes of their unfalsifiability by counterexamples.

What we do not want is a paradigm which, on the one hand, is solidly rooted in a realist interpretation while, on the other, it goes against all we know about the underlying reality that the interpretation is about. This seems to be typically the case with the random-generator paradigm with its random sentence generator. And it is typically not the case with the mediational model. The random-generator view lacks generality in that it conflicts not only with general knowledge but also with other theories or disciplines dealing with the same underlying reality, such as psycholinguistics, sociolinguistics, or speech therapy. The mediational paradigm, by contrast, is perfectly compatible with these and other disciplines dealing with the same underlying reality, provided one is sufficiently cautious in establishing identity relations between the entities postulated in linguistics and those found or postulated in the other disciplines. (Whether it is compatible, in this sense, with brain physiology is too early to say, but that, of course, applies with equal force to the random-generator paradigm.)

This provides one important ground for rejecting the random-generator view in favor of mediationalism. What remains is to see how these two paradigms fare with respect to specific empirical predictions. As regards the random-generator view, the answer to this question would require a thorough inspection of all the different versions in which the random-generator view has been presented over the past thirty or so years—an enterprise that would transcend the boundaries of the discussion here. In the case of minimalism, however, the answer is easy: there are hardly any specific empirical predictions, owing to the overall lack of precision of the grammatical mechanism envisaged. All one can do is point at predictions of a general nature.

Thus, the minimalist version of random-generator grammar would be falsified in a general sense if it were to be convincingly shown that a representational (declarative or filter-based) style of analysis and description had empirical or explanatory advantages over a derivational style. But that has not been shown so far. Minimalism (but not random-generator models of grammar in general) would also be in empirical danger if it were to be convincingly shown that the semantic interpretation of sentences depended, wholly or partially, on phonologically defined surface structure, since the MP grammatical model happens not to have any feeding line from phonological surface structure to whatever may be taken to be "logical form." Fortunately for minimalism, no such surface elements of semantic interpretation appear to exist, as is argued in chapter 7, contrary to Chomsky's own repeated assertions, strangely enough.

Moreover, if it were to be convincingly shown that a grammar will gain in predictive power and simplicity if it takes semantically well-defined structures as input to the rule system and be weakened to the extent that it does not, then not only the minimalist version but all versions of random-generator grammar will be in jeopardy, since that would ipso facto establish the superiority of mediational grammar. Again, any such inquiry would transcend the boundaries of the discussion in this book. It would, in fact, constitute an extensive program of linguistic research. But what is clear is that such a program would be a further extension of what was started in Katz and Postal (1964). If the arguments presented there can be upheld and extended, random-generator grammar will have to go. The discussion thus inevitably takes us back to the birth of generative semantics. It also shows how relevant the points and arguments raised in Katz and Postal (1964) still are.

4.2 Chomsky as a higher authority

There is a persistent trait in Chomsky's way of approaching questions of adequacy of grammatical analyses. It began with *Current Issues* (1964a) and was continued in *Aspects* (1965) (see in particular Chomsky 1965:24–27). The crucial text is (Chomsky 1964a:28–29):

> Within the framework outlined above we can sketch various levels of success that might be attained by a grammatical description associated with a particular linguistic theory. The lowest level of success is achieved if the grammar presents the observed data correctly. A second and higher level of success is achieved when the grammar gives a correct account of the linguistic intuition of the native speaker, and specifies the observed data (in particular) in terms of significant generalizations that express underlying regularities in the language. A third and still higher level of success is achieved when the associated linguistic theory provides a general basis for selecting a grammar that achieves the second level of success over other grammars consistent with the relevant observed data that

do not achieve this level of success. In this case, we can say that the linguistic theory in question suggests an explanation for the linguistic intuition of the native speaker. It can be interpreted as asserting that data of the observed kind will enable a speaker whose intrinsic capacities are as represented in this general theory to construct for himself a grammar that characterizes exactly this linguistic intuition.

For later reference, let us refer to these roughly delimited levels of success as the levels of *observational adequacy*, *descriptive adequacy*, and *explanatory adequacy*, respectively.

This text is full of problematic aspects, one of which is the incomprehensible notion of "achieving a level of success." In normal science one hardly ever "achieves" such levels. One only has levels of elimination: elimination of theories on grounds of evidence or data (counterexamples), elimination on grounds of comparative simplicity, elimination on grounds of consistency with other sciences dealing with the same object of enquiry, or elimination on grounds of internal or methodological inconsistency. To assume that a level of success can be "achieved" presupposes a higher authority endowed with superior knowledge and insight and sitting in judgment over the scientist's work.

But the problem that concerns us here is to do with the second "level of success"—descriptive adequacy—which is "achieved when the grammar gives a correct account of the linguistic intuition of the native speaker, and specifies the observed data (in particular) in terms of significant generalizations that express underlying regularities in the language." Clearly, a description that gives a correct account of its object of description is adequate in any possible sense. But who is to tell? Again, presumably, a higher authority in possession of insights and information not shared with ordinary mortals. The second condition, implying that a grammar must strive for maximal generalizations and thus optimize simplicity of description, is, of course, standard procedure, but no one will be able to say whether or when this level of success has been achieved. In actual fact, all that earthly mortals can do is advance cautious hypotheses and test them on factual correctness and degrees of generalization.

What we now see, in the MP, is the same all over again, but with one additional aspect. Whereas in the old days the superhuman, metaphysical outlook had no direct consequences for the daily practice of work, it is now claimed that the actual content of linguistic analyses and descriptions should be determined, or constrained, by criteria whose satisfaction can only be adjudicated by a higher being gifted with superior powers of knowledge and judgment.

In ordinary science one applies the criterion of the simplest theory covering the largest range of facts—Ockham's razor. But this only answers the question of *how* language is best thought to function, not *why* language is made that way.

Ordinary scientific method, therefore, does not elucidate what could be meant by saying or suggesting that "language is very well designed, perhaps close to 'perfect' in satisfying external conditions" (Chomsky 1998:16), and that the language faculty is "beautifully designed, a near-perfect solution to the conditions imposed by the general architecture of the mind-brain in which it is inserted, another illustration of how natural laws work out in wondrous ways" (1998:17). The latter suggestion is, one remembers from section 3.4, part of a "fable," but at the same time it is implied that the fable might "turn out to have some elements of validity" in that it "helps us pose a problem that could turn out to be meaningful and even significant: basically, the problem that motivates the minimalist program, which explores the intuition that the outcome of the fable might be accurate in interesting ways" (1998:17). The question is: who is to judge?

For ordinary mortals, the fact that the language faculty is saddled with many features, in particular the "displacement property," that have so far escaped attempts at explanation on grounds of conditions imposed by "external systems," suggests that it is highly unlikely that "the outcome of the fable might be accurate in interesting ways." In the light of available human knowledge and insight, it is, therefore, a rather unrealistic enterprise to "explore this intuition." For the moment, language must, to the best of our knowledge, be characterized as suffering from considerable imperfection. Whether this (apparent) imperfection serves a higher purpose of functionality is a question whose answer escapes our present powers of judgment.

Therefore, the first conclusion must be that the methodology as presented on page 1 of *The Minimalist Program* is unrealistic because it is unworkable, counterproductive, and contrary to established practice and, above all, that the question "How perfect is language?" or the notion of an "optimal language design," though perhaps meaningful in a metaphysical sense, is without any practical meaning as long as the environmental conditions are not fully known. Since it is not to be expected that they will be fully known in the foreseeable future, we must conclude that the question "How perfect is language?" is unrealistic given the circumstances.

All we can do at the moment is what we have done for the past decades: look for descriptions of the facts of languages that show maximal uniformity, and try to formulate the general or universal principles underlying such descriptions. The functionality of these principles with regard to environmental conditions of language use is a secondary matter, to be decided on after the universal principles in question have been established to a reasonable degree of certainty. (This question is taken up again in section 5.2.)

The minimalist method is, moreover, conducive to bias, in that it carries a built-in tendency (a) to be selective with regard to the observation of data and (b) to bend observed data and perceived regularities in such a way that it might look as if they fit the mold of the theory, which is constrained by a priori considerations of what would constitute a perfect language system. It will come as no surprise, therefore, that this is exactly what is happening. This aspect of the minimalist program is discussed in the following section.

4.3 Ecologism and formalism

Several authors have pointed out that there is a twofold risk threatening sound scientific methodology: overanxious data collecting and overanxious theory building. The point was eloquently put by the philosopher Charles Travis some years ago with regard to the study of language. Travis distinguishes between what one may call *ecological* and *formalist* approaches to language (1981:1):

> One approach to the study of language views its subject as weird and wonderful, the storehouse of unimaginable complexities and surprises, to be discerned by looking very closely; another views language (or a language) as something we probably could have cooked up one day, along with the soup, had this not, in effect, already been done (perhaps none too well). These are both attitudes, not theses, but each at times may fit comfortably enough, and each guides investigation along rather different paths. The second approach has the virtue, perhaps, of constantly yielding proposals (or guesses, depending on one's view) about how things are done, with the demand that it be *proven* that this isn't how it happens. To an adherent of the first approach, these proposals are apt to seem fanciful and arbitrary. He will want to ask: why *think* that's how it is done (or even that one could guess at all)? The first approach has the virtue of

bringing many particular facts about language to attention, if not into focus, and tends not to assume, prematurely, that problems have been solved. To an adherent of the second approach, this is apt to seem anti-systematic bias—mere dallying over the important business of constructing a tidy theory, with loss of the insight that only a comprehensive and comprehensible picture can bring (though there is room for disagreement about what *insight* would consist in). On the first approach, the primary goal is exactness—describing the phenomena as they are. On the second, it is precision—describing whatever phenomena in a way that leaves no blurred edge—at least in the description.

In an ideal world, it would no doubt be unnecessary to distinguish ecologism and formalism, since good science is both ecologist and formalist. But in the world as it is, the distinction labels two frequently occurring aberrations in the practice of scientific investigation in general, and in the study of language in particular.

Proper science is both ecologist and formalist, both "exact" and "precise," but it should avoid extremes. The extreme ecologist easily gets lost in mere data collecting, setting up a curiosity shop of preferably rare findings, without much in the way of explanatory theory. The extreme formalist quickly develops a tendency toward blindness for evidence, putting the neatness of his formal system above all else and thus losing contact with reality. Neither the extreme ecologist nor the extreme formalist will succeed in explaining anything or in gaining real insight—the former because he has no theory, the latter because he ignores too many relevant facts.

There is, understandably, a strong correlation between ecologism and realism on the one hand, and formalism and instrumentalism on the other (see section 3.3). It is impossible to take full account of the natural habitat of language, as ecologists do, while avoiding some form of realism. And if one is a realist in science, one inevitably looks at language's natural environment. Likewise for formalism and instrumentalism. When one looks upon language as merely a formal system of symbols laden with information, as formalists do, both hardware and non-hardware realism are in principle incompatible with this attitude, even though the boundary line between formalism and non-hardware realism is perhaps less strict. Conversely, when one is an instrumentalist by conviction, whether of the moderate or the mathematical variety, one can hardly espouse any form of ecologism.

The history of linguistics since the late eighteenth century has made it a thoroughly ecologist, and hence realist, discipline. Whenever there was a tendency to leave the natural habitat of language out of consideration, corrections were made, famously in the late 1870s by the Young Grammarians (see Seuren 1998:89–104). Comparative philology, dialectology, anthropological linguistics, and sociolinguistics have flourished in this ecological climate. And twentieth-century theoretical linguistics, fed by comparative philology, psychology, and anthropological linguistics, has likewise been mainly ecological in outlook. The behaviorist onslaught, which took place in America and lasted from the 1920s till about 1965, was unable to change that, as language was still considered to be the product of "natural" processes of stimulus-response conditioning. Only insofar as linguistics was influenced by logic, as in formal semantics, has the ecological orientation been weakened or lost.

Chomsky, however, as we have seen repeatedly and will see repeatedly later, is a special case, in that he has always been eclectic with regard to methodological oppositions, thereby risking charges of methodological inconsistence.

4.4 What to do with evidence?

Despite its overall realist stance, the MP shows features of extreme formalism, in the sense that the formalism, once established, is made to prevail over available (counter)evidence. Chomsky and his school have developed a tendency to ignore or write away unwelcome evidence, as appears, for example, from the following. In the middle of an exposition on the nature of the operation Move, he says (Chomsky 1995:266):

> The empirical questions that arise are varied and complex, and it is easy enough to come up with apparent counterevidence. I will put these problems aside for now, simply assuming the best outcome, namely that UG [i.e., universal grammar] settles the matter—hardly an innocuous step, needless to say.

One notes, to begin with, that any counterevidence that might be presented is immediately branded as being "apparent," which does not sound very encouraging if one was hoping for a fair assessment of the evidence. Then one notes that problems of the kind are unceremoniously put "aside for now, simply assuming the best outcome, namely that UG settles the matter," though it is unclear exactly *how* universal grammar might settle the matter (see section 6.2). Next, one notes the admission that this is "hardly an innocuous step," even though nothing further is done about it and no justification is given for what must be considered a serious flouting of the rules.

There are many such passages in the book, where it is conceded that there is or may be counterevidence or where it is said that the issue ultimately depends on empirical considerations, while nothing is done about such real or possible counterevidence. For example (Chomsky 1995:187):

> The empirical justification for this approach [Government and Binding], with its departures from conceptual necessity, is substantial. Nevertheless, we may ask whether the evidence will bear the weight, or whether it is possible to move toward a minimalist program.

Other such passages abound. One reads, for example, that "the abstraction I am now pursuing may require qualification. I will continue to pursue it nonetheless, merely noting here, once again, that tacit assumptions underlying much of the most productive recent work are far from innocent" (1995:220), or that assumptions are, in the end, "empirical; in the final analysis, [their] accuracy depends on factual considerations" (1995:220), or that the minimalist program "is just that: a research program concerned with filling the gaps and determining the answers to the basic questions raised in the opening paragraph of the introduction, in particular, the question 'How perfect is language?'" (1995:221), or that "these questions too are ultimately empirical, turning basically on explanatory adequacy" (1995:223), and so on.

But there is no serious discussion of empirical issues that might have a bearing on the tenability of the expectations fuelled by the MP. Chomsky never enters into a balanced discussion, keeping open the possibility that, perhaps, the evidence might get the better of the minimalist expectations. The reader must make do with the unsubstantiated reassurance that one should trust in the results of "much of the most productive recent work" (1995:220), or that "what is known about the phenomena seems to me to support this expectation" (1995:222), or that "work of the past few years suggests that these conclusions, which seemed out of the question a few years ago, are at least plausible, quite possibly correct" (1998:21), or that "these questions are currently being investigated in interesting ways, which I cannot go into here" (1998:24), to quote just four of the many passages that are encountered.

There is even the occasional intimation that those who might have doubts or questions do not understand properly (Chomsky 1995:168):

Another recurrent theme has been the role of "principles of economy" in determining the computations and the SDs [i.e., structural descriptions] they generate. Such considerations have arisen in various forms and guises as theoretical perspectives have changed. There is, I think, good reason to believe that they are fundamental to the design of language, if properly understood.

Frequent appeals are also made to an "inner nature" or some "deep sense," whose true character, however, remains concealed (Chomsky 1995:221):

> These requirements might turn out to be critical factors in determining the inner nature of C_{HL} in some deep sense, or they might turn out to be "extraneous" to it, inducing departures from "perfection" that are satisfied in an optimal way. The latter possibility is not to be discounted.

A case in point is the discussion of the well-known process of Subject-to-Object Raising (SOR; see section 8.1) occurring in sentences like (16):

(16)   I expected John to be the winner.

The apparent direct object *John* has been raised from its semantic position as subject in the embedded clause (*John be the winner*) to the direct object position of the matrix clause. For reasons that are irrelevant here, SOR seems to have been causing problems in Chomsky's theories since 1969. For many years this form of raising was denied, the theory being that the embedded subject simply stayed in place but was, "exceptionally," assigned accusative case. Now, however, the raising analysis is accepted, even though it still causes problems in the theory. An appeal is made to unexplained "plausible assumptions of some generality," while it is suggested that we have to do with "a fairly 'deep' property of language." But no attempt is made to solve these problems (Chomsky 1995:174):

> Exceptional Case marking by V is now interpreted as raising of NP . . . to [Spec, Agr_o], the analogue of familiar raising to [Spec, Agr_s]. If the VP-internal subject hypothesis is correct (as I henceforth assume), the question arises why the object (direct, or in the complement) raises to [Spec, Agr_o] and the subject to [Spec, Agr_s], yielding unexpected crossing rather than the usual nested paths. We will return to this phenomenon below, finding that it follows on plausible assumptions of some generality, and in this sense appears to be a fairly "deep" property of language.

No "plausible assumptions of some generality," however, are found in the book, from which the SOR phenomena could be seen to follow. (As regards the methodological aspects of the procedure of raising to [Spec, Agr$_o$] or [Spec, Agr$_s$], see section 8.1.2.)

More startling even than the frequent appeals to results not mentioned or to unrevealed deeper insights is the unexpected denial of "empirical justification" to judgments of grammaticality (Chomsky 1995:213):

> One might be tempted to interpret the class of expressions of the language L for which there is a convergent derivation as "the well-formed (grammatical) expressions of L." But this seems pointless. The class so defined has no significance. The concepts "well-formed" and "grammatical" remain without characterization or known empirical justification; they played virtually no role in early work on generative grammar except in informal exposition, or since.

This statement is odd in the extreme. Right from the start, transformational generative grammar has owed its empirical success to the fact that it identified grammaticality judgments as the central class of observable data required for an evaluation of a theory's adequacy. Throughout *The Minimalist Program* itself, appeals are made to grammaticality judgments for factual support. To deny their role as empirical data is to deny historical fact in a way so blatant as to defy belief, as was pointed out in Pullum (1996). One wonders, moreover, how a denial of empirical status to grammaticality judgments can be regarded as consistent with the frequently made statements to the effect that issues should be decided on grounds of factual or empirical considerations.

Empirical evidence has been a perennial source of discomfort in Chomskyan linguistics since 1970. A concern with the status of empirical data is, of course, a necessity for any discipline that is worth its salt. In this case, however, the concern appears to spring from a desire to immunize the theory against falsification by what are obviously facts of language. As is shown in section 8.1, a distinction has sometimes been made between "core" and "peripheral" phenomena, the latter being considered of no relevance to the theory. Yet the distinction was never based on independent grounds and has, in fact, always corresponded with what the theory could and could not account for, respectively. Counterevidence has also frequently been characterized as "contaminated" or insufficiently "idealized," or due to "performance errors" or the like, again without independent criteria and always in the interest of the current theory. Occasionally, clear counterevidence was even branded as being "dialectal" and not "standard," which was not only contrary to the evidence but also irrelevant, as dialects, too, have their grammars (even if the relation with the standard language is often unclear).[3] A further way of discarding counterevidence consists in treating it as irrelevant as long as the other party does not come up with an alternative theory covering the same range of phenomena as are allegedly covered by the current Chomskyan theory. Clearly, such a measure is illegitimate with regard to specific, small-scale grammatical analyses, since counterevidence remains what it is, even if there is no alternative theory.

It now looks as if a further step has been taken along this road. Not only is unwelcome evidence branded as being merely "apparent" counterevidence, one now also notices an attempt to seek refuge in *method* rather than *theory*. A method cannot be falsified the way a theory can be. The soundness of a method is judged by a variety of criteria, some of which stand in a long and distinguished tradition. Ockham's razor is one of them, and so is compliance with observable evidence, not only the facts that prompted the first causal questions but also those predicted by the theory. Furthermore, a method should make the scientist strive for conceptual clarity and formal precision of the theories constructed in its name. But conceptual necessity is not one of the established criteria in the empirical sciences, though it is in the a priori sciences of mathematics and logic.

Chomsky's statements (1998:16) that "there are minimalist questions, but no specific minimalist answers" and that "the answers are whatever is found by carrying out the program" are misleading, in that it should be possible to characterize answers as either minimalist or nonminimalist,

---

3. Consider, for example, Chomsky and Lasnik (1977), where the question is discussed of why English should have obligatory *that*-deletion in sentences like *Who do you think (*that) killed the butler?* and not in *Who do you think (that) the butler killed?* This fact was attributed to an allegedly universal "*that*-trace" filter, which would rule out all *that*-clauses where the complementizer *that*, or its equivalent in other languages, is immediately followed by a position left empty by a constituent that has been moved away. First, however, the fact that *that* is also inadmissible when the fronted constituent is predicate nominal, as in *Who do you think (*that) you are?*, was not taken into account. But then it also soon became clear that Dutch, Icelandic, Italian, and some other languages do not have any such filter and freely allow for the counterpart of *that* to occur before positions that have been left empty. This fact was ruled irrelevant on the grounds of being "in fact restricted to certain dialects" of Dutch, for which "there seem to be reasonable alternative analyses" (Chomsky and Lasnik 1977:452). But this fact is not dialectal. It is a normal part of standard Dutch and of all its dialects. Moreover, the "alternative analyses" have never seen the light of day. Even so, the *that*-trace filter has never been revoked and still figures in Chomsky (1995:86–87).

provided the minimalist method is well defined. Moreover, the MP is, in fact, much more than that. It does provide a number of answers, albeit under the illegitimate shield of "conceptual necessity," and it also presents a number of "expectations," all of which are said to be supported by results of recent work, neither the results nor the work being specified. The MP thus represents an extreme formalist deviation, but without a formal theory. It would seem that one is allowed to conclude from this that the MP lacks explanatory value and is, therefore, not in a position to provide insight.

The MP, as carried out in practice, can be seen as a reversal to a variety of Cartesian a priori science. For Descartes, good science consisted in grounding scientific procedures in "clear and distinct" notions that were part of self-evident, consistent deductive theories based on mathematics, in particular Euclidean geometry. The aversion to empirical verification justifies a verdict of extreme formalism for this method. But Descartes had at least the advantage of being able to claim the support of mathematics as a grounding theory. Chomsky's "minimalist" practice shows an equal unease with regard to evidence, but it lacks the support of an independently motivated formal theory.

Paradoxically, the minimalist method represents extreme formalism but has not led to any formal theory of the language faculty. One is reminded of Pullum's (1989) criticism that linguistic theory under Chomsky's direction is becoming fuzzier and fuzzier. Chomsky's (1990) reply has not been able to remove that charge. On the contrary, the charge is confirmed by his repeated flirtation with the vague and imprecise, as when he speaks of a "more obscure but quite interesting matter" (1995:222), or when he says that some "questions are not only imprecise but also rather subtle" (1995:223), or when he appeals to "deep" properties of language (1995:174). Pullum's judgment that "the implied epistemology is one of miraculous revelation" (1996:138) and that "the level of explication . . . is risible" (1996:141) may be hard, but it is not without justification.

Another paradoxical conclusion is that the MP does not follow the minimalist method. What one sees happening in practice, in the book and elsewhere, is that evidence that does not conform to the analysis presented as being "minimalist" is written out of the piece one way or another. It is either branded in advance as constituting only "apparent counterevidence" (1995:266) or relabeled as "morphology-driven" (1995:222), or it is simply "swept under the rug" (1995: 220). In general, as we have seen, the impartiality required by the method with regard to both confirming and disconfirming evidence is not found in the actual way the program is pursued: positive evidence is gratuitously invoked; negative evidence is spirited away; and the success of the program is anticipated throughout, even though there is no way of knowing what any such "success" would consist of.

4.5 Conclusion

The overall conclusion is that Chomskyan linguistics in its various guises—the MP in particular—suffers from a crucial lack of empirical support. No crucial positive evidence appears to exist, and possible falsification by counterexample is avoided by all sorts of illegitimate means. The question of how *not* to falsify the theory seems to be of greater concern than the question of how to falsify it. The tendency to ignore the role of evidence has increased over the years; it has now become cavalier dismissal, based on an implicit claim to higher authority. Chomsky's theorizing is seen to be methodologically inconsistent in that it is formalistic in principle, despite the many claims to ecologism and despite the fact that the formalism has become fuzzier and fuzzier over the years. Across the board, the impression is that any form of critique is ruled out of court in advance: those who disagree have not understood the message.

5

What Is Functional
about the MP?

5.1 The minimalist version of functionalism

Since the primary goal of the MP is to show that the central notions developed in Chomskyan grammar over the years are determined by and thus derivable from boundary conditions on meaning and pronunciation, minimalism must be taken to be a form of functionalism, if the latter is seen as an attempt at reducing the properties of human language as much as possible to the demands imposed by the functions it is meant to serve in its natural habitat.

Although for Chomsky this is a recent direction of research, the idea itself is as ancient as linguistics itself. From Plato and Aristotle to the early nineteenth century, the only function of language was taken to be the expression of propositional thought, and theories of language concentrated exclusively on that aspect. Over the past two centuries, however, as knowledge of both the system and the physical, mental, and social habitat of language increased dramatically, functionalist reduction became more and more complex. Modern functionalist theories take into account a wide variety of environmental demands to be satisfied by language, including the given facts of human anatomy and physiology, the physical nature of sound, the structure of the human mind, and the facts of social organization. Any of these, as far as they are known, may conceivably be considered to have been a determining factor in the shaping of the human language system, as far as that is understood. The mainstream of modern linguistics, however, has not been functionalist. American structuralism, with transformational grammar as its offshoot, has been mainly concerned with finding out *what* the language system amounts to and *how* it functions, regardless of any possible functionalist rationale. In itself this is good method, since the more adequate one's insight into the workings of the language system, the more sense it makes to investigate possible environmental influences or functional adaptations. The same goes for the ecological environment: the more is known about the natural habitat of language, the greater the possibility to correlate environmental factors with features of language. Modern developments in psycholinguistics, sociolinguistics, phonetics, and related fields have dramatically increased our knowledge of the conditions under which language is supposed to operate.

Clearly, therefore, initiatives to look at language from a functionalist point of view, such as the new minimalism, should be welcomed. The "minimalist" version of functionalism, however, stands out from the others on a number of counts. First, it is more restricted than most other varieties in that it looks exclusively at meaning and pronunciation requirements, leaving other environmental factors, such as social structure, out of account. In section 5.7 it is shown that this omission vitiates the MP considerably.

Then, Chomsky's variety of functionalism is different in that it is unusually ambitious: it aims at strengthening a theory already developed on different grounds (the EST tradition as developed since 1970) by showing that it follows from natural necessities. Other forms of functionalism are less known for ambitions to provide such post hoc justifications. Clearly, if the minimalist perspective could indeed show Chomskyan syntax in a light of perfect functionality, that would be a great success. In fact, however, the very architecture of the minimalist model defeats any functionalist reduction (see section 5.1). Moreover, minimalist claims as to maximal computational efficiency come to nothing, even when the formal gaps left in *The Minimalist Program* are filled in, as Johnson and Lappin (1997) have shown.

This point is closely related to Chomsky's concept of "perfection." In his view, language is more "perfect" to the extent that it is determined by external factors of functionality and has no unmotivated autonomous principles of its own. Although most functionalist theories also like to say that language has no unmotivated features, the prevailing view in linguistic theory has, so far, been that the autonomy and proper nature of language set it off from the rest of nature. Up to his minimalist turn, Chomsky supported this attitude by promoting the idea that the problem of language acquisition can be solved if the FoL is seen as a specific innate linguistic "organ" with its own stock of autonomous and otherwise unmotivated restrictions, separate from other cognitive functions, which would make the FoL *imperfect* rather than *perfect*. Now, however, the perspective has shifted: the search for universal constraints is replaced by the search for compliance with "external" requirements. This history is unique to Chomskyan functionalism.

Finally, Chomsky's version of functionalism stands out for its emphasis on model building. Whereas less extravagant varieties of functionalism take language bit by bit, minimalism depicts the theoretical linguist as a "superbly competent engineer" building an ideal language faculty according to a set of design specifications.

This chapter is concerned mainly with the aspects in which Chomsky's minimalism stands in contrast with what one would expect of a functionalist approach.

5.2 How perfect is language?

This section takes a closer look at Chomsky's notion that language is more perfect to the extent that it is determined by external conditions of use. His central statement in this regard, in the context of the general motivation of the MP, is found right at the beginning of *The Minimalist Program* (Chomsky 1995:1):

> This work is motivated by two related questions: (1) what are the general conditions that the human language faculty should be expected to satisfy? and (2) to what extent is the language faculty determined by these conditions, without special structure that lies beyond them? The first question in turn has two aspects: what conditions are imposed on the language faculty by virtue of (A) its place within the array of cognitive systems of the mind/brain, and (B) general considerations of conceptual naturalness that have some independent plausibility, namely, simplicity, economy, symmetry, nonredundancy, and the like?

Question (B) is not precise, but not without content; attention to these matters can provide guidelines here, as in rational inquiry generally. Insofar as such considerations can be clarified and rendered plausible, we can ask whether a particular system satisfies them in one or another form. Question (A), in contrast, has an exact answer, though only parts of it can be surmised in the light of current understanding about language and related cognitive systems.

To the extent that the answer to question (2) is positive, language is something like a "perfect system," meeting external constraints as well as can be done, in one of the reasonable ways. The Minimalist Program for linguistic theory seeks to explore these possibilities.

Yet matters are not that simple. Question (2) causes problems in that we have a very incomplete idea of what "the general conditions that the human language faculty should be expected to satisfy," mentioned in question (1), amount to (Chomsky 1995:168):

> The language is embedded in performance systems that enable its expressions to be used for articulating, interpreting, referring, inquiring, reflecting, and other actions. We can think of the SD as a complex of instructions for these performance systems, providing information relevant to their functions. *While there is no clear sense to the idea that language is "designed for use" or "well adapted to its functions," we do expect to find connections between the properties of the language and the manner of its use.* [italics mine]

If taken literally, Chomsky seems to say that question (2), like his question (1B), is imprecise. He certainly says that the functionality aspects of the language faculty are unclear. The question of what to do about aspects of functionality, to which "there is no clear sense," is answered as follows in *The Minimalist Program* (Chomsky 1995:222–223):

> The question is imprecise: we do not know enough about the "external" systems at the interface to draw firm conclusions about conditions they impose. . . . The problems are nevertheless empirical, and we can hope to resolve them by learning more about the language faculty and the systems with which it interacts. We proceed in the only possible way: by making tentative assumptions about the external systems and proceeding from there.

In the Brasilia lectures it is said more explicitly (Chomsky 1998:18–19):

> The external systems are not very well understood, and in fact, progress in understanding them goes hand-in-hand with progress in understand-

ing the language system that interacts with them. So we face the daunting task of simultaneously setting the conditions of the problem and trying to satisfy them, with the conditions changing as we learn more about how to satisfy them. But that is what one expects in trying to understand the nature of a complex system.

And two pages later (Chomsky 1998:20–21):

> We also try to show that no structural relations are invoked other than those forced by legibility conditions or induced in some natural way by the computation itself.

This seems to imply that somehow descriptions and analyses that favor an explanation in the light of the "legibility conditions" imposed by the "external systems" should be considered preferable to those that do not do so, all things being equal, one supposes.

What is one to make of this? It is true that scientists often face "the daunting task of simultaneously setting the conditions of the problem and trying to satisfy them, with the conditions changing as we learn more about how to satisfy them." Science is largely a bootstrapping or feedback operation, and any theoretical linguist who has investigated the problems at issue to any depth will agree that the inquiry consists largely in discovering facts and generalizations about language and languages and using these as support for constrained hypotheses about the workings and the functionality of cognition and communication. An example of this method is provided in section 5.6 in connection with the Creole language of Mauritius.

In normal scientific procedure, whenever such "bootstrapping" is going on, the scientist may, as often happens in the study of nature, be impressed with the beauty, the simplicity, the ingenuity of the system he is gradually discovering, and he may be inclined to attribute some relevant aspects of his object of inquiry to environmental conditions of functionality. But he will most definitely not try to constrain his theory in such a way that the object of inquiry should preferably be taken to be "determined by these conditions, without special structure that lies beyond them," since such a procedure would immediately lead to a biased treatment of the available facts. As long as the bootstrapping or feedback process is going on and the scientist has no clear idea of the demands imposed by environmental conditions on the object of inquiry, any pressure to maximize, in the theory under development, the determining power of the demands discovered so far enhances the risk that the scientist in question may become blind to any further aspects, whether functional or not, he might conceivably discover. Conditions or constraints of this kind are aprioristic in that they are based on the presupposition that human language is, or strives to be, optimally functional. They are also arrogant in that they are based on the presumption that the scientist who poses these conditions has an adequate overall idea of the functional demands to be met by his object of inquiry.

5.3 Optimal language design and model building: the "fable"

Let us have a look at the notion of an "optimal language design." The idea of a minimalist, optimally functional language design is presented in the Brasilia lectures with the help of a fable: "How closely does language resemble what a superbly competent engineer might have constructed, given certain design specifications" (Chomsky 1998:15). The fable setting is needed because in actual reality the design specifications required are not available: as shown in section 5.2, these are still largely to be developed "hand-in-hand with progress in understanding the language system that interacts with them" (1998:18). A real-life engineer, no matter how superbly competent, would therefore be wise to decline the invitation. What remains without the fable element is the supposition that the language faculty is a device that provides optimal conditions for the development, given appropriate stimuli, of maximally efficient grammars.

Authors such as Botha (1997b, 1999) or Johnson and Lappin (1997) have pointed out that this supposition lacks independent motivation, largely because experience tells us that products of nature are usually far from perfect in the engineering sense, though they often also unexpectedly show up features that are remarkably functional. Moreover, although theories about the object of inquiry should satisfy norms of simplicity and elegance, there is no good reason to expect that the object of inquiry itself should be maximally simple and efficient. As Johnson and Lappin put it: "An obvious question, then, is what reason do we have for attributing optimality of design to biological systems" (1997:327). For them, Chomsky's claim of optimal design is "acutely problematic" (1997:329). From this point of view, our comment can therefore be brief: the supposition of optimal language design is unfounded.

Does that mean that it is also useless and uninteresting? Not necessarily, because the construction of minimalist, maximally efficient models or machines can be useful in that they are supposed to work and do the job for which they were designed, unlike theories which, if they are fully formalized (which they seldom are), require a human calculator to to do the work a machine can do much better. An implemented model functioning as a piece of input-output machinery has the advantage of demonstrably meeting at least some of the requirements that the object of inquiry must satisfy, and thus of being likely to show up unexpected obstacles or complications. The idea of an optimal language design can therefore be useful in the context of actual model building.

Unfortunately, Chomsky does not give any indication of what a language faculty (or a specific grammar) constructed according to minimalist principles would look like. He invites his readers to imagine a "superbly competent engineer" but not what such a person could possibly come up with. The grammatical machinery that he does propose is not only heavily underspecified but, more important, also unrelated to any "minimalist" principles or assumptions (see section 6.2.1 for further comment). Moreover, to the extent that actual implementation is envisaged, its coverage is limited to a small range of phenomena that, taken together, do not come close to defining anything that would constitute a real language. Given the absence of any form of model building or formal explicitation of his minimalist idea of a language faculty, Chomsky's appeal to an optimal language design specifying a perfect language faculty constructed by a "superbly competent engineer" remains without substance.

Model building serves a number of purposes in the nonapplied, theoretical sciences. If the problem to be solved is well defined with regard to both the task to be performed by the machinery in question and the input and output conditions to be met, it is a useful way of forming hypotheses. Also, as has been said, the construction of an actually working model may show up hidden snags or complications that had been overlooked in the handwritten version of the theory. It is for that reason that implementations of grammatical rule systems are useful: it often turns out that an abstract rule system, when actually implemented, unexpectedly leads to a blockage or some other undesirable consequence. Moreover, implementations may provide a measure for the evaluation of computational complexity that a nonimplemented formalism is less likely to provide. (It must be noted, in this context, that Chomsky has never shown much enthusiasm for computer implementations of grammatical rule systems.)

Sometimes it is felt that a model may well reflect some properties of the object of inquiry. For example, a sophisticated information retrieval system with its tasks competently defined and implemented in terms of a computer program may well serve as a tentative model of how the brain actually performs tasks of that nature, and crucial experiments may show to what extent the model can be taken to be realistic. If, then, the model turns out to be a reasonably accurate copy of what actually happens in the brain, we would say that the model maker did a pretty good job, rather than that the brain was pretty well designed. Yet Chomsky turns the tables and rather feels that nature deserves a pat on the back: "to the extent that the answer is positive, language is something like a 'perfect' system" (1995:1).

A model is also often used less to *understand* the object of inquiry than to *be applied*, so that it can take over certain tasks or improve the functioning of the object in more general ways. As long as nothing more is involved than the performance of menial tasks and morally relevant aspects of the lives of animals or humans are not encroached on, this is technological progress. But when modeling goes further, extreme caution is required.

Examples are found in the history of society making. The first serious attempt in this direction known in history was Plato's attempt at modeling the society of the Greek city of Syracuse in Sicily in the early fourth century BC according to his ideas of the perfect state. The enterprise soon turned into a total disaster, costing many lives. More recently, we have witnessed truly large-scale attempts at implementing socialist or Marxist theories of what would make for the perfect society. Again, history has shown repeatedly that such a priori attempts are bound to fail, apart from the often awsome consequences. Even so, modern forms of sociological theory have tried the same under the banner of "social engineering," using behaviorist conditioning techniques. These attempts have also proved dismal failures, and politicians and scientists alike appear to have understood now, or so one hopes, that human societies, along with the humans that make them up, are far more complex than the "scientific" theories of sociology and behaviorist psychology had tried to make them believe.[1] All of which goes to show that belief in the perfection of a manmade model usually amounts to hubris.

---

1. For more discussion of attempts at social engineering, see Popper (1945).

As regards the search for the "perfect language" (often identified with the "Adamic" language) as a kind of model building, there is a long tradition going back to the beginning of our culture and heavily spiced with kabbalism (Eco 1995), which fares no better than any of the other naïve modeling traditions. A lone exception, however, is formed by the language of Predicate Calculus created by Bertrand Russell in the early years of the century and based on principles developed by Giuseppe Peano, Gottlob Frege, and himself. This language is a monumental achievement. It is the best instrument available so far for the systematic expression of both mathematical and truth-conditional content, as well as for the calculus of logical entailments. It is the logicians' answer to the logical imperfection of surface sentences and their unsuitability for correct formalized reasoning—the fact that makes it necessary to postulate a transformational mapping procedure between semantic analyses and surface structures in the study of grammar and meaning (Chomsky's "displacement property"). And one must acknowledge that it has proved its mettle in mathematics and all its applications, and also, to some extent, in the study of linguistic meaning. For if present ideas about semantic analysis have any empirical foundation, the language of Predicate Calculus is a surprisingly good model for the mental language of semantic representations.

One may disagree with the logicians' verdict that natural language is unsystematic and suitable only for mundane talk, but one must grant them that *in their perspective of conceptual necessity*, from the point of view of a formal calculus of necessary consequence, the surface structures of language are indeed less than perfect. The logicians failed to see the systematicity and richness detected in language by linguists. But *from their point of view* they were right. And something was done about it: a formal language was developed on grounds of the logical notion of conceptual necessity, instantiating the logical version of a minimalist program. Although the formal language of Predicate Calculus is much poorer than natural language, as it lacks the full expressive power of the latter in a number of centrally important ways and is hardly usable as a means of daily linguistic interaction, it is a prime example of successful model building on the basis of a competent design specification and well-defined tasks.

Although the theoretical significance of the language of logic has been enormous, it was in principle set up as a model language to be applied, especially in logic and mathematics. But in fact, its applicational ambitions went well beyond these two subjects. There was, for some time, a widespread belief that it could also be of great use to society. Russell himself believed that the use of the language of logic gave freedom, and he was not alone in this. Until not too long ago it was thought by many that if people could be induced to use this formal language in their daily dealings, the world would be a better place and eternal peace would descend on earth. This is now generally taken to be naïvely optimistic, but vestiges of the belief that language barriers are an obstacle to world peace are still found.

Compared to logic, minimalism cuts a poor figure. Cool scrutiny relegates it to the somewhat curious tradition discussed in Eco (1995). Whereas the logical notion of conceptual necessity is grounded in a solid theory of logical entailment, Chomsky's "conceptual necessity" is nothing but the vague idea that it is difficult to imagine that things could be different. The minimalist criteria of what would constitute a perfect language are confused and inconsistent, with the result that the MP does not come close to the construction of a minimalist "model language," whether in an applied or a theoretical sense.

5.4 Language and communication

Chomsky's theory of language is badly deficient on the issue of the communicative function of human language, a fact that has seriously impaired his entire vision of the functionality of language and of the language faculty as a whole. To begin with, he does not distinguish linguistic from nonlinguistic communication, as appears from, for example, the following quote (Chomsky 2002:76–77):

> Language is not properly regarded as a system of communication. It is a system for expressing thought, something quite different. It can, of course, be used for communication, as can anything people do—manner of walking or style of clothes or hair, for example. But in any useful sense of the term, communication is not *the* function of language, and may even be of no significance for understanding the functions and nature of language. Hauser quotes Somerset Maugham's quip that "if nobody spoke unless he had something to say, . . . the human race would very soon lose the use of speech." His point seems accurate enough, even apart from the fact that language use is largely to oneself: "inner speech" for adults, monologue for children.

This is distinctly odd. Sober reflection on the well-known fact that sentences, and therefore also their token realizations as utterances, never come without a speech act component immediately makes the communicative function of the language faculty stand out among any other functions it may have. Likewise for the obvious fact that the external motor-perceptual component has been considerably adapted in the course of recent evolution to the production and perception of speech sounds and hence to public use (a fact that is systematically either denied or belittled in Chomsky's writings, against all evidence; see section 3.5.2 and also the following quote).

One does need, of course, some more or less precise idea of what is meant by "linguistic communication," but there are few signs in Chomsky's writings that he is interested in the question at all. Rather than consider the question of what linguistic communication amounts to and how it relates to the architecture of the language faculty, Chomsky resorts to the rhetorical devices of (a) replacing the question with a different one and (b) answering that by means of false association and analogy, as appears from the following passage (Chomsky 2002:106–108):

> So instead of asking the standard functionalist question, is it well designed for use?, we ask another question: is it well designed for interaction with the systems that are internal to the mind? It's quite a different question, because maybe the whole architecture of the mind is not well designed for use. Let me see if I can make an analogy: take some other organ of the body, say, the liver. You may discover that the liver is badly designed for life in Italy because people drink too much wine and they get all sorts of diseases of the liver; therefore, the liver wasn't well designed for function. On the other hand, the liver might be beautifully designed for interaction with the circulatory system and the kidney and so on, and those are just different things. . . . The use of language for communication might turn out to be a kind of epiphenomenon. . . . And then we can ask: how do people use it? It might turn out that it is not optimal for some of the ways in which we want to use it. . . . But there's a totally separate question: is it well designed with regard to the internal systems with which it must interact? That's a different perspective and a new question; and that's the question that the Minimalist Program tries to answer.
>
> The way I would like to think of it now is that the system is essentially inserted into already existing external systems: external to the language faculty, internal to the mind. So there's a sensori-motor system which is there, independently of the language; maybe it is somewhat modified because of the presence of language, but in essence it is there independently

of language. The bones of the middle ear don't change because of language. And there is some kind of system of thought (conception, intention and so on) which is sort of sitting there. . . . The language faculty has to interact with those systems, otherwise it's not usable at all. So we may ask: is it well designed for the interaction with those systems? Then you get a different set of conditions. And in fact the only condition that emerges clearly is that, given that the language is essentially an information system, the information it stores must be accessible to those systems, that's the only condition.

This is a textbook example of false and misleading argumentation. Leaving aside the probably unintended implication that the motor-perceptual system is "internal to the mind," note that, first, the question of the communicative use of language is denied and replaced with a different, much less obvious, question, which, of course, makes sure that "you get a different set of conditions" but leaves the original question unanswered.

Then an analogy is drawn with an organ, the liver, although the liver is not "used" in the sense that language is used but is physiologically involved in all kinds of uses that we make of our bodies. It would have been more enlightening to draw an analogy with, for example, the hand as an organ of the human body. Hands are used in a way that is, to a certain extent, analogous to the way language is used: to attain a purpose under conscious control. They are also linked up with other functions of the body, such as the motor-command and tactile parts of the nervous system, and, of course, with the circulatory and muscular systems, and a few others as well. Given its opposing thumb, it is obviously designed for the prototypical use of grasping under standard conditions, not, for example, for the grasping of water or hot coals (we make tools for those purposes). And repetitive use for certain specific purposes may lead to malfunction, as in the case of repetitive stress injury (RSI). Would one now conclude that the hand is not well designed for use because it fails to grasp water or hot coals and may be subject to RSI, or that the primary function of the hand is not grasping but its interaction with the nervous and circulatory systems of the body? Of course not. Nor does one conclude that language is not well designed for use because it does not function in a vacuum or under water (we make tools for such uses), or because it doesn't work very well for the expression of strictly private experiences, or because one may fall into a stammer under conditions of stress.

Meanwhile, the fact is totally neglected that language use is primarily a question of committing oneself—"putting oneself on the line," so to speak—socially and even in some cases legally, vis-à-vis the listeners or readers with regard to a given proposition (see section 3.5.7). So is the "softer" side of language use, its "grooming" function enhancing social cohesion (Levelt 1999:83): one says something kind just to make it clear that there are no problems—or the opposite. Given these basic deficiencies in Chomsky's analysis of the conditions of use of human language, one is justified in discarding his views on the matter as irrelevant.

5.5 The minimalist program is not minimalist

Right at the beginning of *The Minimalist Program*, Chomsky speaks about the possibility that language will, in actual fact, turn out to suffer from imperfections, but he does so without providing any *null hypothesis* expressing minimal assumptions regarding the external conditions: "To the extent that the answer to question (2) is positive, language is something like a 'perfect system,' meeting external constraints as well as can be done, in one of the reasonable ways. The Minimalist Program for linguistic theory seeks to explore these possibilities." We remember that the questions (1) and (2) have been phrased as: "(1) what are the general conditions that the human language faculty should be expected to satisfy? and (2) to what extent is the language faculty determined by these conditions, without special structure that lies beyond them?" (Chomsky 1995:1). Chomsky thus appears to be saying that the degree of perfection of the language faculty is to be measured against the extent to which the FoL makes resulting languages satisfy general conditions of functionality, including external conditions imposed by the motor-perceptual and cognitive interfaces. However, he also states, as we have seen, that the interface conditions are not well known, and that a better understanding of the "external systems" goes "hand-in-hand" with a better understanding of the language system as work proceeds.

But if that is so, it will be impossible in principle to brand any feature of the language system as being in any way "imperfect," since the feature in question may turn out, during the feedback or hand-in-hand or bootstrapping process, to have a certain functionality value with regard to the way language meets the interfaces in the environment or architecture in which it is embedded, in which case the feature would confirm the perfection, not the imperfection, of the language faculty. As long as there is no independent evidence or a minimalist *base line* regarding the demands imposed by these interfaces, it is logically impossible to apply the predicates of perfection or imperfection. Even so, however, the suggestion is that the main source of imperfections is located in the way language in general, or a specific language, meets the external conditions of delivering satisfactory products at the motor-perceptual and cognitive interfaces.

The matter becomes really tangled when the discrepancy is discussed between the overt surface form of sentences and the covert form postulated for the purpose of semantic interpretation. It is a universal property of language (called "displacement property" by Chomsky) that the surface form of sentences is often misleading with regard to their meaning and in general unfit for direct semantic interpretation. We shall simply assume here, with Chomsky and the majority of professional linguists, that this discrepancy is real. This means that a device is needed to relate the surface structure of sentences to what we have called their semantic analysis or SA. The need for such a device, usually called "grammar," is central to the language faculty and has dominated the study of grammar from the ancient philosophers of the Stoa to the present day.

For Chomsky the need for such a device is an "imperfection," whose source may well have to be sought in "external conditions" of expressibility and interpretability. At the same time, however, the presence of two interface *levels*, one for expression or perception and one for interpretation, is considered to be conceptually necessary (Chomsky 1995:169):

> So far we are within the domain of virtual conceptual necessity, at least if the general outlook is adopted. UG must determine the class of possible languages. It must specify the properties of SDs and of the symbolic representations that enter into them. In particular, it must specify the interface levels (A-P, C-I), the elements that constitute these levels, and the computations by which they are constructed. A particularly simple design for language would take the (conceptually necessary) interface levels to be the only levels. That assumption will be part of the "minimalist" program I would like to explore here.

But if language did without the "displacement" property, then *one level of representation* would be sufficient, which could be fed into both the motor-perceptual and the interpretative system. With one level and two interfaces, no Spell-Out, with all it involves, would be called for. Chomsky has apparently failed to see that the notions "level of representation" and "interface" are only loosely related. Notionally, there may be fewer levels than interfaces because one level may serve any number of interfaces. But there may also be more levels than interfaces, since it is not necessary for a level of representation to serve an interface.

Therefore, the assumption of two structurally different levels, separated by Spell-Out and resulting from different sets of rules or operations, is *not* conceptually necessary, which means that the substantive proposals made in the minimalist *program* are not in accord with the principles defining the minimalist *method*. The minimalist assumption of two structurally different levels is part of an "imperfect" system. Moreover, as we have seen, Chomsky's "conceptual necessity" is not a clear or precise notion but is, in fact, no more than an intuition to the effect that, as far as he can see, things could not have been otherwise.

Staying within Chomsky's frame of thought, one will naturally accept that the motor-perceptual interface and the conceptual interface must impose different legibility conditions, but that does not require different levels of representation, connected by an operation "Move." One can easily imagine one and the same level of representation, some of whose features are legible to the one and others to the other interface. It is a priori strange or even absurd to suppose that, for example, parsing at the motor-perceptual end, or cognitive processing at the conceptual end, would be facilitated by moving elements away from the position they occupy on the basis of lexical "merging." Mere Merge, without any Move or Displacement, is the best guarantee for both parsing and cognitive processing. One is, therefore, somewhat amazed at finding Chomsky suggest that Move or Displacement might be seen as possibly motivated by either the conceptual or the motor-perceptual interface (Chomsky 1995:317):

> The second question—why do natural languages have such devices?—arose in the early days of generative grammar. Speculations about it invoked considerations of language use: facilitation of parsing on certain assumptions, the separation of theme-rheme structures from base-determined semantic (θ) relations, and so on. Such speculations involve "extraneous" conditions of the kind discussed earlier, conditions imposed on C_{HL} by the ways it interacts with external systems. That is where we would hope the source of "imperfections" would lie, on minimalist assumptions.

> Our concern here is to determine how spare an account of the operation Attract/Move the facts of language allow. The best possible result is that bare output conditions are satisfied in an optimal way.

Incidentally, contrary to what Chomsky says, the functionalist question of why natural languages have such devices hardly arose at all in the early days of generative grammar. If it did, it was marginal and not considered to be of much relevance. Then, what Chomsky names "our concern here"— that is, answering the question "how spare an account of the operation Attract/Move the facts of language allow"—differs in no way from what has been tried in theoretical grammar since the 1960s.

Again one wonders what it could mean to say that language is in any sense "perfect" regardless of the external conditions mentioned, or that "there seems to be a second and more dramatic imperfection in language design: the 'displacement property' that is a pervasive aspect of language." Chomsky admits that the question "why language should have the displacement property is interesting" and "has been discussed for many years without resolution" (1998:24). However, if it is not known how or why language needs this property on account of external conditions, what sense does it make to speak of "imperfection" at all? The justification given is that the formal languages of logic and mathematics, or those used in computer science, which lack such imperfections, are "free to disregard the legibility conditions imposed on human language by the architecture of the mind/brain." But this is not so: all these formal languages need some interface with the human mind/brain, or else they would be useless. The language of Predicate Calculus, in particular, needs precisely the same cognitive interface as is required for natural language, in addition to the interface needed for writing. Perhaps not for speaking, but there, too, one may maintain that it is possible to pronounce Predicate Calculus formulae in some regimented form of natural language. The difference with the MP is that the designers of the formal languages of logic, mathematics, and computer science have taken the external legibility conditions for granted, not assigning them any special importance beyond the obvious.

To speculate that "the best possible result is that bare output conditions are satisfied in an optimal way" is equally vacuous given the scarcity of independent evidence about these output conditions, and given the fact that whatever little evidence is available strongly suggests that language does not instantiate the "best possible result." We remember that "the external systems are not very well understood, and in fact, progress in understanding them goes hand-in-hand with progress in understanding the language system that interacts with them" (Chomsky 1998:18). On the one hand, Chomsky asserts (1995:221–222):

> This property of language might turn out to be one source of a striking departure from minimalist assumptions in language design: the fact that objects appear in the sensory output in positions "displaced" from those in which they are interpreted, under the most principled assumptions about interpretation. This is an irreducible fact about human language, expressed somehow in every contemporary theory of language, however the facts about displacement may be formulated.

On the other hand, he continues (1995:222):

> We want to determine why language has this property . . . and how it is realized (our primary concern throughout). We want to find out how well the conditions that impose this crucial property on language are satisfied: "as well as possible," we hope to find. Minimalist assumptions suggest that the property should be reduced to morphology-driven movement. What is known about the phenomena seems to me to support this expectation.

The situation is at least curious, given that (a) the external conditions are said to be insufficiently understood, so that it is not known why language has the "displacement property"; (b) available knowledge suggests that we have to do with "a striking departure from minimalist assumptions"; (c) even so, it is hoped that language satisfies the hitherto unknown external conditions that impose this property as well as possible, so that this property would *not* be a striking departure from minimalist assumptions but fulfill minimalist expectations; (d) what is known about the phenomena is said to support minimalist assumptions; but (e) no such evidence is shown, although it would play a crucial part in the discussion, which now appears eerily out of touch with tangible reality.

Seen in this light, the MP position is without any interest. It would have some interest if clear data or analyses were provided, showing the explanatory power of the position. But, as has been said more than once, no such evidence is shown at all. As it is, every oddity found in some language can be interpreted as the result of some as yet unknown output condition.

What we do have is an abundance of negative evidence. Languages differ in so many mutually incompatible ways, that, prima facie, no conclusion ought to be drawn at all about external conditions imposed on language. This would explode the vicious circle and eliminate all talk about functionality. Fortunately, however, the situation does not have to be that bad. For there is a good chance that the *format of syntactic rules* is subject to universal constraints. Moreover, it looks as if there are general *overall tendencies* in grammatical rule systems, such as Matrix Greed (see section 8.1). This allows one to ask whether these universal constraints and tendencies may perhaps be seen to make some sense in the light of external conditions of functionality. In these cases it does make sense to pose the functionality question, though it still makes no sense to speak of optimal solutions.

This does not help the MP, however, for the MP has jettisoned the notion of syntactic rule. All it has (besides "stylistic" rules; see section 8.1) is Move—that is, obligatory raising induced by lexical ("morphological") features. More traditional analyses, which use the notion of syntactic rule, leave at least some room for a functionalist perspective. The MP, however, which does without syntactic rules, not only lacks empirical support, as we have seen, but it also defeats functionalist reduction as long as the options that are taken to exist in the selection of the "morphological" features that are said to determine the way elements are raised by the operation Move are not set out on some comparative functionality scale, no matter how rudimentary or intuitive. The MP, however, has not even begun to do so.

Let us consider a few concrete examples. The first is the analysis of complementation systems in terms of Subject Raising (SR) and Predicate Raising (PR) as discussed in section 8.1. If the MP could account equally simply and convincingly for the facts that are accounted for in terms of SR and PR as distinct obligatory or optional rules, it would be in business. At the moment, however, the SR/PR analysis is the only satisfactory generative account we have, and it does not stand reduction to a unified raising procedure. Given this account, it makes no sense to optimize functionality in the theory, for if the one choice is more functional than the other, why does the FoL have the other, if it is to be optimally functional? What does make sense is the observation that both are forms of *raising* into the lexical matrix frame of the sentence, which may suggest a general functionality of such raising procedures.

Or take the position allocated to adjectival or adverbial modifiers. In some languages they are placed before, in other languages after the constituent they qualify, and in others again both positions are allowed (though usually with some restrictions).[2] This is typically a matter of choice on a parameter. But the question of how to evaluate the functionality of either choice makes no sense in the absence of independent criteria of functionality. All one can say is that there appears to be some functionality in the fact that attributive adjectives are generally placed in the immediate proximity of their nouns.

More problematic is the canonical position of the verb in sentences. Some languages are standardly verb-final, others verb-first, and in other languages again the verb stands in the middle or the position of the verb is free. It is hardly to be expected that all positional variants are the optimal answer to "external output conditions." In fact, it may well be that the SVO (=NP-VP) order is easier to process and thus more functional than either VSO or SOV. Still, variations such as these cannot be caught in an overall tendency that would show some higher-level functionality. Here functionality does not seem to be a valid criterion.

5.6 Why choices? The case of Mauritian Creole

Even if some functionality can be detected in some general aspects of universal grammar, there is still the question of why choices should be allowed. This question is the more pressing since some choices are clearly not so functional. The operation Predicate Raising, for example, discussed in section 8.1, can hardly be called functionally optimal, since it may lead to multiple embeddings with crossing dependencies, which are notorious for the difficulties they create for comprehension. A Dutch clause like (1), for example, where PR has been applied three times in succession, is hard to process, largely owing to the crossing dependencies (though a proper context and a rapid presentation have a considerable facilitating effect on comprehension). The synonymous sentence (2), in contrast, where PR has applied only once (on the *laten*-cycle; PR on the *leren*-cycle and the *proberen*-cycle is optional and has not been applied in (2)), offers no special processing difficulties, just like the English translation added to (2):

(1)   . . . dat   zij Leo de hond het bot probeerde te leren laten halen
       . . . that she Leo the dog the bone tried   to teach let fetch

2. For example, as Paul Postal (personal communication) pointed out, English has *large enough* along with *sufficiently large*, but not **enough large* or **large sufficiently*.

(2)   . . . dat zij probeerde Leo te leren de hond het bot   te laten halen
       . . . that she tried   Leo to teach the dog the bone to   let fetch
       '. . . that she tried to teach Leo to get the dog to fetch the bone'

Yet both (1) and (2) are equally grammatical in Dutch. Therefore, if one looks for functionally optimal explanations of grammatical phenomena, the PR facts of Dutch (and many other languages) are highly problematic.

In general, any effort at supplying functional explanations for the phenomena relating to (universal) grammar will be up against the fact that natural languages do not, on the whole, optimize semantic transparency, in the sense that they do not facilitate the transition from SA to surface structure and vice versa as much as possible.

The optimization of semantic transparency is reasonably taken to be a defining feature of Creole languages, which came into being in circumstances of extreme deprivation, with personal liberties heavily restricted by conditions of slavery or other forms of servitude, and an immediate and vital necessity to communicate with fellow slaves and with masters without a common language being available (Seuren and Wekker 1986). The study of Creole languages shows that normally most of their lexical items, along with some grammatical aspects, have been taken from the superstrate language of the (mostly European) masters, whereas the grammars tend to retain, next to elements from the superstrate language, also areal features common to the (mostly African) substrate languages of the Creole speakers. But all grammatical elements, whether taken from substrate or superstrate languages, are recast in formats that suggest an optimization of semantic transparency. The constraining or possibly creative role of universal grammar or the human language faculty in these historical processes of language creation and language change is constantly mentioned, for obvious reasons, by specialists in Creole languages, but it has not, so far, proved possible to give it an even remotely precise definition.[3]

An example of how the drive for semantic transparency might be seen to influence the transfer and re-use of elements taken from the grammar

---

3. An extreme view is defended in Bickerton (1981 and other publications), to the effect that Creole grammars are entirely determined by the creative powers of the innate language faculty, without any substrate influence exerted by the languages already spoken by the mostly adult slave population. This extreme view has proved open to too many conceptual and factual reservations to be considered tenable.

of the superstrate language is the case of PR (Predicate Raising) versus SR (Subject Raising) in the French-based Mauritian Creole, the lingua franca of the Indian Ocean island of Mauritius. Since Creole languages do not, on the whole, favor rules like PR that are, in principle, counterproductive with regard to semantic transparency, it seems safe to assume that Mauritian Creole has not developed PR on its own, as a result of the built-in faculty of language, but has taken PR from the syntax of its superstrate language, French. However, it is found that in many cases where one would expect PR since it is already there in the language, the PR rule is not applied and SR is applied instead. In (3a), for example, PR has applied, but not so in (3c), which has SR. Application of SR in (3a) results in the ungrammatical (3b), while PR applied in (3c) gives the ungrammatical (3d). (3e,f) allow for both PR and SR:

(3) a. √Serzã-la pa ule $_v$[fer vin] èn dokter.
        sergeant-the not wants $_v$[make come] a doctor
        'The sergeant does not want to send for a doctor.'
     b. *Serzã-la pa ule fer èn dokter vini.
        the sergeant does not want a doctor come
     c. √Mo kuzẽ pu fer mwa gagn èn bõ travay.
        my cousin will make me get a good job
     d. *Mo kuzẽ pu $_v$[fer gagn] mwa èn bõ travay.
        my cousin will $_v$[make get] me a good job
     e. √Mo fin $_v$[tan dir] so papa sa nuvel-la.
        I have $_v$[heard say] his father that news
     f. √Mo fin tan so papa dir sa nuvel-la.
        I have heard his father say that news

Why these differences? Let us assume, for a start, that the SVO linear surface order is more transparent than either VSO or SOV, perhaps because in the SVO order the subject term and the object term are separated by the verb and thus are more conspicuously identifiable by their position. The basic SVO linear surface order is, in fact, a Creole universal, and is also the basic linear surface order in Mauritian Creole. Note that SR always results in the SVO linear order for the embedded clause, whereas PR never does.

Inspection of the data reveals that PR is obligatory in Mauritian Creole only when the verb of the embedded clause has at most one argument, either because it is intransitive, as in (3a), or because Passive has applied. This minor deviation from the SVO linear order for the embedded clause may perhaps be seen as a concession to the superstrate language French, from which the PR rule was taken. When the lower verb has more than one overt argument term, as in (3c), the default alternative SR must be used, so that the SVO order is saved.

Cases like (3e) are problematic, since they have a VSO surface linear order with respect to the elements of the embedded S, with both overt subject and overt object: 'dir so papa sa nuvel-la'. (3e) would thus be incompatible with (3d), which is considered ungrammatical for that reason. The answer to this problem may be this.

Assume that (3e,f) have the underlying form (4a) (specified as far as relevant), with obligatory Subject Deletion (SD). After SD we have (4b), which corresponds to (3f). At this point, PR is optional. If PR applies, the result is (4c), which is identical to (3e):

(4)   a.   mo fin tan so papa$_x$ $_S$[x dir sa nuvel-la]   SD $\rightarrow$
            I have heard his father$_x$ $_S$[x say that news]
      b.   mo fin tan so papa $_{VP}$[dir sa nuvel-la]   PR $\rightarrow$
      c.   mo fin $_V$[tan dir] so papa sa nuvel-la

Since both (4b = 3f) and (4c = 3e) are grammatical, one can posit that when the lower subject has been deleted under SD and precisely one further overt argument term—the direct object—is left, PR is optional. This may then be seen as the most serious deviation from semantic transparency allowed in the language or, alternatively, as the extent to which Mauritian Creole is prepared to go with regard to the superstrate language French.

The general rationale behind the apparently odd collection of restrictions on PR in Mauritian Creole thus seems to be that the damage done to semantic transparency by PR is kept to a workable minimum, whereby we realize that the notion of "absolute minimum" cannot be made precise (see Seuren 1990 for a detailed analysis).

This analysis, incidentally, is a clear case of what was called "bootstrapping" in section 5.2. But note that any tentative ideas about the influence of semantic transparency are brought to bear a posteriori and have in no way influenced or directed the analysis. There is, in particular, no a priori expectation of optimal semantic transparency ("perfection"), even though the fact that we are dealing with a Creole language might, to some extent, justify such an expectation. The furthest we would be prepared to go in this respect is to allow considerations of semantic transparency to play a role in a final evaluation of an analysis of a Creole construction compared to possible alternative analyses that cover the facts to an equal degree of completeness, simplicity, and generality but without the perspective of semantic transparency. These are elementary matters of good method.

5.7 Sociolinguistic factors

This still leaves open the question of why languages should develop features that run counter to semantic transparency. On minimalist assumptions, semantic transparency should be a main determining factor in the growth of grammars, since it should contribute in the most direct manner thinkable to a state of perfection. Yet this is not what is found. What is found, in the languages of the world, is a combination of, or trade-off between, two opposed tendencies. On the one hand, languages tend to favor semantic transparency, especially during times of profound social upheaval, such as occurred when the Roman Empire collapsed taking the national language Latin with it, which rapidly turned into a variety of new Romance vernaculars. The new languages that arise in such circumstances have to satisfy the most basic needs first, just like Creole languages. On the other hand, languages tend to develop features that go against transparency, such as ad hoc exceptions or unexpected complications in grammatical rule systems occurring without apparent reason or motivation. This tends to happen especially when a language is spoken by a large community that has known a long period of relative political stability, cultural continuity, and economic well-being.

Work by sociolinguists on the mechanisms of sound change (e.g., Weinreich et al. 1968, Labov 1972, 1980, 1994) has shown that social position, attitudes and aspirations are a dominant determining factor (Labov 1980:261–262):

> It appears that the speakers who are most advanced in the sound changes are those with the highest status in their local community, as the socioeconomic class patterns indicate. But the communication networks provide additional information, discriminating among those with comparable status. The most advanced speakers are the persons with the largest number of local contacts within the neighborhood, yet who have at the same time the highest proportion of their acquaintances outside the neighborhood. Thus

we have a portrait of individuals with the highest local prestige who are responsive to a somewhat broader form of prestige at the next larger level of social communication.

Although most work in this area has been done on sound change, there seems to be no reason why the conclusions should not be extrapolated to other parts of the language system, including grammar. In fact, some of the work done by Labov strongly suggests that the same social mechanisms are at work in grammar (Labov 1969).

The psychological mechanism is clear. Speakers in an enviable social position want to distinguish themselves from the rest by dressing and behaving differently, and language use is one form of behavior. At the same time, the less privileged often, but not always, have the wish to be somehow associated with their social models, with the result that either they dress and behave in the same way (or try to do so anyway), or else they adopt forms of attire and behavior that show their positive attitude toward their models. The latter, again, still wanting to distinguish themselves, will introduce further innovations. This can go on ad infinitum, but usually social processes interfere and assign prestige to different groups, where the same phenomena will occur. The reason that most linguistic changes are not traceable to their causal sources is precisely the fact that the often minute and complex social movements causing the changes have almost always remained hidden from the historian. It is easily understood that such a mechanism is conducive to the introduction into the language of elements that are the opposite of semantically transparent. For it is in the interest of the model groups to make their variety of the language more difficult, not easier.

The very fact that such a mechanism exists takes the bottom out of Chomsky's MP, with its expectation to find a "perfect" language. For it does not seem possible to treat the sociological parameters involved in the building up of social positions, attitudes, and ambitions as part of the "external systems" behind the motor-perceptual and the semantic interfaces, even though they belong to the wider context of language use. Redefining these external systems in such a way as to incorporate the sociological parameters in question would not help, since it would then be necessary to recognize that there are contrary forces at work in these systems, which would defeat the notion of an optimal answer to conditions imposed from outside.

What was said at the end of section 1.3 with respect to different languages applies with equal force to different dialectal or sociolinguistic language varieties: if each specific language variety is defined by the values selected on a set of universal parameters, it is hardly thinkable that each value selected will result in an equal degree of functionality. Chomsky's suggestion that "every possible language meets minimalist standards" (2002:130) has not been backed up by any kind of serious analysis.

5.8 Conclusion

What we see in Chomsky's MP is a combination of an unrealistic random-generator view and an untenably narrow functionalist view, together with a lack of any specification of what makes for an optimal solution to the demands imposed by boundary conditions of meaning and sound, a fatal lack of necessary formal and empirical detail, and the absence of any relation between minimalist premises and the grammatical theory proposed. Moreover, and perhaps most fatally, not a single actual *argument* is found in Chomsky's presentation of his MP. There are plenty of vague promises and assurances, but no cogent or coherent argument that would convince even the unwilling reader that a particular conclusion is inescapable. This makes it hard to subscribe to the opinions quoted in the first paragraph of section 1.3, to the effect that we have here a "masterpiece" or a "major break-through to a new level of abstraction" or "one of the most fascinating conceptual adventures of our time." On the contrary, what we do have is a fanciful fabrication invoking a grammatical machinery without presenting the facts that it should account for and assigning it properties of functionality that are demonstrably absent.

6

What Is Conceptually Necessary about the MP?

We now come to the question of what conceptual motivation for the random-generator position taken in the MP could be provided. Recall that the random-generator position entails the random generation of sentences. In minimalist terms this means that syntax is regarded as a random generator of sentential structures, each consisting of a pair (SA,PR) in such a way that SA (semantic analysis) and PR (phonological representation) are instructions to "external" systems of semantic interpretation and phonetic realization, respectively. (For a flowchart representation of this model of grammatical description, see fig. 6.3 later in this chapter.)

In chapter 7 it is shown in detail that the only potential empirical support for the general random-generator position—namely, the existence of certain structural elements that codetermine semantic interpretation but cannot be regarded as being part of syntactic deep structure and must, therefore, be taken to originate in an autonomous process of surface structure construction—comes to nothing, in that the alleged instances of surface structure semantic interpretation are seen to be best located in the underlying or "deep" structure that is fed into the transformations that generate surface structures.

Furthermore, although in a general sense these surface-driven elements of semantic interpretation support random-generator models of language generation (as shown in figs. 6.1 and 6.2 later in this chapter), they are an embarrassment in the specific random-generator model that forms part of the MP, since that model lacks a feeding line from the level of phonetic form to that of semantic interpretation (logical form). Yet, for reasons that are not made clear, Chomsky still insists on the reality of the elements in question, in the face of arguments to the contrary and in spite of their incompatibility with the program he proposes.

6.1 Conceptual motivation for the random generator?

Assuming now that the arguments of chapter 7 are correct, which means that the only empirical support for the random-generator view in a general sense has disappeared, we must consider the question of whether this view, and in particular the version proposed in Chomsky (1995), can be upheld on grounds of conceptual necessity. This is what Chomsky maintains (1995:168–169):

> Another standard assumption is that a language consists of two components: a lexicon and a computational system. The lexicon specifies the items that enter into the computational system, with their idiosyncratic properties. *The computational system uses these elements to generate derivations and SDs.* The derivation of a particular linguistic expression, then, involves a choice of items from the lexicon and a computation that constructs the pair of interface representations. So far we are in the domain of virtual conceptual necessity, at least if the general outlook is adopted. [italics mine]

And again (Chomsky 1995:186):

> Recall the (virtual) conceptual necessities within this general approach. UG determines possible symbolic representations and derivations. A language consists of a lexicon and a computational system. *The computational system draws from the lexicon to form derivations, presenting items from the lexicon in the format of X-bar theory.* Each derivation determines a linguistic expression, an SD, which contains a pair (π,λ) meeting the interface conditions. [italics mine]

The first observation to be made is that the notion of random generation is slipped in surreptitiously. This is done in the sentences that have been italicized in the preceding quotes. A closer look will help.

One has no difficulty in accepting that it is conceptually necessary to hold that there must be an algorithmic computation enabling speakers to produce sentences, if, as is widely agreed, the set of possible sentences in a language is denumerably infinite, since only an algorithmic generator can produce a denumerably infinite set of strings of symbols. This much is not just conceptual but mathematical necessity, complete with the requirement that there must be a lexicon (usually called "vocabulary" in the mathematical literature) to provide the symbols that make up the strings.

One can thus accept without any problem that lexical items, with their idiosyncrasies (though there is a great deal of regularity also in the lexicon), enter into computations that produce sentences. The question, however, is whether it is appropriate to say that the computational system *uses* the lexical elements to generate sentences, or *draws from* the lexicon to form derivations. The terms *use* and *draw from* induce a presupposition of causal origin, and this presupposition is not conceptually necessary, neither in a mathematical nor in any other sense. Yet it is precisely this implicit presupposition that is the foundation of the random-generator position put forward in *The Minimalist Program*.

Suppose we reformulate the italicized sentence in the first of the two quotes given above as follows:

> These elements are fed into the computational system
> to generate derivations and SDs.

Under any interpretation, mathematical or otherwise, of the notion of conceptual necessity, the reformulated sentence is as necessary, or unnecessary, as the italicized sentence in the quote given above. (One recalls from section 1.5 that recent formulations in Hauser, Chomsky, and Fitch 2002 and Chomsky 2002 come close to this reformulation.) Both procedures are conceptually or mathematically possible, but neither is necessary. The natural question to ask is: which of the two is correct in a realist sense?

6.1.1 The transition from random-generator to mediational grammar

6.1.1.1 The combination of structuralism and behaviorism.   Before we turn to this question, let us first trace the historical origins of the random-generator view of language, to have a better idea of the historical context. This concept of grammar seems to have a double origin, stemming from a confluence of two intellectual currents around the middle of the twentieth century. One current was the combination of structuralism and behaviorism, a combination which, as one knows, has profoundly affected linguistic thinking during much of the past century. A major result of the structuralist-behaviorist thinking prevalent in linguistics at the time was a strong and sometimes exclusive focusing on linguistic form, combined with an attitude of uneasiness with regard to semantic phenomena. There was a tendency to ignore semantic facts as much as possible and look the other way. Leading theoretical linguists like Leonard Bloomfield and, for a while, Zellig Harris even held that meaning should be kept out of linguistics altogether.

This attitude of repression of semantic aspects in the study of language was transferred to early transformational grammar, even though, by that time, behaviorism was clearly on the wane and meaning was looked upon with less suspicion than before. As a matter of historical fact, we can say that linguists working within most varieties of generative grammar continued to be uneasy in the presence of semantic phenomena and remained entirely focused on linguistic form, even though there clearly was a greater openness toward semantic phenomena. The rise of logic-based model-theoretic semantics as a formal theory of meaning did not do much to improve the situation in linguistics. Chomsky is a clear representative of this manner of linguistic thinking. His main concern has always been syntax, while his notions with regard to semantic or pragmatic theory have been much less noteworthy and have, in fact, lacked any influence whatsoever.

6.1.1.2 Algorithms in linguistic theory. The second current leading to the random-generator position presented in Chomsky (1995) is the mathematical theory of algorithms developed during the 1920s and 1930s by eminent mathematicians like Emil Post and Kurt Gödel (see Rosenbloom 1950:ch. 4, for a detailed exposition). Around 1950, Harris was driven to the theory of algorithms on the basis of his recently gained insight that the set of constructions that make up the sentences of a language, down to the primitive lexical elements, can be characterized by an algorithmic generative device. He formulated this new insight as follows (Harris 1951:372–373):[1]

1. The abstruse terminology should be seen, of course, against the background of the time this was written. Note that Harris's expression "geometric models (diagrams)" refers to the tree diagrams that now make up the central illustrative device in the study of grammar.

The work of analysis leads right up to the statements which enable anyone to synthesize or predict utterances in the language. These statements form a deductive system with axiomatically defined initial elements and with theorems concerning the relations among them. The final theorems would indicate the structure of the utterances of the language in terms of the preceding parts of the system. There may be various ways of presenting this system, which constitutes the description of the language structure. The system can be presented most baldly in an ordered set of statements defining the elements at each successive level or stating the sequences which occur at that level. Compactness, inspectability, and clarity of structure may be gained at various points by the use of symbols for class, variable member, and relation, or by the construction of geometric models (diagrams).

This is how the theory of algorithms found its way into linguistics, forming the basis of the new theory of generative grammar.

Although the mathematical theory of algorithms is extremely general and allows for any formally well-defined manipulation of strings of symbols, the kind of algorithm envisaged in early generative grammar was an initial or primitive algorithm, and not a derived algorithm. An initial or primitive algorithm simply generates strings of symbols (sentences) on the basis of a vocabulary and a finite set of "rewrite" instructions, which are constrained in such a way as to produce a new piece of branching structure every time they are applied. The production or generation of the strings of symbols in question is either random or weighted by some external measure, such as, for example, statistical frequency conditions on certain combinations of symbols. No form of external weighting, however, was ever considered in the theory of grammar as presented by Harris and those who took over his ideas, including Chomsky.

In Harris's instrumentalist perspective, this was a way of characterizing the set of sentences of a language and their structure that far exceeded anything in existence in clarity and precision. Given the absence of any form of weighting, this early concept, where a grammar consists entirely of "rewrite" or tree-expansion rules, is unequivocally of the random-generator type and instrumentalist. A generative grammar of this type randomly generates sentences, merely as a formal procedure, regardless of any semantic or other "external" considerations.

Then, however, two things happened. First, Harris soon found, as an empirical matter, that this method of generating sentences was not maximally economical. It proved simpler and more efficient to generate sentences in two steps: (a) an initial tree-expansion or rewrite grammar to generate "kernel sentences" (soon to be replaced with "deep structures"), and (b) a noninitial or derived algorithm consisting of transformational rules that take an already generated tree structure as input and deliver a tree structure as output (i.e., functions from tree structures to tree structures). This, as is well known, became the concept of transformational generative grammar, which gained ascendency in linguistics around 1960. Note that this transformational concept of grammar still took no account of meaning and was still entirely of the random-generator type, as well as instrumentalist.

By this time, however, the theoretical horizon of linguistic theory began to widen, in the sense that it became accepted, in the context of new insights in cognitive science and the philosophy of science in general, to view a grammar of a language as a theory of the native speaker's linguistic competence.

6.1.1.3 The reintroduction of meaning: mediational grammar. Thus, the second thing that happened was the realization, around 1963, by Jerrold Katz and Jerry Fodor that the notion of linguistic competence—that is, knowledge of a language—could not be limited to a native speaker's ability to produce well-formed sentences at random, without any knowledge of what these sentences should mean. Knowledge of a language L must be taken to imply also the ability to understand sentences in L, besides the ability to produce them, and understanding implies some form of knowledge of what the sentences in question mean. It was therefore proposed (Katz and Fodor 1963, Katz and Postal 1964), that the existing model of grammatical description should be extended, not just with a phonological component, which was becoming standardly accepted, but also with a semantic component, which would have to account for the meanings of the sentences generated by the syntactic generator. One notices that the perspective is still that of a random-generator grammar: the syntax generates, and the two components do the "interpretation."

The proposal was thus that next to the syntax or grammar there should be a "semantic component," which was taken to consist of "interpretative rules" taking syntactically defined structures as input and delivering semantic analyses of whatever kind. In Katz and Fodor (1963), the syntactic structures that should serve as input to the semantic component were taken to be both deep and surface structures. In Katz and Postal (1964), however, it was argued that deep structures should be the sole input to the semantic component. This would keep the transformations semantically invariant, since the semantic properties of the structures concerned were already fixed at the deep structure level of representation. This theory was subsequently adopted by Chomsky in *Aspects* of 1965, but given up soon afterward in favor of the position proposed in Katz and Fodor (1963), renamed extended standard theory or EST, schematically rendered in figure 6.1 later in this chapter.

At the time, much of all this was still unclear and ill defined. Thus the format of the semantic analyses was, for some time, totally opaque. Not until it was convincingly argued by McCawley in (1967) that semantic analyses are likewise linguistic structures but cast in the mold of (an enriched variety of) the language of Predicate Calculus did it become clear that the intended semantic component was, in fact, another derived transformational algorithm, turning tree structures of one kind into tree structures of another kind.

About that time, in the wake of the Katz and Postal hypothesis of the semantic invariance of the transformational rules in syntax, the idea caught hold that there was no need to distinguish the semantic analysis from the deep structure level of representation, which made the entire notion of a separate semantic component superfluous. This idea was based, on the one hand, on notional or conceptual grounds, in that if the deep structure already contains all semantic information there is no need to assume that the semantic analysis is distinct from it, and, on the other hand, on a number of empirical arguments, similar to those presented in chapter 7. This new development was christened *generative semantics*, even though it was not a semantic but a syntactic theory.

Most readers will be familiar with the story. Yet it is not generally recognized that the transition from Katz and Fodor (1963) via Katz and Postal (1964) to generative semantics was, in fact, a transition from a random-generator to a mediational concept of language. Whereas in Katz and Fodor (1963) and Katz and Postal (1964) the syntax is still viewed as the autonomous "starter" of the generative process, randomly producing sentences, the generative semantics model is naturally interpreted as implying a cognitive origin of sentence structures, with the (transformational) syntax merely mediating between semantically defined deep structures on the one hand and surface structures on the other. The old tree-expansion or "rewrite" rules can now be reinterpreted as structural constraints imposed on nascent SA-structures by the language and its lexicon. The generative principle, held responsible for the infinity of the set of sentences of a language, is no longer located in the recursive properties of the algorithmic device constituting the grammar, but in the faculty of thought, with its infinite powers of combining ideas and forming propositions. The generative semantics model thus provides a formalization of the traditional concept of language as a system that expresses thoughts by means of sounds. (It will be clear, as mentioned in section 1.5, that Chomsky's recent public statements to the effect that, in his theory, language is seen as a system whose "core property" is "the use of finite means to express an infinite array of thoughts" (2002:45) are seriously misleading, implying as they do that his theory is mediational, which it emphatically is not.)

All the production grammar has to do, in this mediational view, is provide the technical means required for the transformation of an infinitely variable input into an infinitely variable output. This it does by building on a principle known in more traditional forms of linguistics as the principle of "double articulation" mentioned in section 3.5.3, in combination with the transformational system. We reinterpret the principle of double articulation as follows. First, there is the lexicon. A small inventory of speech sound types (made up from an even smaller universal inventory of sound features) is sufficient to form an infinite variety of possible morphemes, some of which are noncomplex (monomorphematic) words. A selection of these may be combined, by means of processes of derivational morphology, into larger units, usually complex words. Sometimes also also idiomatic combinations of words, normally formed with the help of rules that are borrowed from the syntax, must be stored in the lexicon. The lexicon is thus the first level of articulation, involving several sublevels.

Any given thought, out of the infinite array of possible thoughts, drives a particular selection of lexical items, including idioms, from the lexicon on grounds of semantic satisfaction conditions. Since each item in the lexicon has associated with it a specification of the kind of structure in which it can or must appear, normally called its argument structure, which allows for recursive occurrences of propositional or S-structures, an infinite array of tree structures can thus be built up, driven by whatever thought needs to be expressed. The restriction to propositional or S-recursion (introduced by Chomsky in the early 1960s and adopted as a central principle in generative semantics, but rather neglected in subsequent forms of Chosmkyan linguistics) reflects the notion that this is the only form of recursion that makes for the infinity of possible thought structures. The structures built up by following the argument structure frames associated with the lexical items chosen are the semantic analyses (SAs) of the language. They form the second level of articulation.

These infinitely variable SAs are then transformed into corresponding surface structures by the grammar of the language, which includes a syntactic component and a component for flectional morphology (derivational morphology being located in the lexicon). The output of the grammar, the surface structure, is then fed into a phonological component, which is responsible for turning the surface structure into a recipe for sound (or writing). A mediational production grammar is thus not a sentence *generator* but a sentence *transformer*, which must satisfy certain technical specifications for it to function properly. The overall architecture of mediational grammar is shown in figure 6.4.

Chomsky, however, wouldn't have any of it. In the late 1960s he first reverted to the random-generator position of Katz and Fodor (1963) with a shared deep and surface input to the semantic component (see fig. 6.1, depicting his EST-position), and then turned to his post-EST position where the semantic component is fed exclusively from the surface structure (see fig. 6.2). That the random-generator view prevails in EST and post-EST theorizing, such as the Government and Binding framework, is clear from the following passage (Chomsky 1995:187):

> The EST framework adds additional structure; for concreteness, take *Lectures on Government and Binding*. . . . One crucial assumption has to do with the way in which the computational system presents lexical items for further computation. The assumption is that this is done by an operation, call it *Satisfy*, which *selects an array of items from the lexicon* and presents it in a format satisfying the conditions of X-bar theory. [italics mine]

What prompted Chomsky to give up the Katz and Postal hypothesis of semantically invariant transformational rules, still adopted in *Aspects* of 1965, by the time it became clear that this would lead automatically to a mediational position and what made him steadfastly uphold a random-generator position (at least in his more technical writings, but much less in his recent public performances, as shown in section 1.5), is, again, a question that eludes an explanation in strictly academic terms.[2]

2. See Huck and Goldsmith (1995) for a thorough discussion of this bizarre episode in the history of modern linguistics.

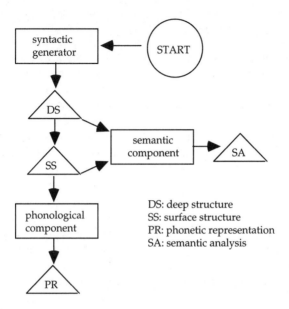

FIGURE 6.1. Architecture of an EST grammar

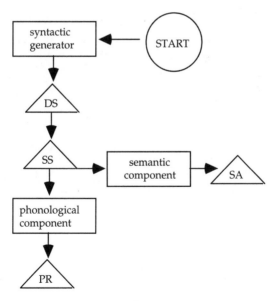

FIGURE 6.2. Architecture of a post-EST grammar

6.1.2 What drives the sentence generator?

Thus, after thirty years, we are still stuck with the question: which of the two is correct, the random-generator or the mediational view? One great advantage of the appearance of *The Minimalist Program* is that this question can now be discussed at a global notional and methodological level. To the extent that this issue has been discussed during the past quarter century, it was in terms of perennial and fruitless contests of who gains most points on account of observations, rule systems, or the like. On the whole, this has proved less successful than one might have hoped. The new minimalist position, however, is not so much of an empirical as of a methodological and conceptual nature. This opens up a more restricted battle area, where the issues are under better control and where the debates can no longer be endlessly protracted on account of undecidable differences over the status of observations or the explanatory power of specific descriptions. Now at least there is a clear choice between a realist and an instrumentalist interpretation of the minimalist model depicted in figure 6.3.

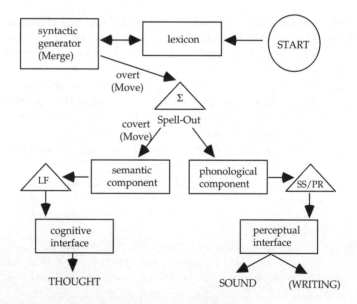

FIGURE 6.3. Architecture of a minimalist grammar

The realist interpretation implies that the structures and operations postulated correspond to what takes place in the brain, under a sufficiently cautious formula of interpretation (see section 3.3). In such an interpretation, the model is a flowchart representing the system of causal relations presumed to be at work in the use of language. It hardly needs arguing that the MP model, if seen in this light, is absurd, not only in the technical sense adopted here. One merely needs to ask the question "What drives the sentence generator?" to see the absurdity of the answer that the sentence generator is driven by a process, activated by a start signal, that randomly selects lexical items and casts them into a grammatical structure. Equally absurd is the notion that a randomly generated sentence structure should be taken to pass an instruction to the cognitive system of the same organism for the sentence to be interpreted. Clearly, outgoing signals are driven by a decision to express cognitive content, as seems to be increasingly recognized by Chomsky in his latest public performances (see section 1.5). Therefore, as far as production is concerned, there is no way in which this model stands a chance of being adequate in any realist sense. Yet, as shown in section 3.3, Chomsky's overall attitude with regard to the model tends to realism, notwithstanding a few mysterious remarks that would point the other way. (On the comprehension side, the model makes no attempt at any account at all, which, given the uncertainty regarding the compositionality of the parsing process, may be considered harmless in the present context.)

This being so, one is left with either a moderate or a strictly mathematical form of instrumentalism. Under a moderate instrumentalist interpretation, the model must be considered "perverse" in the sense defined in section 3.3. For there is a perfectly reasonable alternative model, in terms of mediational grammar (fig. 6.4), which follows more closely the causal direction of the processes reasonably presumed to be at work in the use of language. The only option that remains is a strictly mathematical interpretation, which lands the random-generator model in the most extreme form of instrumentalism, typically found in the camp of computational linguistics.

It is thus clear that unless the random-generator model presented in *The Minimalist Program* is regarded as an instance of mathematical instrumentalism, which would take it further away from realism than ever, it is indeed trapped between absurdity and perversity, no matter whether it is thought to follow from minimalist principles or from any other consideration brought to bear on account of Chomsky's notion of universal grammar.

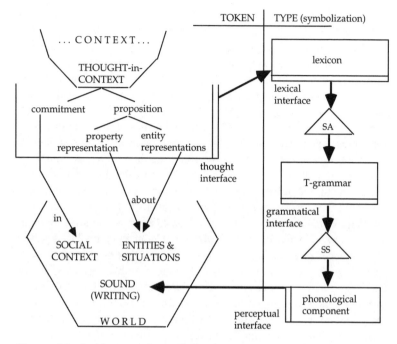

FIGURE 6.4. Architecture of a mediational top-down grammar

6.2 Is the "displacement property" conceptually motivated?

The final issue to be looked at in the context of "conceptual necessity" is that of what Chomsky calls the "displacement property" of language, or the fact that surface structures must be taken to differ in nontrivial ways from their underlying semantic analyses. We have seen (sections 5.2, 5.3, and 5.5) that this is considered an "imperfection" of language, although it may also be taken to be proof of how perfect language is, since what looks like an imperfection may eventually turn out to result from conditions imposed by "external systems." These, however, "are not very well understood" and their understanding should go "hand-in-hand with progress in understanding the language system that interacts with them" (Chomsky 1998:18).

It has already been pointed out that these are fruitless speculations that cannot possibly form a basis for a sound methodology. But if one probes a little deeper, one sees that this ambiguous position of the displacement property with regard to its being a sign of perfection or imperfection of language reveals a further ambiguity in the application of the minimalist method, to do with the position of universal grammar (UG) in the minimalist model.

We recall that, on the opening page of *The Minimalist Program*, the work is said to be "motivated by two related questions: (1) what are the general conditions that the human language faculty should be expected to satisfy? and (2) to what extent is the language faculty determined by these conditions, without special structure that lies beyond them?" (Chomsky 1995:1). UG comes into play on p. 167 of the book: "The theory of languages and the expressions they generate is Universal Grammar (UG); UG is a theory of the initial state S_0 of the relevant component of the language faculty" (Chomsky 1995:167). Since UG is said to be a theory of part of the language faculty, question (2) applies, and we are entitled to ask: to what extent is UG determined by the general conditions that the human language faculty should be expected to satisfy, without special structure that lies beyond them? Moreover, since UG is said to *determine* possible linguistic analyses and descriptions ("Recall the (virtual) conceptual necessities within this general approach. UG determines possible symbolic representations and derivations" (Chomsky 1995:186)), it follows that one is entitled to ask: to what extent are possible symbolic representations and derivations determined by the general conditions that the human FoL should be expected to satisfy, without special structure that lies beyond them?

The implication is clear: the study of universal constraints on grammatical descriptions, together with the typology arising out of it, is part of the MP and therefore subject to the minimalist method. This, however, makes it very hard to understand what could be meant by saying that "UG settles the matter" when counterevidence is presented with respect to a particular grammatical analysis. Recall from section 4.4 that, in the middle of an account of the operation Move, Chomsky appeals to UG as an answer to possible counterevidence: "The empirical questions that arise are varied and complex, and it is easy enough to come up with apparent counterevidence. I will put these problems aside for now, simply assuming the best outcome, namely that UG settles the matter—hardly an innocuous step, needless to say" (Chomsky 1995:266). The only way, it seems, that UG can "settle the matter" is by integrating counterevidence into UG and putting it down to a conceptually unnecessary "imperfection" in the system (if one accepts that Chomsky's account of Move is determined by minimalist assumptions, which it is not). But then the "best outcome" amounts to a rejection of the account of Move presented by Chomsky owing to counterevidence, which is clearly not what is intended. What actually is intended remains one of the puzzling questions one is left with on reading *The Minimalist Program*.

6.2.1 X-bar theory

In fact, the position of UG in the MP is unclear generally, despite the assurances that UG falls in the scope of the two questions that are said to motivate the program. In chapter 3, once the generalities are over and a beginning is made with the technicalities of grammar, the opening paragraph of the section on X-bar theory reads as follows (Chomsky 1995:172):

> The computational system takes representations of a given form and modifies them. Accordingly, UG must provide means to present an array of items from the lexicon in a form accessible to the computational system. We may take this form to be some version of X-bar theory. The concepts of X-bar theory are therefore fundamental. In a minimalist theory, the crucial properties and relations will be stated in the simple and elementary terms of X-bar theory.

No reason is given why one "may take this [computationally accessible] form to be some version of X-bar theory," nor why X-bar theory should be taken to satisfy the criteria of the minimalist method. If there is any "conceptual necessity" to X-bar theory, it is not shown. Nor is it made clear that X-bar theory represents an optimally functional solution to the question of sentence structure. Readers have to make do with the assurance that X-bar theory is "simple and elementary." Nothing more is said on the matter (see section 2.2.1 for comment).

Once again, one cannot help wondering how seriously Chomsky takes his readers when he tells them first that "the concepts of X-bar theory are fundamental" (1995:172), subsequently that "standard X-bar theory is largely eliminated in favor of bare essentials" (1995:246), then that "there should be no phrasal units or bar levels, hence no phrase structure rules or X-bar theory" (1998:20), and finally that "X-bar theory, I think, is probably wrong" (2002:151)—all that without any analysis or argument, let alone any precise definition of what is rejected and what is to take its place. The saga of X-bar theory, from its beginning in the late 1960s till its extinction in the late 1990s, becomes even more interesting when one realizes that it was shown in Kornai and Pullum (1990) not only that X-bar theory was never properly defined but also that all of its possible well-defined varieties contribute hardly anything to the descriptive power of grammars and turn out to have very little substance for the theory of grammar in general. By now the reader will no longer be surprised to hear that this eminent and well-known work by Kornai and Pullum has never been referred to in any of Chomsky's writings.

For the sake of clarity it may be noted that if conceptual necessity is invoked, X-bar theory is not a very likely first candidate as a determiner of "simple and elementary terms" of structural relations, lacking as it does any independent support from any of the disciplines occupying themselves with the study of a priori necessity. A much stronger first candidate is found in the semantics of Predicate Calculus, where the leading principle of structural composition consists in the combination of a predicate with its argument terms—that is, in what may be called the *propositional principle* (see sections 3.5.1 and 3.5.6). As pointed out in McCawley (1972), this propositional principle is naturally upheld throughout the structures of the language of Predicate Calculus. It includes structures created by quantificational and other operators (like negation, conjunction, disjunction, modalities, tenses, and adverbial or clausal modifiers), since all these operators are naturally regarded as predicates over propositional structures (see Seuren 1998:348, 363). Clearly, the propositional principle has the backing of modern logic, with all it entails in the way of conceptual necessity.

Conceptual necessity, as worked out in the age-old tradition of philosophical and logical analysis, demands that sentential structures consist in principle of a predicative element expressing a property P and one or more argument terms referring to entities to which P is assigned. That being so, X-bar theory is not very enlightening, since it does not indicate where the predicate element and the argument terms are to be found. Nor does it provide the simplest possible terms for the expression of a predicate-argument structure.

Moreover, the internal structure of canonical lexically filled argument terms is, in general, determined by the Fregean principle that the entities referred to by the terms in question are identified by means of a predicate and a determiner. The predicate limits the class of entities where the term referent is to be located. The determiner determines the manner of location. Again, none of this is found anywhere in X-bar theory.

It is possible, of course, that the transformational machinery converting semantic analyses into surface structures is constrained by an X-bar type structural format, but it is not clear that this is so, nor would any such constraining format have the status of being conceptually necessary. Since X-bar theory is not supported by conceptual necessity (or, for that matter, criteria of functionality), the decision, in minimalist theory, to state the "crucial properties and relations in the simple and elementary terms of X-bar theory" is unwarranted on the best of minimalist grounds, and any support it has will have to come from elsewhere.

The same applies to what is said to be the "basic structure of the clause," presented in (1). This is motivated by an appeal to "standard assumptions" and is based on "an elaboration of Pollock's (1989) theory of inflection" (Chomsky 1995:173). But even if this structure had the strongest empirical support drawn from overwhelmingly successful analyses of relevant phenomena in a vast number of languages, that would still not make it conceptually necessary in any sense of these terms.

(1)

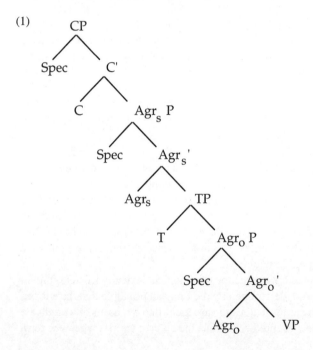

Since the same is found with regard to virtually the entire grammatical apparatus presented by Chomsky, one can only say that the concept of UG as presented in *The Minimalist Program* has no relation to any of the minimalist assumptions formulated in that work or to any aspect of the minimalist method. What one has is a random-generator, nonsemantic way of practicing grammar that has its roots in a quarter-century-old history of searching for autonomous syntactic generalizations and constraints. The minimalist approach has added nothing to that. Whatever merits that way of practicing grammar may have had in the past, it has meanwhile become clear that we now have at our disposal vastly superior ways of doing grammar.

6.2.2 The "deep structure" argument

An example of the irrelevance of minimalist assumptions with regard to the syntactic analyses presented in *The Minimalist Program* is provided by the case against deep structure as an "internal interface between the lexicon and the computational system" (Chomsky 1995:187):

> The EST framework adds additional structure; for concreteness, take *Lectures on Government and Binding*. . . . One crucial assumption has to do with the way in which the computational system presents lexical items for further computation. The assumption is that this is done by an operation, call it *Satisfy*, which selects an array of items from the lexicon and presents it in a format satisfying the conditions of X-bar theory. Satisfy is an "all-at-once" operation: all items that function at LF are drawn from the lexicon before computation proceeds and are presented in the X-bar format.
>
> We thus postulate an additional level, D-Structure, beyond the two external interface levels PF and LF. D-Structure is the *internal* interface between the lexicon and the computational system, formed by Satisfy. Certain principles of UG are then held to apply to D-Structure, specifically, the Projection Principle and the θ-Criterion. The computational procedure maps D-Structure to another level, S-Structure, and then "branches" to PF and LF, independently. UG principles of the various modules of grammar (binding theory, Case theory, the *pro* module, etc.) apply at the level of S-Structure (perhaps elsewhere as well, in some cases).
>
> The empirical justification for this approach, with its departures from conceptual necessity, is substantial. Nevertheless, we may ask whether the evidence will bear the weight, or whether it is possible to move toward a minimalist program.

Any force the argument may have is independent of specifically minimalist assumptions and depends solely on well-known and generally accepted standards of scientific explanation, in particular the criterion of simplicity, even though the argument is presented as a "move toward a minimalist program." One witnesses here a confusion, already signaled in section 5.3, between the standard requirement of maximal simplicity and generality of the *theory* on the one hand, and the assumption of maximal simplicity or functionality of the *object of inquiry* on the other. The latter is, of course, not a standard theoretical requirement. If there is "special structure that lies beyond" the "general conditions that the human language faculty should be expected to satisfy" (1995:1), one simply has to accept that as a fact, and then construct the simplest possible theory to account for it. In any case, the fact that the "general conditions" mentioned are largely unknown means that the entire question is without significance.

In sum, all attempts made by Chomsky to make it appear as if his grammatical machinery (to the extent that it is formally explicit) follows from or is subject to criteria of conceptual necessity come to nothing. The "minimalist" element brought into play is just rhetoric.

6.3 Conclusion

It is unrealistic and overambitious to think that one can set up on a priori grounds of conceptual necessity a design specification for a product of nature of the complexity of natural language. It is equally unrealistic to try and develop a methodology on the basis of such an illusory design specification. What we know about language is not much, compared to what there is to know. But we know enough to realize that language is profoundly complex. It is complex in itself as it consists of a number of interlocking subsystems that work together to form the "language system" that is beginning to come into view. It is complex also in the ways it links up with its ecological embedding in the mind-brain, in the motor-perceptual system or systems, and in society. There still is a long way to go before we can say with justified confidence that we have an adequate overall grasp of the parameters and dimensions involved. There is an even longer way to go before anyone may pretend to have found the universal Einstein-formula for human language, if there is such a thing. The MP has not changed that situation. It has grossly overreached itself, and in doing so it has added nothing but unnecessary confusion to what we already knew and were doing.

7

Surface-Driven Elements of Semantic Interpretation

In this chapter an extended analysis is presented, showing that the argument of surface-driven elements of semantic interpretation—the one potentially relevant argument against the mediational view of the FoL and in favor of the random-generator view (though not the version instantiated in the MP)—is invalid, since all cases of alleged surface-driven semantic interpretation quoted are seen to be better handled in terms of deep structure semantic interpretation. There is some irony in this conclusion, as is conceded by Chomsky himself, in that the MP happens to represent a variety of random-generator grammar that is incompatible with at least those surface-driven elements of semantic interpretation that are lodged in phonetic form and not in Spell-Out (such as accentual focusing devices), since the MP contains no provision for a feeding line from phonetic form to logical form. The conclusion that the alleged surface-driven elements of semantic interpretation are, in fact, not surface-driven but must be assumed to be present at the level of semantic analysis thus not only reinforces the position of mediational grammar but should, unintentionally, also reinforce the MP position, were it not that the latter simply lacks the means to account for the elements in question, in particular to the extent that they are to do with intonation. As so often, Chomsky's position in this respect remains ambiguous and noncommittal. In any case, this should now put to rest an old controversy that has existed since the early 1970s and has come up again in the present context.

7.1 The question stated

Around 1970 a hotly debated issue was whether what was then called deep structure should be considered to carry all semantic information of the corresponding sentence, so that subsequent transformations would have no semantic effect, or whether semantic interpretation was to some extent codetermined by surface structure elements. The former view instantiates the mediational position and was defended by the generative semanticists, the latter, random-generator, view was defended by Chomsky and his autonomists, who called their approach the extended standard theory, or EST. The issue is relevant because the mediational position is incompatible with any surface structure elements that (co)determine meaning.

The semantic elements that, according to Chomsky, must be derived from the surface structure rather than from the deep structure of a sentence were (a) focusing strategies, including topic-focus modulation, contrastive or emphatic (i.e., heavy) accent, and displacement phenomena like fronting or postposing; (b) presuppositions; and (c) the determination of operator scope according to the linear order of scope-bearing operators. As regards (a) and (b), Chomsky's comment was (1972:99–100):

> To summarize these remarks, we seem to have the following situation. Rules of phonological interpretation assign an intonational contour to surface structures. Certain phrases of the surface structure may be marked, by grammatical processes of a poorly understood sort, as receiving expressive or contrastive stress, and these markings also affect the operation of the rules of phonological interpretation. If no such processes have applied, the rules assign the normal intonation. In any event, phrases that contain the intonation center may be interpreted as focus of utterance, the condition being perhaps somewhat different and more restrictive when the intonation center involves expressive or contrastive stress, as noted. . . . The notions "focus," "presupposition," and "shared presupposition" . . . must be determinable from the semantic interpretation of sentences if we are to be able to explain how discourse is constructed and, in general, how language is used.

Chomsky did concede that it is possible to build markers or other structural elements into semantically defined deep structures, so that the generative semantics position could be upheld: "Technically, it would now be the case that deep structure fully determines meaning, even so far as focus and presupposition is concerned" (1972:101–102). But such a step would, in his view, be "merely a notational variant of a theory that determines focus and presuppositions from the surface structure" (1972:102). Moreover, "the attempt to express the latter concepts in terms of deep structure seems to me to have led to considerable artificiality in the construction of grammars, in recent work" (1972:103). No further argument was given, nor was any attention ever paid to subsequent work showing that to express the concepts in question in terms of deep structure was far from artificial but, on the contrary, highly motivated and natural.[1]

In the light of section 3.3, we now understand that Chomsky's vaguely instrumentalist position of those days made it possible to depict the mediational or generative semantics account of grammar as a "perverse" description in the sense specified in section 3.3 ("considerable artificiality"), though at the time this implication was not clear. No actual *arguments* or *analyses* were provided by Chomsky to support these statements or suggestions. There were equivocations of notions and terms that were poorly understood by all concerned, with the result that opponents were easily nonplussed. The suggestion that the mediational position of generative semantics was "merely a notational variant" of the random-generator position of EST diverted attention from the real issue, which was whether any charge of "artificiality" or perversity (in the sense defined) could be leveled against either EST or generative semantics. Now that, in the context of the MP, the real issue has come to the fore with much greater clarity than before, it is no longer difficult to decide that the charge of perversity should not be leveled against the mediational theory of generative semantics but against EST and its random-generator successors.

---

1. It was shown—for example, in Lakoff (1971) and McCawley (1972; in circulation since 1969)—that the nontrivial correspondence between operator scope and linear ordering was naturally accounted for by a rule or process of Operator (Quantifier) Lowering. No account was taken of these and similar proposals. Yet, when rules of semantic interpretation, in the spirit of Chomskyan grammar, were proposed in May's (1977) study on quantification, the proposals made by McCawley, Lakoff, and others in this respect were adopted (though, for obvious reasons, with the directionality inverted: quantifier *raising* instead of *lowering*) without any attribution.

In subsequent versions of Chomskyan grammar, the EST position was pushed to an extreme in that an architecture was proposed that takes surface structures as the only input of semantic interpretation delivering a semantic analysis ("logical form") as output—that is, the framework underlying May (1977) mentioned in note 1. This is what is found in the versions that passed under names like Revised Extended Standard Theory (REST), Filters and Control, Government and Binding, Principles and Parameters, and others. Since, in those models, it is always the autonomous syntactic generator that starts sentence production, such an architecture strictly rules out any variety of mediational grammar.

In the minimalist framework the position has again changed somewhat, shifting in the direction of the generative semantics position of a quarter century ago. As we have seen, the minimalist position implies that a language is a generative system constructing pairs (PF-LF) of representations that are interpreted as instructions to the two external performance systems, LF being interpreted or "read" at the conceptual-intentional (C-I) interface by the "language use" or conceptual system.

Although, as has been said, this means that a presumed syntactic generator produces sentential structures that receive a phonological interpretation on the one hand and a semantic interpretation on the other (the same random-generator position as is found in EST and its successors), it is now no longer surface structures that are taken to be the input to the phonological and the semantic components. In the new setup, the partition between phonological and semantic interpretation is placed at the earlier stage of Spell-Out. Surface structures are now part of the phonological component and should no longer be accessible to the covert computation yielding a semantic analysis (LF). Therefore, the phenomena cited above under (1) and taken, around 1972, as instances of surface-driven elements of semantic interpretation, are, in the MP model, computed in what is now called the phonological component, while semantic interpretation is reserved for the covert semantic component, both components being strictly separated by Spell-Out. Since this makes surface-driven elements of semantic interpretation impossible, these elements have now become an embarrassment. A look at figure 6.3 of the preceding chapter will make this even clearer.

The status of any surface-driven elements of semantic interpretation in the minimalist program is rightly recognized by Chomsky as a problem. For, as appears from the diagrams in figures 6.1 to 6.4 in chapter 6, apart from being incompatible with a mediational position, such elements also destroy any rationale for the minimalist version of random-generator grammar. In EST- and post-EST-type grammars, surface structure feeds the semantic component, which rules out any form of mediational grammar. But in the minimalist concept shown in figure 6.3, the semantic component is not fed by phonetic form, only by Spell-Out, and only in a way that cannot involve phonetic features. The result is that the random-generator position put forward in the minimalist framework is left without independent support. It now rests solely on the criterion of "conceptual necessity," and, as has been shown in chapter 6, there is little conceptual necessity to be found in the minimalist framework.

Chomsky's own comment on the matter is the following (1995:220):

> Notice that I am sweeping under the rug questions of considerable significance, notably, questions about what in the earlier Extended Standard Theory (EST) framework were called "surface effects" on interpretation. These are manifold, involving topic-focus and theme-rheme structures, figure-ground properties, effects of adjacency and linearity, and many others. Prima facie, they seem to involve some additional level or levels internal to the phonological component, postmorphology but prephonetic, accessed at the interface along with PF (Phonetic Form) and LF (Logical Form). If that turns out to be correct, then the abstraction I am now pursuing may require qualification. I will continue to pursue it nonetheless, merely noting here, once again, that tacit assumptions underlying much of the most productive recent work are far from innocent.

No answer is given in *The Minimalist Program*, other than that "the abstraction I am now pursuing may require qualification." In Chomsky's (1998) work, the presumed surface-driven elements of semantic interpretation are tentatively presented as one reason for the displacement property of language—the fact that the meaning-bearing elements in sentences often do not occur in a position in which they allow for semantic interpretation. The relevant text runs as follows (Chomsky 1998:24):

> Why language should have the displacement property is an interesting question, which has been discussed for many years without resolution. One early proposal is that the property reflects processing conditions. If so, it may in part be reducible to properties of the articulatory and perceptual apparatus, hence forced by legibility conditions at the phonetic interface. I suspect that another part of the reason may have to do with phenomena that have been described in terms of surface structure interpretation: topic-comment, specificity, new and old information, the agentive force that we find even in displaced position, and so on. These

seem to require particular positions in temporal linear order, typically at the edge of some construction. If so, then the displacement property also reflects legibility conditions at the semantic interface; it is motivated by interpretive requirements that are externally imposed by our systems of thought, which have these special properties, so it appears. These questions are currently being investigated in interesting ways, which I cannot go into here.

Not much of an answer, one has to fear. The burden of explanation is shifted on to "our systems of thought," which are supposed to have "special properties" implying an external imposition of "interpretive requirements," "so it appears." But nothing of the kind appears. All that appears is that even if the presumed surface-driven elements of semantic interpretation were "externally imposed by our systems of thought," they would still violate the Spell-Out principle. The simple truth is that the minimalist model as it stands is incompatible with the assumption of surface-driven elements of semantic interpretation.

Given the absence of cogent arguments in favor of such elements, a simple solution would be to abandon the random-generator position of the 1970s and later and admit that there are, after all, no surface-driven elements of semantic interpretation. One might take the side of formal semantics and maintain (though that would be wrong, as will be shown in a moment) that the phenomena in question are, for the most part, not truth-conditional and belong to pragmatics rather than semantics. Or, more sensibly, one might accept the phenomena in question as being represented in a structure Σ before Spell-Out in the form of features that are preserved in both components. In either case the minimalist model would be out of trouble. In its present form, however, the model cannot work. One cannot hold on to elements of surface interpretation and at the same time propose a random-generator model that has no place for them and is thus deprived of just about the only motivation that might be given in its favor.

Let us look into the matter a little more deeply, even if that involves a rather detailed empirical and theoretical analysis. The elements at issue, we recall, are (a) focusing strategies, including topic-focus modulation, contrastive or emphatic (i.e., heavy) accent, and displacement phenomena like fronting or postposing; (b) presuppositions; and (c) the determination of operator scope. They will be discussed, in that order, in the following three sections.

In all three cases, the first question is whether these are really semantic or just pragmatic elements. If they are pragmatic, as is standardly assumed in formal semantics and pragmatics, there is no problem, since then they need not be structurally derived but may be seen as resulting from the context of use, which would deprive them of any relevance in the present context. Unfortunately, however, we have to admit, against accepted opinion, that they are not pragmatic but semantic. This makes it necessary to face the second question: are they determined by surface structure, or can they with equal or greater justification be regarded as being determined at the level of semantic analysis? This question must be answered because, if the elements in question can only be derived from surface structure and have no place in semantic analysis, the mediational position is untenable and the theory will be in serious jeopardy. A thorough revision of all the basic notions and arguments developed to date will then be required.

What the rather detailed digression in the following three sections shows is that the worry raised by presumed surface-driven elements of semantic interpretation (Chomsky 1995:220, 1998:24) is unjustified, since all instances quoted are naturally accounted for as elements that are identifiably represented in any reasonable version of semantic analysis and hence derivable from it. In other words, the MP could proceed without that worry if it made the necessary formal means available. Yet even then it could not proceed safely. For although the need for surface-driven elements of semantic interpretation has been removed, the MP is still clearly of the random-generator type, and as such finds itself without just about the only arguments that would show that the mediational view is not viable. That is, it is caught not only between the absurd and the perverse, as we have seen, but also between the impossible and the unmotivated.

7.2 Focusing strategies

Focusing strategies are complex and still badly understood. For that reason their discussion inevitably requires a relatively large amount of space. The first thing to be shown is that, for the most part, they are semantic and not pragmatic, and must therefore be expressed at the level of semantic analysis (SA). This conclusion is syntactically supported by sentences that are ungrammatical *with* certain heavily accented or clefted constituents (see (6)–(7)), as well as by sentences that are ungrammatical *without* a heavily accented or clefted subject (see (23)). In all these cases, SA-configurations provide an immediate solution. Chomsky's

(1972) objection that bound morphemes and phonemes can be singled out for heavy accent but not for clefting is countered by the observation that in all such cases there is a metalinguistic meaning, which has syntactic effects, even though little is known about them.

The most important focusing strategies are (a) the use of focusing particles like *only* or *even*; (b) contrastive or emphatic (heavy) accent; (c) various forms of clefting; and (d) topic-comment modulation. These are semantic phenomena in the full truth-conditional sense. To show that this is so, I will systematically apply a test whereby sentences (clauses) containing a focusing element are placed under an emotive attitudinal operator like *be surprised*, *hope*, *be angry*, *worry*, and the like. When the sentences in question are truth-conditionally different from their counterparts without any focusing element, the difference must be semantic and cannot be pragmatic.

This is a refinement of a similar test that has been basic to semantics since Frege, who showed that the difference brought about by the substitution of co-referring terms must be semantic, even though it makes no truth-conditional difference in simple clauses, because it does make a truth-condtional difference when these clauses are embedded under an intensional operator like *think* or *believe*. Given that the terms *the evening star* and *the morning star* refer to the same planet, Venus, substitution of one term for the other in simple clauses like (1a,b) makes no truth-conditional difference, and may thus be thought to be semantically irrelevant: co-referring terms may be substituted *salva veritate*. Since, however, it does make a truth-conditional difference in sentences like (2a,b), where the original sentences are embedded under the intensional operator *believe*, the conclusion must be that substitution of co-referring terms does bring about a truth-conditional semantic effect:

(1) a. The evening star is inhabited.
     b. The morning star is inhabited.

(2) a. John believes that the evening star is inhabited.
     b. John believes that the morning star is inhabited.

Clearly, if (1a) is true, or false, (1b) must be. But the truth (or falsity) of (2a) does not make it necessary that (2b) is likewise true (or false), for John may mistakenly believe that the morning star is not identical with the evening star.

In the same way, we find that, although there seems to be no observable truth-conditional difference between, for example, (3a) and (3b), there is an observable truth-conditional difference between (4a) and (4b):

(3) a. Not even JIM laughed at the joke.
     b. Jim didn't even laugh at the JOKE.

(4) a. What worried Sue was that not even JIM laughed at the joke.
     b. What worried Sue was that Jim didn't even laugh at the JOKE.

Clearly, (4a) can be true while (4b) is false, and vice versa. In (4a) Sue's worry concerns the joke, whereas in (4b) it concerns Jim. For example, if Sue had hoped to find that Jim's depression wasn't so serious after all, (4b) may be true while (4a) does not even make sense.

Analogously, one sees that sentences like (5a) or (5b) are not inconsistent, which they would be if the focusing device had no truth-conditional effect:

(5) a. Sue was angry that JIM had sold the car, not that Jim had sold the CAR.
     b. Sue was angry that it was Jim who had sold the car, not that it was the car Jim had sold.

There is thus, besides the Leibniz-Frege principle of substitution of co-referring terms *salva veritate*, an analogous principle of substitution of focus-comments *salva veritate*. Both principles hold in extensional contexts, but fail to hold in intensional contexts. Since both principles are metaphysically necessary in the Aristotelian theory of truth, the problem posed by intensional contexts must be solved by semantic theory. Frege's semantic solution for the problem of nonsubstitutivity of co-referring terms in intensional contexts consisted in defining the extension of clauses embedded in an intensional context as the underlying thought, while letting thoughts vary with choice of (co-referring) terms.[2] The semantic solution for the problem of nonsubstitutivity of focus-comments in intensional contexts is, analogously, taken to reside in the fact that thoughts differ according to their (discourse-dependent) topic-comment structure. The latter, unlike different choices of co-referring terms, must then be made visible in the meaning descriptions

---

2. See Seuren (1998:372–382) for ample comment.

of sentences, which is easily done by taking topic-cleft structures as part of their SA-structure.[3]

The next point to be shown is that the semantic effects at issue are best derived from the SA of the sentences involved. As regards focusing particles this is trivial, since these are lexically realized and lexical insertion is uncontroversially a "deep" process. But heavy accents and forms of clefting are not so quickly dealt with. It has been suggested (e.g., Chomsky 1972:99–100) that phonological rules may assign heavy accent to any arbitrary element in the sentence. The semantic interpretation of this accent would then not be traceable to the SA underlying the sentence in question. Likewise for cleft and pseudocleft constructions. It has been proposed (e.g., Akmajian 1970) that clefting processes result from the transformational extraction of any arbitrary nominal or prepositional constituent and are thus not derivable from a semantically given structure.

A quick way to show that such proposals are incorrect consists in providing examples where heavy accent assignment or extraction should be possible, according to the proposals in question, but in fact is not. Consider, for example, the following cases ("*" marks ungrammaticality, "√" marks grammaticality):

(6)   a. √John isn't in the least interested.
      b. *JOHN isn't in the least interested, PETER is.
      c. *It isn't John who is in the least interested, it's Peter.

(7)   a. √I don't think John is in the least interested.
      b. *I don't think JOHN is in the least interested but PETER.
      c. *It isn't John I think is in the least interested, it is Peter.

These sentences revolve around the negative polarity item *in the least*. *In the least*, just like *the slightest*, belongs to a strong class of negative polarity items that require a full negation (including negative quantifiers like *none*) in simple assertive clauses for grammaticality, unlike, for example

---

3. The most commonly held view is that these phenomena are determined by the kind of (implicit) question the sentence is intended to be an answer to. A sentence like *John had fish for lunch yesterday* may be an answer to 'What did John have for lunch yesterday?' in which case the nuclear accent will be on *fish*. But if the question was 'When did John have fish for lunch?' the nuclear accent will be on *yesterday*.

yet or *any*, which are negative polarity items belonging to a weaker class and can do with a semi-negative adverb like *hardly*, as in (8a):

(8) a. √John has hardly written anything yet.
     b. *John is hardly in the least interested.
     c. *John has hardly shown the slightest interest.

Moreover, *in the least* and *the slightest* cannot occur in negative questions, unlike *any* or *yet*, which can:

(9) a. √Hasn't John written anything yet?
     b. *Isn't John in the least interested?
     c. *Hasn't John shown the slightest interest?

Then, *in the least* and *the slightest* cannot occur in conditional clauses, unlike *any*, which can, but like *yet*, which also cannot:

(10) a. √If John has written anything, it must be about tigers.
      b. *If John has arrived yet, he must be tired.
      c. *If John is in the least interested, he will listen.
      d. *If John has shown the slightest interest, he will listen.

(Note that (10c,d) are all right with the counterfactual verbal forms *were*, *had*, and *would*.)

Finally, *in the least* and *the slightest* have to occur *within the same clause* as the required negation, again like *yet* but unlike *any*:

(11) a. √I didn't know that John had written anything.
      b. *I didn't know that John had arrived yet.
      c. *I didn't know that John was in the least interested.
      d. *I didn't know that John had the slightest interest.

However, there are cases where *in the least* or *the slightest* may occur in a lower clause than the negation, as in (7a). To save the generalization, it has been proposed that the negation constructed with *think* in a sentence like (7a) should be construed as originating in the subordinate clause in the semantic analysis, as is indeed suggested by the normal meaning of the sentence. An optional but preferred process of Negative Raising would then be responsible for the fact that the negation is raised into the main clause with verbs like *think* or *expect*. The generalization that expressions like *in the least* or *the slightest* must occur with the negation *in the same clause* can then be reformulated for the SA level of semantic analysis as the generalization that these expressions must occur in clauses immediately commanded by the negation operator.

This hypothesis is reinforced by the oberservation that *in the least* and *the slightest* cannot occur when they are separated, in the semantic interpretation of the sentence, by an intervening scope-order-sensitive operator. Thus, sentences like (12a,c) and (13a,c) are well-formed, but their counterparts (12b,d) and (13b,d) are not:

(12) a. √Many people are not in the least interested.
      b. *Not many people are in the least interested.
      c. √Many people don't show the slightest interest.
      d. *Not many people show the slightest interest.

(13) a. √John is often not in the least interested.
      b. *John isn't often in the least interested.
      c. √John often doesn't show the slightest interest.
      d. *John doesn't often show the slightest interest.

This is readily explained when one realizes that in the SA of (12a,c) and (13a,c) *not* takes direct scope over the clause containing the negative polarity item in question, whereas in (12b,d) and (13b,d) there is an intervening scope-order-sensitive operator (*many* or *often*). (13a), for example, is analyzed as: 'often [not [John is in the least interested]]'. Here *not* is separated from the clause containing the expression *in the least* by a single pair of square brackets, whereas in the ungrammatical (13b) the order of the two operators is reversed, so that *not* is separated from *in the least* by two pairs of square brackets, violating the conditions of the negative polarity item *in the least*: 'not [often [John is in the least interested]]'. In these cases Negative Raising cannot come to the rescue.

Facts like these, incidentally, reinforce the overall mediational position, defended by generative semantics and its successors, that the deep structure of semantic analysis has, by itself, explanatory value with regard to phenomena of syntactic well-formedness.

Reverting now to (6) and (7), we see that the ungrammaticality of the (c)-sentences is explained when their cleft form is considered to be part of their SA, and not the result of an extraction transformation. The SA of

(6c) would then correspond in the relevant respects to: 'not [the x [x is in the least interested] is John]', where the clause "x is in the least interested" is removed from the operator *not* by two pairs of square brackets, and not by one, as prescribed by the generalization.

The ungrammaticality of the (b)-sentences of (6) and (7) can now be explained if it is assumed that heavy accents in surface structures are derived from an underlying cleft by a (meaning-preserving) transformational rule of Cleft Predicate Lowering, or CPL. This rule takes the cleft predicate ('John') and lowers it into the position of the variable *x* of the embedded clause, while assigning it heavy accent (reinforcing the normal nuclear sentence accent that goes with predicates), and deleting all remaining structure of the cleft construction. An underlying cleft like (14), with the cleft predicate 'John' is then transformed by CPL into (15):

(14)   the x [x is interested] (is) John $\rightarrow$ (CPL)

(15)   JOHN is interested.

A higher negation can now be incorporated in the standard way, resulting in (6b) without *in the least*. It is clear that in this case *in the least* cannot be selected from the lexicon because it would be separated from *not* by two pairs of square brackets. The same analysis, but placed under 'I think', with the additional process of Negative Raising, accounts for (7c).

Chomsky (1972:88–99) objects to the CPL analysis, observing that clefting is limited to cases that allow for syntactic extraction in general, whereas heavy accent can be assigned to just about any constituent, even to single morphemes or phonemes. The cleft (16a) is thus ungrammatical due to violation of an island constraint. But (16b), with heavy accent instead of clefting, is well-formed:

(16)   a. *It isn't 'd' that he sold irty pictures, it's 'th'.
       b. √He didn't sell Dirty pictures but THirty pictures.
       c. √It isn't DIRTY pictures that he sold but THIRTY pictures.

Jackendoff (1997:77) adds to it by presenting the case of (17a,b):

(17)   a. *It is paint that John ruined the book by smearing on it.
       b. √John ruined the book by smearing PAINT on it.
       c. √It is by smearing PAINT on it that John ruined the book.

But (17c) is well-formed and CPL applied to (17c) also leads to (17b). The only relevant cases are thus those like (16a), with contrast on (morphological or phonological) elements within islands.

To answer Chomsky's objection, note, first, that languages differ in the conditions under which CPL (heavy accent) is allowed. In French, for example, high NPs cannot be lowered to heavy accent, and a surface cleft form is obligatory:

(18) a. *PIERRE a écrit la lettre, pas JEAN.
          PIERRE has written the letter, not JEAN.
      b. √C'est Pierre qui a écrit la lettre, pas Jean.
          'It is Pierre who has written the letter, not Jean.'

The principle seems to be that in French the surface cleft form is obligatory whenever it is not blocked by any island constraint. When it is blocked, CPL is the only option left. In English and many other languages, however, CPL is the default option for all cases, but a surface cleft is also possible unless it is blocked by an island constraint. Since island constraints work both ways, top-down and bottom-up, the question that must arise for a cleft SA origin of cases like (16b) is: why can CPL override island constraints in such cases?

In answering this question we must appeal to a bit of theory that has not been worked out yet but is required in virtue of a set of relatively clear observations. The point is that cases like (16a), where clefting appears impossible, all require a metalinguistic interpretation. They express a comment on a lexical selection just made or a form just pronounced, as also in the following sentences:

(19) a. He was an unhappy, or rather unfulfilled, person.
      b. Not LIZZY, stupid , but the QUEEN was wearing a red hat.

(19a) does not say that the man in question was either an unhappy or an unfulfilled person, but expresses a correction of a lexical selection just made. Analogously, (19b) can be read not only as saying that the person wearing a red hat was not Lizzy but the queen, but also as saying that the expression *Lizzy* is inappropriate and should be replaced with the more polite *the queen*.

This being so, an SA must be postulated expressing metalinguistic propositions as such. That is, there must be an SA containing quoted elements and metalinguistic predicates like 'be an appropriate expression'. This again requires a rule system mapping the metalinguistic SA onto the surface structure and vice versa. There must be, in other words, both a grammar and a semantics of quotes.

According to Larry Horn (1985) and others, metalinguistic interpretation is based on a general inferential faculty of speakers and is thus pragmatic. Yet the pragmatic solution does not seem to work, again because there clearly are purely grammatical restrictions on metalinguistic interpretation. Consider (20a–c). They are all syntactically well-formed, but only (20a) is coherent, though only in a metalinguistic interpretation with heavy accent on *not*, which implies a correction of what has been said before. (20b,c) are incoherent no matter what kind of accent is placed on *not* (the exclamation mark indicates incoherence):

(20)   a. He did NOT only lose $1,000. He only lost $100.
      b. !He not only lost $1,000. He only lost $100.
      c. !Not only did he lose $1,000. He only lost $100.

A pragmatic theory of reinterpretation on general inferential grounds fails to explain why pragmatic inference does not work for (20b,c).

Or consider two speakers, A and B, discussing a politician considered by A to be a crook but by B to be an honest man. A says: "And Brutus is an honorable man!" quoting Anthony in Shakespeare's *Julius Caesar* and thus implying a similarity between the politician in question and the treacherous Brutus in the play. Speaker B strongly disagrees, but he cannot express his disagreement by uttering (21), although it would be clear on general inferential grounds what he would have meant. What B could have said is something like (22):

(21)   Brutus is NOT an honorable man!

(22)   My foot / The hell Brutus is an honorable man.

General inferential powers are therefore insufficient to explain the facts concerned. Grammatical constraints are clearly involved.

A pragmatic analysis combined with a surface-based interpretation of the phenomena at hand thus does not stand much chance of being correct. A "grammar of quotes" mapping SAs expressing metalinguistic propositions onto correct surface structures and vice versa is needed. The fact that such a "grammar of quotes" has not so far been actually developed does not affect this conclusion.

For cases like (16a) this means that we assume, in the absence of any further theory, that the metalinguistic SAs that must be postulated for such cases are indeed (special) cleft structures, which are of such a nature that the island constraints that hold in ordinary, non-metalinguistic cases do not apply because quoted elements are structurally detached from the construction they belong to in non-metalinguistic use.

We therefore conclude that proposals implying a surface assignment of heavy accent or a transformational extraction of clefted elements are incorrect. The same conclusion follows from cases with heavy accent or clefting whose unaccented or noncleft version is ungrammatical. Consider a father telling his son not to cry because, as he says, "well-educated boys don't cry." Now the boy says (23a), thus putting the blame on his father. Without heavy accent the sentence *I didn't educate me* is ungrammatical, and the grammatical *I didn't educate myself* does not express what the boy wants to say. He could also have used the cleft forms (23b) or (23c):

(23)   a. √*I* didn't educate me, *YOU* did!
       b. √It isn't me who educated me, it's you.
       c. √Who educated me isn't me but you.

What is at issue here is reflexivization. The general principle is that object pronouns are obligatorily reflexive when they are coreferential with the clause-mate subject term. On the whole, this principle is correct, despite problems with prepositional phrases (Kuno 1987). It fails, however, to explain the grammaticality of (23a). On the assumption that heavy accent is assigned by a surface rule, (23a) should be ungrammatical. In (23b,c) it is unclear whether the clause-mate subject *who* is coreferential with the object pronoun *me*. A solution is found if we let the reflexive principle apply to SA-level subjects only and not to derived subject terms. (23a) then has the underlying cleft SA: 'not [the x [x educated me] be me]]' and all is well.

As regards the non-truth-conditional "weak" variants of the topic-comment distinction, they are best looked on as resulting from a correspondence between (implicit) questions and their answers. The comment is regarded as the answer to a specific question reflected in the topic. A grammatical analysis readily presents itself, again in the form of SA-cleft structures. Given a (possibly implicit) question like (24a), with an underlying semantic form roughly like (24b), the answer (25a), with *Bob* as comment and 'x wrote the letter' as topic, is given the strictly parallel underlying semantic form (25b), but with only a nuclear, not a heavy, accent:

(24)   a.   Who wrote the letter?
      b.   the x [x wrote the letter] is *who*?

(25)   a.   Bob wrote the letter.
      b.   the x [x wrote the letter] is Bob

The overall conclusion as regards focusing strategies is, therefore, that there is no compelling argument supporting the view that they are surface-based. On the contrary, the evidence shows that they are best derived from a level of semantic representation expressing them in terms of cleft structures. This conclusion is of central importance in the present context, since it takes away the most important category of elements adduced by Chomsky to support his thesis that some semantic elements must be regarded as having a surface-driven interpretation.

7.3 Presuppositions

The second class of phenomena considered by Chomsky to have a surface-driven semantic interpretation are presuppositions. Here we can be brief. Four types of presupposition can be distinguished:

> *Type i*: existential presuppositions (induced by the main predicate for definite terms)
> *Type ii*: factive presuppositions (induced by the main predicate for factive clauses)
> *Type iii*: categorial presuppositions (induced by the main predicate)
> *Type iv*: remainder category (induced by heavy accent, cleft constructions, focusing particles)

Types i to iii are illustrated in (26a–c), respectively; type iv is illustrated in (26d–f) ("»" stands for "presupposes"):

(26)   a.   The king of France is bald.   »   there is a king of France
      b.   She realized that John had died.   »   John had died
      c.   She was divorced.   »   she had been married before

    d. Only John laughed.   »   John laughed
    e. JOHN didn't laugh.   »   someone laughed
    f. It wasn't John who laughed. »   someone laughed

Types i and ii are naturally regarded as subclasses of iii. That is, the existential and factive presuppositions of types i and ii, respectively, are easily derived from the satisfaction conditions of the main lexical predicates involved. Existential presuppositions derive from the extensional character of the predicate with regard to the term in question, which means that real existence of the referent of that term is required for the truth of the sentence formed with it. *Bald*, for example, is extensional with regard to its subject term, because a sentence like (26a) is automatically false when there is no king of France. By contrast, a predicate like *famous* is not extensional but intensional with regard to its subject term, because a sentence like *Sherlock Holmes is famous* is true, even though the (imaginary) person denoted by the term *Sherlock Holmes* does not exist. Existential presuppositions are thus directly derivable by the otherwise necessary specification of extensionality or intensionality of any given predicate with respect to each of its terms (see Seuren 1985, 1988, 2000 for extensive comment).

Since the same is naturally done for factive and nonfactive predicates, the former inducing factive presuppositions as exemplified in (26b), we may posit the generalization that for types i–iii the presuppositions are induced by the main lexical predicate of the sentence, which, in all existing theories, is introduced at the deep level of lexical selection. As regards type iv, it has just been argued, in the previous section, that these cases, too, are best treated as induced by elements that are part of the semantic analysis of the sentences concerned. There is thus no reason to presume that presuppositions are semantically interpreted on the basis of elements introduced in surface structure or during the transformational process. In minimalist terms, this means that there is no reason to presume that presuppositions are introduced in the phonological component, beyond Spell-Out.

7.4 Operator scope

Finally, we come to the determination of operator scope (see also section 4.1.1.1). Prima facie it might seem that operator scope can be determined either at the semantic or at the surface level, since in surface structure scope corresponds nontrivially to left-to-right linear ordering:

(27) a. *Some* children do *not* know *all* rugby players.
      b. ∃x:child – not – ∀y:rugby player [x know y]

(28) a. *No* children know *all* rugby players.
      b. ¬ ∃x:child – ∀y:rugby player [x know y]

(29) a. *Every* morning I read *some* poem.
      b. ∀x:morning – ∃y:poem [I read y on x]

(30) a. I read *some* poem *every* morning.
      b. ∀x:morning – ∃y:poem [I read y on x]
      c. ∃y:poem – ∀x:morning [I read y on x]

The (a)-sentences are normal English surface structures (the elements printed in italic type represent scope-bearing operators; *no* represents underlying 'not some'). The (b)-sentences are the corresponding (simplified) semantic analysis, or, for the ambiguous (30), semantic analyses. "∃" stands for "some," "∀" for "all," and "¬" for "not." Although the semantic analyses are given here in linear order, they really are tree structures of the following kind (for (27b); compare the tree structures in (12)–(14) of chapter 4):

(31)

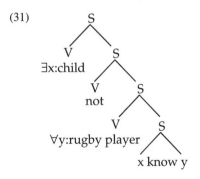

In (27)–(29) the order of the operators corresponds exactly to the hierarchical order in the logico-semantic analysis: they obey the scope ordering constraint (SOC) discussed in section 4.1.1.1. It would thus make no difference whether operator scope is determined on the basis of the surface structures or their logico-semantic analyses. Sentence (30a) is ambiguous between the two readings indicated, owing to the fact that "high" prepositional adjuncts like *every morning* are allowed to override the linear order constraint (see section 4.1.1.1). But this would not make any difference, either, because the ambiguity will have to be identified in any theory. There thus seems to be no compelling reason to say that the elements that signal operator scope are present only in surface structure and not in the logico-semantic analysis. If there were a compelling reason to say that, the determination of operator scope would indeed be a case of surface-driven semantic interpretation.

This point is implicitly recognized in May (1977), where the rule schema of Operator Lowering, developed in the framework of generative semantics, is simply reversed into Operator Raising (but without attribution), as was mentioned in note 1. Interestingly, the determination of operator scope is not mentioned in Chomsky's later writings.

There are, however, good reasons for assuming that the assignment of operator scope is not neutral between top-down or bottom-up, but is actually fixed at the SA-level of description and that the corresponding surface structure is causally derived from the SA-level. We have just seen, in connection with the negative polarity item *in the least* in (13a) and (13b), repeated here for convenience as (32a,b), that the ungrammaticality of (32b) is best explained by an appeal to the corresponding SA-structure, where the negation is at two removes from the clause into which it has to be incorporated, while it should be at no more than one remove:

(32)   a.   √John is often not in the least interested.
       b.   *John isn't often in the least interested.

Another argument for considering logical relations in SA-structures causally responsible for grammaticality phenomena is the following. Whereas a sentence like (33a) is ungrammatical on account of incorrect number agreement, (33b) is fully grammatical:

(33)   a.   *Either Harry or Fred were late.
       b.   √I don't think either Harry or Fred were late.

The explanation appears to lie in the fact that (33b) is *interpreted* as (34a)—that is as 'I think that (a) Harry was not late and (b) Fred was not late', where the predicate 'be late' has two distinct subject terms under the conjunction *and*, and should therefore take plural number when constructed with both subject terms at the same time:

(34) a. I think [and [not [Harry be late]], [not [Fred be late]]]
      b. I think [not [or [Harry be late], [Fred be late]]]
      c. I think [not [either Harry or Fred be late]]
      d. not [I think [either Harry or Fred be late]]

In virtue of the fact that the conjunctor *and* induces Negative Raising with simultaneous relexification into *or*, (34a) is first transformed into (34b). Then Disjunction Reduction produces (34c), and Negative Raising on the *think*-cycle gives (34d). Final Operator Lowering of *not* gives (33b). On the assumption that the conjunctor *and* in (34a) places a feature on the identical predicate *be late* of its two argument clauses to the effect that in case the two occurrences of the predicate are reduced to one by a reduction operation during the transformational process the predicate must be plural, the plural form *were* is fixed in (34c), after the operation of Disjunction Reduction.

In the old days there was a great deal of resistance to such "global rules," mainly fueled by a priori but unfounded considerations of economy of description. Nowadays, however, with the appearance of features that "trickle down" through trees and derivations, such objections have, on the whole, vanished. Therefore, in the absence of a better explanation, one may take it that, indeed, the grammaticality of (33b) is to be explained by an appeal to its underlying SA-structure.

7.5 Conclusion

The conclusion of these excursions into details of grammar and semantics is clear. First, the elements listed in Chomsky (1972) and still referred to in Chomsky (1998) as requiring a semantic interpretation based on the surface structure rather than on the semantic analysis of the sentences in which they occur—namely focusing devices (including topic-focus modulation), presupposition and scope differences—do not require surface-structure interpretation procedures but are securely lodged in any empirically adequate form of semantic analysis that is fed into the grammar to produce the corresponding surface structures. Second, if the elements in question were indeed instances of surface-driven semantic interpretation, then such a fact would be a direct threat to the MP, which is incapable of handling such phenomena, owing to the absence of any feeding link from the phonetic representation of sentences to their logical form.

8

The Embarrassment
of Evidence

Let us finally take a closer look at the actual complexity of grammar and
try to decide whether the differences taken to exist between the surface
and the semantic levels of representation (or whatever levels are invoked
in the MP) are adequately described by the term "displacement." This might
seem a matter of minor terminological importance, yet a closer look will
provide a clearer insight into what exactly is involved. While discussing
actual structures and processes, I will try to remain as theory-neutral as
possible, given the circumstances. To the extent that there may be a bias
toward my own, mediational, way of analyzing and presenting syntactic
structures, it is restricted to simple assumptions that are either well established or natural, or both. In line with the assumption that the semantic input
structures to the mediational grammar are cast in the format of the language
of Predicate Calculus, or LPC, it is assumed that the basic form of underlying S-structures is verb-subject-object or VSO (for languages with a right-
branching syntax; languages with a left-branching syntax have SOV). The
syntactic advantages of this assumption are set out in McCawley (1970).

For Chomsky, the displacement property consists in "the fact that
objects appear in the sensory output in positions 'displaced' from those
in which they are interpreted, under the most principled assumptions
about interpretation" (1995:221–222). As we have seen, the absence, in

Chomsky's theory, of any principled notion of semantic structure makes the appeal to "assumptions about interpretation" entirely empty. But if we take the expression "the most principled assumptions about interpretation" literally and seriously, then the real question is whether on current standard principles, not found in Chomsky's work, "displacement" is all there is to the difference between surface and semantic structure. In this chapter we will see that a mere displacement notion of the mapping procedure between semantic content and phonetic realization is woefully inadequate. As a result, one must conclude that the fact complexes discussed in this chapter are beyond the analytical and descriptive powers of the MP, which thus turns out to be empirically deficient.

8.1 Deletion and Raising in infinitival complements

This section looks at the complementation systems of the languages of the world, in particular at the infinitival forms of complementation. The purpose of the investigation is to see to what extent the MP is capable of accounting for the phenomena observed in relation to forms of infinitival complementation.

In some cases the term *displacement* (or *movement*) describes accurately enough what seems to be the case. In a sentence like (1a), the element *John* is "displaced" in that in surface structure (I shall continue to use this term)[1] it figures as the subject term of the verb *tend*:

(1)   a. John tends to be accurate.
       b. $_S$[tend $_S$[be accurate (John)]]

The semantic interpretation of the sentence, however, requires that *John* be the subject term of the predicate *be accurate*, so that the semantic structure of the sentence would be something like (1b), where the main predicate is

---

1. I recognize surface structure as a level of representation for the simple reason that it is conceptually necessary: sentences, in the form in which they occur in daily life, must have a structure, or else they would not be sentences at all. Moreover, in many languages there are efficient tests for determining at least the main elements of surface structure (constituent fronting, for example, in surface V-second languages such as German or Dutch). Given these reasons, the burden of proof lies with those who wish to deny surface structure as a level of representation, not with us. And no compelling arguments have so far been advanced in favor of that position.

the verb *tend*, which has as its subject term the embedded S-structure [be accurate (John)]. The grammar of English is thus responsible for the movement of *John* from the position of subject to *be accurate* to the position of subject to *tend*. This form of movement is part of the grammar of English and is known as Subject-to-Subject Raising. In cases such as this it is not unnatural to speak of displacement, though one must realize that this displacement is not a one-dimensional operation applied to strings of symbols but a two-dimensional operation applied to tree structures.

There is, however, much more to the relation between sensory output and semantic structure. The system that maps semantic analyses (SAs) onto surface structures (SSs) involves more than just movement. There is also *deletion* of elements that are taken to figure in SA but have disappeared in SS. Sometimes it is found that specific lexical items need not be expressed in SS, as their deletion is part of their lexical specification. Shakespearean English has sentences like *I must away*, with the verb *go* deleted. Analogous phenomena are found in modern standard Dutch and German. Such purely lexical deletions have a certain universality, in that it is often verbs of motion that are deleted, and frequently also verbs of having, as in *I want that book*. Expressions like *the greatest victory ever* are instances of deletion that are halfway between grammar and lexicon (though what exactly has been deleted is a matter of debate).

But let us have a more systematic look at what is at issue and concentrate on the grammar of infinitival complementation. Complementation is the universal phenomenon of a sentential structure (S-structure) taking the place of an argument to a predicate. Languages deal with such constructions in different ways, which can be summarized as follows. It appears that fully tensed complement-Ss surface as full subordinate clauses (in English mostly with the default complementizer *that*). Untensed or partially tensed complement-Ss surface as (a) nominalizations (expressions corresponding to, for example, 'I want my/your going'), (b) as infinitivals (e.g., 'I made him leave'), or (c) as participials (e.g., 'I saw him opening the door').

As far as can be ascertained at the moment, infinitival complements in any language appear to result from the application of one or more of the following cyclic rules:

Subject Deletion (*SD*) (= erstwhile Equi–NP–deletion): The subject is deleted under a referential identity condition controlled by a nominal argument term (usually the subject) of the higher verb.
   Example: *I want to go*, from $_S$[want – I_x – $_S$[go – x]].

Predicate Raising (PR): The lower V-constituent is united with the higher V-constituent into a V-cluster and the remaining NP-terms are amalgamated with those of the higher V under the higher S.

Example: *I let go the rope*, from ₛ[let – I – ₛ[go – the rope]].

Subject Raising (SR): The lower subject is raised to the argument position occupied by its own S, where it assumes the nominative or accusative case normally assigned to NP arguments in that position. There are thus two (formally identical) varieties of SR: Subject-to-Subject Raising (SSR) and Subject-to-Object Raising (SOR).

Examples: SSR: *The bird seems to fly*, from ₛ[seem – ₛ[fly – the bird]]
SOR: *I want you to go*, from ₛ[want – I – ₛ[go – you]].

In tree-structure terms (VSO-format), the operations look as in figure 8.1.

The application of SD, PR, or SR is best assumed to be driven by lexical specification: each complement-taking verb is marked in the lexicon for the cyclic rules it induces. Thus, English *expect* (like *want*) will be marked "SD or SR"—that is, SD applies when the higher and lower subject are co-referential, SR applies when they are not, as in *I expect the bird to fly*, taken to be derived from an underlying semantic form corresponding to 'ₛ[expect – I – ₛ[fly – the bird]]'. *Believe* will lack the op-

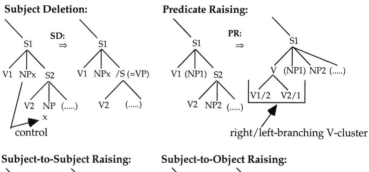

FIGURE 8.1. Schematic rendering of SD, PR, SSR, SOR

tion SD, given the ungrammaticality of **I believe to be right* (its equivalent in most other European languages is fully grammatical), but will be marked for SR, the default raising rule for English.

The three cyclic procedures SD, PR, and SR have one clear overall effect: the maximal unification of the lower clause with the matrix-S. There is, in general, a clear tendency in the complementation systems of the languages of the world for the matrix-S to incorporate as much material as is possible, given the language type and universal constraints. I use the term *Matrix Greed* to denote this tendency.

In the light of the data and the analyses proposed, it seems natural to assume that a complement-S that loses its subject-NP is demoted to /S (i.e., the traditional VP), the resulting S being "deficient" in that it lacks its subject-NP. Moreover, when a complement-S loses its V, its S-node is abolished and any remaining arguments are reattached, in their order of occurrence, to the higher S. Repeated cyclic application of PR leads to complex (right- or left-branching) V-clusters: all verb forms are aligned on one side of the clause and the nominal argument terms picked up from the various cycles aligned on the opposite side.

This general picture is simple and clear enough, and based on meticulous analyses of a fairly large number of languages. It is, however, disturbed by some isolated facts which have so far eluded explanation and show that further refinements of the theory are necessary. A case in point is the phenomenon of inflected infinitives in Portuguese. In Portuguese there exist embedded Ss that probably correspond to infinitival embedded Ss, but with a nominative case subject in place, as in the following sentences:

(2)   a.   Ele lamenta eu ter trabalhado demais.
           he regrets I_{nom} have$_{inf?}$ worked too much
           'He regrets that I have worked too much.'
      b.   Ele entrou em casa sem eu ver.
           he entered in house without I_{nom} see$_{inf?}$
           'He entered the house without me noticing.'

The pronoun *eu* (I) has overt nominative case, the oblique form being *me*. The semantic subject of infinitives may occur in the accusative—a clear instance of SR—but sometimes it may or has to occur in the nominative, as here. The conditions are unclear. But then, it is not clear that the forms *ter* (have) or *ver* (see) are indeed nonfinite, since Portuguese has the curious phenomenon of "inflected infinitives": apparent infinitives receiving a special set of endings under conditions that have so far remained obscure.[2] In (2a,b) the infinitive appears uninflected, but that is because the paradigm has no overt ending for the first person singular. Portuguese has, for example, the following well-formed sentences:

(3)   a. Ele lamenta os trabalhadores ter*em* trabalhado demais.
         he regrets the workers$_{nom}$ have$_{3plur-inf?}$ worked too much
         'He regrets that the workers have worked too much.'
      b. Ele entrou em casa sem os meninos ver*em*.
         he entered in house without the children$_{nom}$ see$_{3plur-inf?}$
         'He entered the house without the children noticing.'

Here the NPs *os trabalhadores* and *os meninos* must be taken to have nominative case (by analogy to *eu* in (2a,b)). The point is that *terem* and *verem* seem infinitival yet are inflected for third-person plural.

Cases like the Portuguese inflected infinitive show that the finite-nonfinite parameter must allow for variations that have so far not found a place in the theory, and, moreover, that the occurrence of nominative case subjects is likely to be conditioned by at least some finiteness characteristic of the verb to which the subject term is an argument. Other than that, however, it does seem to be the case that fully nonfinite clauses exclude nominative case subject terms.

A second, related, complication is the following. What has been called Matrix Greed is so strong that it sometimes even attracts subjects from clauses that appear to be finite. In some Balkan languages, for example, one finds sentences like (4) (taken from a Greek folk song):

(4)   Thélo ton ánthropo na échi kardhiá.
      I want the$_{acc}$ man$_{acc}$ that he-has$_{3sg}$ a heart
      'I want a man to have a heart.'

---

2. Raposo (1987) makes an attempt at fitting the Portuguese inflected infinitive into the framework of Government and Binding, but this attempt is inadequate as it fails to consider the optional inflected infinitive under causative *fazer* (make), as in:

(i)   A nova lei fez os trabalhadores vender(em) a sua casa the new law made the workers sell their house

Here the NP *ton anthropo* (the man) has accusative case, having been been raised from its semantically defined position as the subject term of the finite verb *échi* ((he)-has). Romanian shows a similar phenomenon (Chomsky 1995:285, 385), as well as Bulgarian. Again, however, as with the Portuguese inflected infinitive, there is some doubt as to the status of the embedded clause. Thus, it is impossible for Greek clauses embedded under the subjunctive particle *na* to have an overt subject term in the canonical position preceding the finite verb (Joseph 1990):

(5)   *Elpízo na o ánthropos échi kardhiá.
     I hope that the$_{nom}$ man$_{nom}$ has$_{3sg}$ a heart

One has to say instead:

(6)   Elpízo na échi kardhiá o ánthropos.

Here the subject term has been extraposed to final position.

    Apart from anything else, this would seem to be in violation of MP principles, which, as far as one understands, do not allow for a surface form verb-object-subject, and which rule out left-to-right movement. Although this is not my immediate concern right now, it is both relevant and interesting. It must be mentioned because of the way Chomsky deals with this category of counterevidence. For it appears, surprisingly, that the MP does allow for rightward extraposition (1995:333, 335), but in a way "that may not belong at all within the framework of principles we are considering" (1995:333). One is given to understand, by a reference to p. 325, that extraposition, along with other phenomena that violate the MP framework, belongs to a peripheral "stylistic" component of the FoL. The passage referred to is the following (Chomsky 1995:324–325):

> In early transformational grammar, a distinction was sometimes made between "stylistic" rules and others. Increasingly, the distinction seems to be quite real: the core computational properties we have been considering differ markedly in character from many other operations of the language faculty, and it may be a mistake to try to integrate them within the same framework of principles. The problems related to XP-adjunction are perhaps a case in point: they may not really belong to the system we are discussing here as we keep closely to the first of the two courses just outlined, the one that is concerned with Last Resort movement driven by feature checking within the N $\rightarrow$ π computation. It is within this core

component of the language that we find the striking properties highlighted by minimalist guidelines. It seems increasingly reasonable to distinguish this component of the language faculty.

No further explanation is given regarding this supposed distinction between the "core" component and the "stylistic" extensions of the FoL. The conclusion is, one must fear, that anything not conforming to strict MP principles will be declared "stylistic" and thus not belonging to the "core," even though this escape clause was not mentioned among the "guiding principles" specified in the opening pages of chapter 4 of *The Minimalist Program.*

The lesson to be drawn from this is that for Chomsky the preconceived theory is immune to contrary facts. We have here the Hegelian principle that facts do not matter: if facts belie the theory, then, says Hegel, so much the worse for them. Clearly, such a breach of basic principles of scientific method should be sufficient to disqualify the MP as a whole.

To revert now to the Modern Greek (Bulgarian, Romanian) form of SR out of a clause that appears to be finite, no existing theory explains why this should be possible, but it does seem that there is something amiss with the finite status of *na*-clauses in Modern Greek. Joseph (1990) suggests that *na* is not a complementizer but a preverbal subjunctive marker which cannot be separated from the verb. If so, *na*-clauses lack a complementizer, which may perhaps suggest that such clauses, in a still badly understood way, somehow "stand in" for the infinitives that were lost, over the centuries, in the Balkan languages.

The matter is still quite opaque. In Portuguese we have inflected (quasi)infinitives with a nominative case subject; in Greek we have inflected (quasi-)finite forms with the subject either raised to object accusative-case position or extraposed to the far right. A more refined theory of the finite-nonfinite parameter should create the theoretical space for a satisfactory account of these and similar phenomena. For the moment we must store these facts as "problems to solve."

8.1.1 The typology of Subject Raising and Predicate Raising

Apart from such complications, languages appear to fall into three main groups as regards their treatment of infinitival complements: those that resort exclusively to SR, those that resort exclusively to PR, and those that resort to both SR and PR, under controlled conditions. (SD appears to play no special role in typological distinctions.) English, Russian, Portuguese, Latin, Ancient Greek, most Caribbean Creole languages, and many others belong to the SR group. Dutch, German, Icelandic, Japanese, Turkish, Hindi, and a host of other languages belong to the PR group, as is evidenced by their sometimes extended V-clusters. French, Italian, Spanish, the Creole languages of Mauritius and the Seychelles, and no doubt more languages as well, appear to have both SR and PR, but under controlled conditions. Typical PR-induced V-clusters in French, Italian, and Spanish are those that are formed under causative verbs for 'cause, make' (e.g., French *faire*), and semi-causative verbs for 'let, allow' (e.g., French *laisser*) (Seuren 1996:185–203). Portuguese has no such V-clusters but is similar to English in its application of SR.

SR and PR constructions are typically, but far from exclusively, found with causative verbs, and with verbs of knowing or believing and perception verbs. There often is an ambiguity between a *control reading* (I saw John$_x$ [x sign the letter]), where SD applies, and a *raising reading* (I saw [John sign the letter]), where either SR or PR will apply, depending on the language. When one encounters sentence forms of type (7a), the language in question is likely to be of the SR type, but when the sentences are like (7b), PR is most likely:

(7) a. X believe Y (to) like strawberries
    b. X (believe (to) like) Y strawberries

Thus, the English sentence *I let the rope go* manifests SR (SD, in the control reading, is less likely). But its near equivalent *I let go the rope* is a clear case of PR. (This, incidentally, is the only case of PR so far observed in English, and, as often with PR cases, it has been weakly lexicalized, as appears from the more current *I let go of the rope*, with the partly lexicalized expression *let go of*.)

PR constructions typically lead to the emergence of datives, reflecting original subject terms. This is because when the NP terms of a lower transitive clause are amalgamated with those of the higher clause, the lower subject will find itself between the higher subject and the lower object term—that is, in the canonical position of the indirect object. For example, the Dutch underlying subordinate clause (8a) is transformed by PR into the surface structure (8b), where the NP *de man* has dative case, as is shown by the optional preposition *aan* (to), and where *liet zien* (let see) is a V-cluster (moved to the far right by postcyclic V-Final):[3]

(8) a. . . . dat $_S$[laten-Past zij $_S$[zien de man de brief]]
        . . . that $_S$[let-Past she $_S$[see the man the letter]]
     b. . . . dat zij (aan) de man de brief liet zien
        . . . that she (to) the man the letter let-Past see
        '. . . that she let the man see the letter'

Such PR-derived datives are, of course, frequent in French, Italian, Spanish, Turkish, Japanese, and many other languages.[4]

The main features of these analyses are not in dispute among competent grammarians of the languages in question. No serious alternative has been proposed, although there are considerable variations in the manner and degree of formalization, as well as in the general frame of reference and in the terminology.[5]

3. A diagnostic difficulty arises in Dutch and German main clauses, due to the fact that in main clauses the finite verb form must, in principle, be in second position, while the remaining nonfinite part of the V-cluster comes, in principle, at the end of the sentence. This often creates the erroneous impression that SR, and not PR, is applied in Dutch and German main clauses, which explains why grammarians of these languages often, mistakenly, think that these languages apply SR instead of PR. This mistake is reinforced by the fact that Latin and English, the two languages whose grammatical analyses are best known and have been most influential, are both SR languages. To avoid this mistake, and also to be in a better position to study the V-cluster phenomena in these languages, a convention has now arisen among grammarians of Dutch and German to present the example sentences preferably as subordinate clauses, which display the V-clusters in their full glory, rather than as main clauses, where the V-clusters have been split up. For that reason, the Dutch and German examples here are given as subordinate clauses. For extensive discussion see Seuren (2003).

One notes, incidentally, that these facts of Dutch and German subordinate clauses are in conflict with MP principles, since there is no way in which all NP terms can be raised over V, assuming these languages are right-branching. But if Dutch and German are taken to be left-branching languages, there is no way of getting the structure of the main clauses right, either. Chomskyans, who love stylistics, will probably reply that these facts do not belong to core grammar.

4. German does not have a dative in the corresponding cases, but assigns a secondary accusative case to the original subject term, thus giving rise to double accusative constructions. Baker (1988:164–165) reports the same phenomenon for Chamorro (Austronesian) and a dialect of Chichewa (Bantu).

5. A splendid example is Bech (1983), which contains a masterly though informal analysis of German V-clusters, described in terms of "coherence." More recent, and more formal, approaches to the problems posed by German and Dutch verb constructions are collected in Seuren and Kempen (2003).

Some tentative universals may be ventured. It seems, for example, that a V-final (SOV) language never has SR but may have PR. A sentence meaning 'John may leave the house' would then be structured as 'John–the house–$_V$[leave–may]', and not as 'John–$_{VP}$[the house–leave]–$_V$[may]'. Another tentative universal says that SR from subject position (Subject-to-Subject Raising) never occurs when the higher V is transitive, so that a sentence like **John surprised me to have died* will never occur. But such matters, though undecided, leave intact the generalization that languages make different choices from the triple menu of SD, SR, and PR. The complications that remain, such as the Portuguese inflected infinitives or the Greek form of SR, show that the theory is insufficiently refined, or that additional machinery is required. They do not affect the overall picture, which is that of SD, SR, and PR.

What appears of all this in *The Minimalist Program* amounts to little, and what one finds is truly disappointing. There are two short and inconsequential passages (1995:47, 50), in the context not of complementation systems but of derivational and representational forms of grammar, devoted to the raising of verbs that are adjoined to causative higher verbs and thus form V-clusters of the kind discussed, with reference to Baker (1988).[6] A further short passage, likewise referring to Baker (1988), is chapter 3, pp. 183–184, where the topic is chains of traces. The typical PR dative, mentioned above, is not commented on though it occurs in the example discussed. Yet it needs an explanation in the MP framework. Baker (1988:164–204, 431–439) deals extensively with this topic. In the comprehensive chapter 4 of *The Minimalist Program* no mention occurs at all of PR or of the processes and structures associated with it. How V-clusters could be generated in the MP framework is not explained (an appeal to the earlier chapters is invalid, since the notions and techniques that apply there no longer apply in chapter 4). In fact, in cases where PR would immediately solve a particular problem, as with the word order in the Icelandic existential *there*-sentences referred to in (162a,b) on p. 342 (see section 8.3), the solution is sought not in the application of PR but in terms of MP-related forms of raising determined by different kinds of features, with the result that one is led "into a thicket of complex and only partly explored issues" (1995:344).

---

6. No mention is made of McCawley (1968), where the rule of Predicate Raising was proposed for the first time in a formal transformational context.

8.1.2 Subject-to-Object Raising: nothing "exceptional"

Special attention must be devoted to Chomsky's way of dealing with the facts relating to Subject-to-Object Raising (SOR). On p. 58, the following passage occurs: "Constructions of the form (74a) are rather idiosyncratic to English; in similar languages (e.g. German), the corresponding expressions have the properties of (67bii–iii), (73), and so on" (Chomsky 1995:58). The sentences referred to are the following (one must take into account Chomsky's preference for presenting example sentences adorned with all kinds of formal elements that prejudge their analysis):

(74) a.   John believes [Bill to be intelligent]
(67) b. ii (I prefer) [$_{CP}$ for [$_{IP}$ John to meet Bill]]
          iii (it was decided) [$_{CP}$ C [$_{IP}$ PRO to meet Bill]]
(73)   I wonder who he decided [$_{CP}$ C [PRO to catch t]]

This passage is remarkable for a number of reasons. First, it repeats the extraordinary statement that SOR, as in the quoted (74a), is "rather idiosyncratic to English." In fact, this strange and embarrassingly uninformed statement is reflected in the equally strange term *Exceptional Case Marking* (ECM) that was used for a number of years to denote SOR phenomena, and is still used in *The Minimalist Program* on pp. 108, 112, and even in chapter 4 on p. 345. Both the statement and the term reflect an inexplicable disregard of the fact that SR, in particular SOR, characterizes a well-established and widely occurring typological class. As we have seen, it is found in Latin, Ancient Greek, many Creole languages, Portuguese, Russian, and so on.

It must be observed that for many years Chomsky staunchly refused to accept SOR as a rule of grammar, against not only the tradition but also a barrage of arguments presented in Postal (1974) (see Seuren 1998:509). His term ECM stands for an "exceptional" ("idiosyncratic") accusative marking of the subject of the embedded clause, which should, in the way of subjects, have nominative case. (As we saw in (2a,b), this happens occasionally in Portuguese, in its inflected infinitive constructions, but those cases are extremely rare and the term "exceptional" should apply to them, not to the perfectly normal accusative marking of embedded subjects raised to object position.) But then, in chapter 3 of the book, the raising of embedded subjects to matrix-object position is suddenly acknowledged as a valid process, after many years of denial, without any further comment about this change of mind and without any reference to the well-known earlier debates about the issue, notably Postal (1974). Chomsky comments (1995:174):

> Exceptional case marking by V is now interpreted as raising of NP to the Spec of the AgrP dominating V. It is raising to [Spec, Agr$_o$], the analogue of familiar raising to [Spec, Agr$_s$].

But to revert to the passage quoted from p. 58, besides its other noteworthy features, it also fails to recognize the important typological difference between English and German: German is a PR language, whereas English is an SR language. Chomsky's (74a) has no structurally analogous translation in German. The closest German comes is in sentences like:

(9) Johann läßt Wilhelm intelligent sein.
     Johann lets Wilhelm intelligent be

But this is not SOR at all. The subordinate clause version of this sentence shows that *läßt* and *intelligent sein* form a left-branching V-cluster extraposed to the far right by V-Final (the main clause version results from a cutting up of the V-cluster; see note 3):

(10) ..., dass Johann Wilhelm intelligent sein läßt
      ... that Johann Wilhelm intelligent be lets

As regards the examples quoted as (67bii–iii) and (73), what these sentences have to do with German remains a mystery.

In sum, *The Minimalist Program* fails to pay sufficient attention to the facts regarding the distribution of SD, SR, and PR in the languages of the world. Although the MP is predicated on the notion of universal parameters that take on specific values for individual languages, no serious attempt is made at establishing such parameters on the basis of well-founded analyses and known facts.

8.1.3 The lack of serious typology in the MP

Occasionally, an attempt is made at some sort of typology. For example, on p. 134, one is suddenly confronted, without any introductory comment, with an alleged distinction between "French-type" and "English-type" languages. On p. 159, the "French-English type" is, in turn, contrasted with the West African language Bambara. One would have wished to see a specification of the propinquity measure used, and also some indication of what languages belong to each group, but alas, no such information is supplied. The ad hoc distinction between English-type and French-type languages is invoked, on p. 134, to account for the different behavior of adverbs in the VPs of English and French. Relevant examples are the following:

(11) a. John completely lost his mind.
      b. John has completely lost his mind.

(12) a. Jean perdit complètement la tête.
      b. Jean a complètement perdu la tête.

The difference shows in the (a)-sentences, where English puts the adverb before, but French after, the finite verb. In the (b)-sentences, with the perfect tense auxiliary as finite verb, the adverb follows the finite verb in both languages. To explain this it is assumed that in French V raises to Infl in the structure

$$_{IP}[NP,_{Infl'}[Infl,_{VP}[Adverb,_{VP}[V, NP]]]]$$

whereas in English Infl is said to lower to V, except when V is an auxiliary, in which case V raises to Infl, as in French.[7]

But this is in chapter 2, and chapter 4 forbids lowering. So what to do? On pp. 330ff. some solution is proposed for some related but highly fragmentary facts of English, in terms of raising, as is to be expected. Then, on p. 332, the question of the French way of treating VP-adverbs is brought up again: "Questions remain about other matters, among them: What is the basis for the French-English distinction, and is it somehow reducible to overt V-raising?" Five lines later, the answer is provided: "I leave such questions without any useful comment." Here one hastens to follow suit.

---

7. Baptista (2000) is typical in that she uncritically follows Chomsky's adverb placement criterion for alleged V-Raising in some Creole languages, without any further data analysis. In fact, however, the question of the position of adverbs in many languages, including English and French, is highly complex. Serious formal treatments are rare and still do not achieve complete coverage (for English, see Baker 1991 and Seuren 1996:116–128, 203–206).

8.1.4 Lexical idiosyncrasies

In general, the MP treatment of complementation strategies is fragmentary and, one has to say, confused. A further striking example may illustrate this. In (1995:313), the ungrammaticality of

(13)   *John believes to be intelligent.

(actually presented as 'John [$_{VP}$ *t'* [BELIEVE [*t* to be intelligent]]]', but we have already encountered such instances of tendentious data presentation) is attributed to its "lacking the external argument required by the verb." That is, the verb *believe* needs a direct object, just like the verb *hit*, mentioned in the same context, or else the resulting sentence will be "deviant" or, as we are used to saying, ungrammatical. Fair enough, one would think, because one is fully entitled to consider **John believes* ungrammatical. A few pages later, however, on p. 345, the grammatical sentence:

(14)   I expected to leave early.

(actually presented as 'I expected [PRO to [*t* leave early]]') is discussed. Now the analysis assigns a control structure with SD to this sentence, or, in Chomsky's parlance, "H assigns null Case to the subject, which must therefore be PRO." But surely, **I expect* is as ungrammatical ("deviant") as **John believes*. So, if the latter is ungrammatical on account of its lacking the required object term, why not the former? Why, in other words, is it not possible to represent (13) as 'John believes [PRO to [*t* be intelligent]]', and why is (14) not represented as 'I [$_{VP}$ *t'* [EXPECT [*t* to leave early]]]', which would presumably make it ungrammatical? No answer is provided. One fears that the author is simply forgetful, or careless.[8]

The answer can only lie in a small lexical quirk of the English verb *believe* (and a few other verbs, such as *know*). In most European languages the near-equivalent of *believe* (and in some languages also that of *know*)

---

8. Some carelessness is apparent anyway on the same p. 345, where, in the same context, the sentence (172b) *I expected someone to leave early* is discussed. Five lines below the example presented, one reads: "In the ECM structure (172b), H assigns no case, so *John* raises to the checking domain of Agro in the matrix clause." A little care would have shown the author that, for once, the sentence isn't about *John*, but about *someone*.

is assigned the rule feature SD, forcing it to delete the subject of the embedded nonfinite clause provided that subject is lexically empty and controlled by the higher subject. Thus, in German, French, and Italian one has, respectively (with the infinitival particles *zu* in the German, and *di* in the Italian sentence):

(15) a. Johann glaubt intelligent zu sein.
      b. Jean croit être intelligent.
      c. Gianni crede di essere intelligente.

There does not seem to be any principled reason why English *believe* lacks this rule feature. Other similar verbs, such as *expect* or *want* or *prefer*, do have it. In order to express what the sentences in (15) express, English has to resort to a finite clause: *John believes that he is intelligent*, which avoids all problems to do with nonfinite clauses. This appears to be the sole and simple answer.

Verbs of the appropriate semantic structure show a frequent, but by no means automatic, combination of SD, only applicable with controlled and lexically empty lower subjects, with raising (SR or PR, depending on the language concerned), raising being applicable only if the element to be raised has not been deleted. This combination makes for pairs like the English (16), with SR, or the Dutch (17), with PR:

(16) a. She wanted to leave.
      b. She wanted the man to leave.

(17) a. . . . dat ik wist te ontsnappen
          . . . that I knew to escape
          '. . . that I managed to get away'
      b. . . . dat ik het huis wist te liggen
          . . . that I the house knew to lie
          '. . . that I knew where the house was situated'

It is possible that Chomsky will agree that the difference in syntactic behavior between *believe* and *expect* is due to this kind of lexical quirk. But if that is so, it does not appear from his writings.

There is, however, a moral to the story of verbs like *believe* or *know*. What it shows is that SD must be stipulated as a separate rule and cannot be taken to follow automatically in any structure containing a nonfinite object clause with a subject that is semantically controlled by a higher argument NP. If that were so, the lexical quirk manifest in English verbs like *believe* or *know* would not be possible.

8.1.5 Raising and lowering in the MP

Why does the MP disallow elements to move down the right-branching tree, from left to right, and is the only permissible movement from right to left, up the tree? The question is justified because the MP recognizes, in principle, functional categories like tense, modalities, quantifiers, negation, and others. These are operators and therefore have scope, and scope can only be expressed structurally in terms of a command relation, as in structure (a) of figure 8.2, where the scope-bearing element *Operator* is united with the constituent S2 that forms its scope into one constituent S1. S2 can again consist of an Operator and a smaller scope S3, recursively. The smallest possible scope, at the bottom of the tree, is an S-structure built up from the main surface predicate of the sentence and its argument terms, according to the lexically defined argument structure of that predicate. This latter S is called the *matrix-S* or *lexical nucleus*. In structure (b) of figure 8.2 the matrix-S '[love – she – me]' is the scope of the operator *not*. The grammar of English transforms this structure (neglecting tense) into the simple surface sentence *She does not love me.* The part of the tree above the matrix-S we call the *auxiliary system*. The matrix-S forms the lower end of the tree, unless one of its argument terms is again an embedded (complement-)S. So far we may reasonably consider ourselves to be in the realm of "conceptual necessity," as these are principles of the Language of Predicate Calculus.

Since, in surface structures, most operators are added as extras to the matrix-S, which, as we have seen, is "greedy," the grammar must somehow

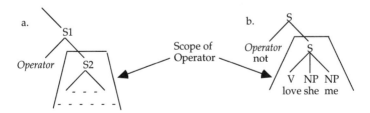

FIGURE 8.2. Operator scope expressed in terms of constituency trees

unite these operators in the auxiliary system with the matrix-S. The question is: is this best achieved by *lowering* the operators into the matrix-S, or by *raising* the latter to the formal LPC-position of operators?

In either case the procedure must preserve the overall structure of the matrix-S. This is so because in almost all cases, the matrix verb becomes the main verb of the surface sentence, and in most cases the NP arguments figure as such in surface structure. In fact, many theories of grammar (dependency grammar, lexical functional grammar, head-driven phrase-structure grammar, and so on) are, each in its specific way, founded on the notion that the surface structure of sentences is dominated by the lexical main predicate (verb) and its argument terms, and not by the abstract elements of the auxiliary system.

If the operators are united with the matrix-S by lowering, then a specification is needed of the "landing site" of each operator. Some operators, such as the quantifiers, have a natural landing site in the position occupied by the (first occurrence of the) bound variable in the matrix-S. In other cases, as with the tenses and often also the negation, the landing site is the matrix-V, so that lowering results in a matrix V-cluster. Often, when an operator lands on the lower V, it is relabelled as a morphological affix, so that it becomes part of the morphological structure of the verb form. This is typically the case with operators expressing tense, modality, and sometimes negation.

Often, however, the landing site is peripheral, in that the operator lands at the far left or the far right of the matrix-S. Examples are prepositional phrases, which never cluster with the matrix-V. Likewise, in most Germanic languages, the negation does not cluster with the matrix-V but is moved, in principle, to the far right of the lower S (as in early modern English *She loves me not*; present-day English inserts the dummy verb *do* with full lexical verbs).

One might conceivably maintain that a raising operation achieves exactly the same result as is achieved by lowering. This appears to be so for those operators that cluster with the matrix-V. For these cases Predicate Raising will ensure the correct result, since PR destroys the S-node immediately dominating the raised V, the remaining material being re-attached higher up in the same order. However, a raising operation makes for considerable formal complications in cases where the operator to be raised stands in a peripheral position. It thus seems that, for an orderly account of the fact that operators are unified with the matrix-S in surface structure, the answer is lowering and not raising.

The MP, however, has banned all forms of lowering and thus depends entirely on forms of raising. Let us see how the MP aims at achieving the correct results, taking into account that the MP setup is entirely different. We remember that the raising operations implied in the MP are partly overt and partly covert and do not map semantic structures onto surface structures, as in mediational grammar. Instead, they map Numerations (i.e., arbitrary selections from the lexicon), merged according to certain X-bar principles into one syntactic object, onto pairs (PF,LF), also called (π,λ), of phonological and logical forms. At Spell-Out the mapping procedure splits up into a covert part producing LF and an overt part producing PF. The notion of surface structure has been eliminated, but, in order to compare the two approaches, I will, just for the moment, identify the structure as it is at Spell-Out with what is normally taken to be surface structure.

Given the restriction to raising and the prohibition of lowering processes, a merged Numeration that will not crash and will successfully make it to (PF,LF) automatically assumes a form in which the lexical content of the sentence in question is concentrated largely at the base of the tree, while the higher parts are occupied by more abstract constituents whose function consists mainly in attracting the appropriate lexical material. These higher "abstract" elements are, for example, Agr_s, which attracts lexical material for the subject-NP, Agr_o, which does the same for the object-NP, or Infl(ection) for verbal lexical material. The MP thus reflects, in its own peculiar way, the distinction drawn above between the lexical matrix-S on the one hand and the auxiliary system on the other. The parallel is not complete, however, as the "abstract" elements in the higher part of MP input trees are, on the whole, not scope-bearing operators but, rather, feature complexes that attract lower, lexical feature complexes on the basis of a matching procedure. In this system of raisings, there is no question of preserving any form of predicate-argument structure. The MP raising system thus destroys whatever may have been available in the way of a lexical matrix structure, and thereby also an obvious structural basis of surface sentences. In the MP, the resulting structure of the sentence *John saw Mary* becomes something like figure 2.1 in chapter 2, which is presented as a logical form, not as a surface form, and we have already commented on the groundlessness of considering anything like it as a "logical" form at all. However, if the only covert raising, that of the direct object *Mary*, is undone, we have the structure of the sentence *John saw Mary* as it is at Spell-Out, and hence, in principle, the surface structure. Such structure assignments are of the quaintest possible kind and lack any justification whatsoever.

The main reason for the quaintness of whatever corresponds to the MP surface structures lies in the postulation in the auxiliary system of agreement constituents such as Agr_s and Agr_o for NPs or Infl(ection) for verbs. It is not clear what could motivate the postulation of Agr_s, Agr_o, or Infl in the higher parts of MP input trees. Such agreement features do not fit into the category of operators (to the extent, that is, that they are agreement features and do not fulfill other, unrelated, functions; Infl, for example, is also meant to give shelter to modal auxiliary verbs, though there is no relation with agreement). So why are they there in the first place? Clearly to provide an anchor ("target") for the raising operations that are part of the MP design. But there are no formal or empirical grounds to assume that NPs or verbs are raised in language the way they are taken to be in the MP. SR and PR, as well as the lowering of operators, are motivated on good syntactic and formal grounds, but the forms of raising conjured up in the MP are merely artifacts of certain a priori formal concepts, unsupported by valid evidence. Agr_s, Agr_o, and to some extent also Infl, are thus postulated to account for nonexistent phenomena.

This is, of course, very serious from a methodological point of view. Although perhaps less immediately obvious, it is in fact worse than the circular ascription of a *virtus dormitiva* (soporific power) to opium to explain its soporific power, as Molière, in his comedy *Le malade imaginaire*, lets his main character do. For it is at least an empirically proven fact that opium is soporific, whereas it is far from proven that NPs or verbs raise the way they are supposed to do in the MP. The assumption of Agr_s, Agr_o, and Infl elements in the auxiliary system therefore appears to violate elementary principles of sound methodology.

8.1.6 Directionality and German V-clusters: the R-condition

This section is a rapid case study of some particularly striking phenomena occurring in German V-clusters—phenomena that are clearly part of syntax, not of some "stylistic" component. The point of the exercise is to show that, given a handful of simple and natural assumptions, the phenomena are effortlessly accounted for in terms of semantic syntax, my own implementation of mediational grammar. Such an account is totally alien to the MP, which is not in a position to rephrase the account given in its own terms and appears to be far too restrictive to offer an

alternative account that does justice to the facts in a non-ad-hoc manner.
Consider the clauses:

(18)   a.   ..., daß sie ausgehen² will¹
           ... that she out-go wants
           '... that she wants to go out'
       b.   ..., daß sie hat¹ ausgehen³ wollen²
           ... that she has out-go want
           '... that she has wanted to go out'
       c.   *..., daß sie ausgehen³ gewollt² hat¹
           ... that she out-go wanted has
           '... that she has wanted to go out'
       d.   ..., daß sie mich ausgehen² sah¹
           ... that she me out-go saw
           '... that she saw me go out'
       e.   ..., daß sie mich hat¹ ausgehen³ sehen²
           ... that she me has out-go see
           '... that she has seen me go out'
       f.   ..., daß sie mich ausgehen³ gesehen² hat¹
           ... that she me out-go seen has
           '... that she has seen me go out'
       g.   *..., daß sie wird¹ ausgehen²
           ... that she will out-go
           '... that she will go out'
       h.   ..., daß sie ausgehen² wird¹
           ... that she out-go will
           '... that she will go out'
       i.   ..., daß sie wird¹ ausgehen³ wollen²
           ... that she will out-go want
           '... that she will want to go out'
       j.   ..., daß sie ausgehen³ wollen² wird¹
           ... that she out-go want will
           '... that she will want to go out'
       k.   ..., daß sie mich das wird¹ haben² tun⁵ sehen⁴ können³
           ... that she me that will have do see can
           '... that she will have been able to see me do that'
       l.   *..., daß sie mich das tun⁵ sehen⁴ gekonnt³ haben² wird¹
           ... that she me that do see can$_{PastPart}$ have will
           '... that she will have been able to see me do that'

m. . . . , daß ich sie habe[1] tanzen[4] gehen[3] lassen[2]
. . . that I her have dance go let
'. . . that I have let her go dance'

One sees that more deeply embedded verbs (superscripts indicate depth of embedding) normally precede less deeply embedded verbs, reflecting left-branching in the V-clusters. Sometimes, however, as in (18b,e,i,k,m), the left-branching order is disturbed, optionally in (18e,i), which have synonymous left-branching counterparts in (18f,j), respectively, but obligatorily in (18b,k,m). Right-branching (18g) and left-branching (18c,l) are ungrammatical. The data are clear, at least for Standard Modern German (the dialects show a great deal of variation).[9]

The MP appears unable to account for such data, Move being obligatory and subject to the Minimal Link Condition. The leapfrogging seen in the data would thus be impossible. (It is not clear anyway if and how the MP can account for V-clusters in general; see section 8.1.1.)

Clause (18a), with its left-branching V-cluster, is straightforwardly accounted for if the following assumptions are made: (a) the rules of SD and PR are cyclic; (b) the tense operator PRES is treated as an abstract predicate Vt inducing both SR and Lowering, and is relabeled "Affix" during the cyclic treatment (the second tense shown in the diagrams of section 4.1.1.1 has been left out so as to simplify the exposition); (c) German V-clusters are typified as left-branching in principle (but see below); and (d) postcyclically, the entire V-cluster is moved to the right (here vacuously), after which the morphology unites *wollen* and PRES. The resulting mapping procedure from SA to the end-cyclic (19e) is shown in (19a–e). (Branching directionality in V-clusters is indicated with heavy lines.) No feature checking is required and no traces are left.

---

9. Example (18m) has an obsolete fully left-branching alternative in . . . *daß ich sie tanzen gehen gelassen habe*, which is considered un-well-formed in Standard Modern German but was still fully acceptable a century ago. *Versuchen* (try), in addition, takes PR optionally, allowing for clauses like

(i)   . . . daß ich das Buch zu lesen hätte1 versuchen3 wollen2
      . . . that I the book to read would-have try want
      '. . . that I would have wanted to try to read the book'

where [das Buch zu lesen] is an embedded VP and the V-cluster consists of [hätte versuchen wollen].

(19)

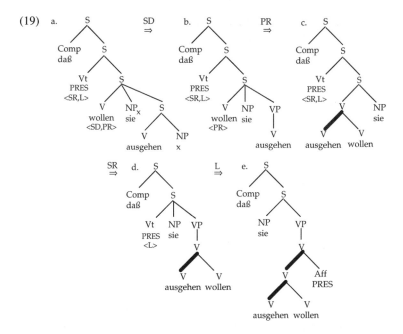

The question is: why has normal left-branching been changed in (18b,e,g,i,k,m)? The facts have been studied systematically by traditional grammarians such as Heidolph et al. (1981:274), Bech (1983), and Sitta (in Eisenberg et al. 1995:786–787), but they provide no principled explanation. It seems that the explanatory principle for these data is to be found in a change of branching directionality of the V-cluster under the following condition (see Seuren 1996:271–280, 2003:279–284).

Assume a class of R-verbs, consisting of the following members (*sehen*, *hören*, and *fühlen* are optional members in some dialects):

sehen 'see' (optional)	*können* 'be able'	*mögen* 'like', 'may'
hören 'hear' (optional)	*müssen* 'must'	*dürfen* 'be allowed'
fühlen 'feel' (optional)	*sollen* 'must'	
lassen 'let', 'allow', 'make'	*wollen* 'want'	

Assume further that these verbs are subject to the *R-condition*, which changes the directionality of further additions to the V-cluster:

When an R-verb V_R is the highest lexical verb and clustered with one or more lower verbs (which are then on its left hand side), then all subsequent lowerings in the auxiliary system are right-branching, i.e. with left-attachment:

- (a) obligatorily when V_R stands directly under a perfective auxiliary (*haben* in all cases), in which case the rule *Past Participle*, producing a past participle from the verb, is inoperative (so that one gets a so-called Ersatzinfinitiv);
- (b) optionally when V_R stands directly under the modal verb of futurity *werden* (will).

This gets all the data right, provided that a class of modal and semimodal predicates, including futurity *werden* but excluding any R-verbs, are taken to occur, in SA, just below Vt and may never occur without Vt. This will be illustrated now.

The assumption that modal auxiliaries occupy the SA-position just below the finite tense operator Vt is strongly supported by empirical facts. In English, for example, the well-known defective paradigm of the modal verbs *may, must, can, will, shall, need, dare*, and *ought to*, which lack all nonfinite forms and occur only in the simple present or simple past, need not be stipulated as an arbitrary fact, under this assumption, but follows from it. This is so because they must take on the tense responsible for the finiteness of a verb form, Vt (PRES or PAST). Verbs occurring in different positions will be nonfinite (infinitive, participle). By restricting the occurrence of the English modals to the position just below Vt, the effect is achieved that they can only become manifest as finite verb forms—that is, in fully tensed clauses.

This is true for those modal verbs that have become auxiliaries—have been through the historical process of *auxiliation*. Not all verbs expressing a modality have undergone auxiliation. Dutch, for example, still has a full morphological paradigm for the futurity verb *zullen*, and nonfinite complement clauses with *zullen* are normal. In this respect Dutch differs from German, where the futurity modal *werden* has indeed been auxiliated. This appears from the following contrasting pair of clauses ("√" indicates grammaticality; "*" indicates ungrammaticality):

(20)   a.   ... dat ik hoop het te √zullen[1]/√kunnen[1] klaren[2]
        ... that I hope it to will$_{INF}$ / can$_{INF}$ manage
        '... that I hope I will/can manage'

    b. ..., daß ich hoffe, es schaffen[2] zu *werden*[1]/√*können*[1]
      ... that I hope it manage to will$_{INF}$ / can$_{INF}$
      '... that I hope I will/can manage'

The fully grammatical Dutch clause (20a) (with right-branching V-cluster) contains the infinitive *zullen* (will) or *kunnen* (can). The German clause (20b) (with left-branching V-cluster) is ungrammatical with the infinitive *werden* (will), but grammatical with *können* (can). The ungrammaticality of *werden* in this position has been observed by traditional German grammarians, but it was always seen as a quirk of the language, never as the automatic result of a system. The semantic-syntax analysis of tenses and modals shows that this fact is an automatic consequence of that system of syntactic analysis and description.

Let us review the data again. Clause (18b) is a direct result of the R-condition: *wollen* is a full member of the R-class, and it stands under the perfective auxiliary *haben*. Change of directionality in the V-cluster is therefore mandatory, and (18c), where the change has not taken place, is ungrammatical. Note that in (18b) the expected past participle *gewollt* does not occur, owing to the fact that the R-condition has applied: whenever the R-condition applies, the cyclic rule Past Participle does not apply and the infinitival form remains (Ersatzinfinitiv).

In (18d) the R-condition has not applied, but in (18e) it has, optionally, because *sehen* is an optional member of the R-class. For that reason (18f) is also grammatical (though dialectally colored). (18f), moreover, contains the expected past participle.

In (18g), the futurity modal *werden* occurs without intervening *haben* but over the verb *ausgehen*, which is not a member of the R-class. Therefore, the V-cluster remains left-branching, as in (18h). Clauses (18i,j), however, have *werden* over the R-class verb *wollen*, which means that the R-condition applies optionally, so that both (18i) and (18j) are grammatical.

Clause (18k) has *haben* over *können*, so that he R-condition applies obligatorily. The fact that *werden* also occurs is not relevant here, since *werden* has larger scope than *haben*, and the V-cluster changes directionality as soon as *haben* is lowered. *Werden* is not relevant when it is followed by the perfective tense, resulting in the perfective auxiliary *haben*. The result is that the top of the V-cluster, *wird*[1] *haben*[2], has to be right-branching, while the tail end *tun*[5] *sehen*[4] *können*[3], has to be left-branching. This is shown in (21):

(21)

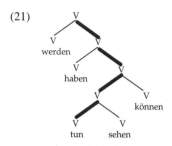

Any other branching directionality, as in (18l), is ungrammatical. Clause (18m) demonstrates the principle for *haben* over the obligatory R-class member *lassen*.

One notes that the analysis of German V-clusters presented here, succinct as it may be (for a complete treatment, see Seuren 2003:279–284), is based on an essentially complete survey of the relevant data of Modern Standard German. A really complete study would require more data, possibly from a reliable corpus, and more verbs to be discussed (see Richter 2000 for additional details).[10] Again, the contrast with the MP, where no reliable data surveys are given or referred to at all, is conspicuous.

8.2 Copying phenomena

Copying is a widespread phenomenon in the languages of the world. Yet it finds no place at all in the MP, which only allows for raising movements forced by feature checking. Despite the MP, however, speakers of some English dialects say things like:

(22)   'E ain't never been no good to no woman, not never.

Here a "literal" interpretation would yield the meaning that the man spoken about has at times been of some use to some woman. But, as anyone

---

10. Head-driven phrase-structure grammar (Hinrichs and Nakazawa 1994) assigns a feature FLIP to the perfect auxiliary *haben*, which will make it jump across the V-cluster in leftward direction when *haben* is placed directly after the verbs of the R-class. The same feature is assigned as an option to *werden*. This analysis, however, misses out on the cases like (18k,l), where the FLIP feature is obligatory, owing to *haben*. A readjustment is possible, but will be ad hoc.

familiar with this dialect will know, this is emphatically not what the sentence means.

Sentence (22) shows a rampant form of *negation copying*, or, according to some, *negative concord* or *negation spreading*. Since, in many languages, negations also crop up in comparative constructions, one would feel inclined to treat those cases as negation copying as well, the original negation having somehow disappeared. The following are good examples, (23a) from Cockney, (23b) from French:

(23)   a.   She ran faster than I *never* thought she would.
       b.   Elle est plus riche que je *ne* pensais.
            'She is richer than I thought she was.'

The hypothesis would be that the comparative construction contains an underlying negation in the semantic analysis of roughly the form (for (23a)) 'she ran fast [to an extent to which not → than] [I ever thought she would run fast]'. Whether such a hypothesis (Seuren 1973) would hold under further scrutiny, is a question that still awaits an answer. Yet the facts are there, and they find no home in the MP.

Whereas negation copying is perhaps the most frequently occurring form of copying, other forms occur as well. Sentence (24) shows pronominal first-person copying in a serial verb construction, observed by Paul Schachter (1974:258–259) in the Akuapem dialect of the West African language Akan:

(24)   Me-de aburow mi-gu nsu-m.
       I-take the corn I-flow water-in
       'I pour the corn into the water.'

In a "literal" interpretation, this sentence should imply that the speaker ("I") "flows" into the water, whereas what the sentence actually says is that the corn flows into the water (to be washed). Serial verb constructions behave as if they were nonfinite complement clauses, although they have the semantic function of indicating concomitant circumstances or ensuing results. The process underlying (24) is clearly, first, SD controlled by the higher object term *aburow* (corn), followed by the (probably postcyclic) copying of the higher pronominal subject term in the complement clause.

A different form of pronominal subject copying is found, for example, in most West-Flemish dialects. There one finds subordinate clauses like:

(25)   ... da' ek-ek-ek naor ø:s welde γaon
       ... that I-I-I to house wanted go
       '. . . that I wanted to go home'

The problem for the MP is that it contains no provision for the copying of elements in a rightward direction. Traces might conceivably be
interpreted as overt or covert copies of an element moved upward—that
is, in a leftward direction—but in this case the movement can only be in
a rightward direction.

Moreover, it would presumably be hard for a feature-checking theory
to account for the fact that in many languages the copying of negation is
conditioned by the occurrence further down the sentence of existential
quantifiers in some form or other: these appear to "attract" negation copies, for reasons unknown so far. To fit out existential quantifiers with a
"negation attraction" feature would seem to be wildly ad hoc and clearly
not at all in the spirit of the MP. What sort of feature might condition
pronominal subject copying is anybody's guess.

From a psycholinguistic point of view, copying phenomena are relatively easy to understand: semantically important elements with a weak
phonological form ask for reinforcement, which often comes in the form
of copying. This, however, does not answer the question of the structural conditions that must be obeyed by copying phenomena. Further
research is clearly indicated, but it would hardly be good policy to take
the MP as the frame of reference.

8.3 Existential *there*

Existential *there* (often also called "expletive" *there*, as in Chomsky 1995
and elsewhere) is one of the most frequently discussed topics in *The
Minimalist Program*, occupying some thirty pages, dispersed throughout the book. The relevance of existential *there* for the MP is obvious:
there is an adverb by trade, but it functions as an almost complete NP,
with features of person, number, and case (nominative or accusative). It
is, moreover, subject to a great deal of raising. The suggestions made in
the sequence of chapters in the book correspond to the different stages
of development of the MP, with a heavy emphasis on feature checking,
Move, and other aspects that are central to the MP.

This situation is not uncharacteristic for the MP. The primary concern is not so much to get a coherent body of facts right, syntactically and hopefully also semantically, as to save the theory—in the state it is in at each moment—in the light of observations that are selected according to their relevance for feature checking, Move, the Minimal Link Condition, and other elements of the MP. Both methods have their merits, but good science will prefer a middle course: look at the theory from the point of view of the facts, and at the same time look at the facts in a theoretical light. The MP, however, appears to emphasize the latter and to neglect the former.

This point is of special importance in the case of existential *there* constructions, since these are plagued by a multitude of uncertainties, mostly of a lexical semantic kind, but also, at a deeper level, to do with higher-order quantification over actions or events. The exact delimitation of the classes of verbs that allow for the existential *there* construction in the various languages turns out to be fraught with difficulties. The lexical semantic distinctions are often vague or as yet undefinable, and often (as in English) the limits differ according to sociolinguistic register. The widely known distinction of (un)ergative and (un)accusative verbs may be of some use in this case, but it is far from sufficient. Moreover, some languages, such as Dutch and German, have impersonal passives with (their equivalent of) *there*, illustrated in (34) and (35) below, which suggest higher-order existential quantification over actions or events. Yet the machinery for making that intuition syntactically explicit is simply not available.

Let us have a closer look. In English the existential *there* construction appears to be limited to a class of main verbs that are somehow connected to existential being in a wide sense, including verbs with inchoative and negative aspects: *be* (in an existential sense, but also *be* of the progressive form), *come, go, arrive, be absent, be missing, fail,* and a few more. The exact delimitation of this class of verbs has so far not been achieved, also because of vague boundary cases reflecting an earlier but not quite extinct stage of the language where more verbs were included. English thus has existential *there* sentences like the following:

(26) a. There are two men in the room.

   b. There were two books missing.

   c. There were five people working.

Dutch has the same existential "there" (Dutch *er*) construction as English, but with a much wider range of main verbs, which includes, in principle, action and process verbs, as in (27d,e):

(27)   a.   Er zijn twee presidenten.
          there are$_{plur}$ two presidents
          'There are two presidents.'
     b.   Er arriveerden twee vreemdelingen.
          there arrrived$_{plur}$ two foreigners
          'Two foreigners arrived.'
     c.   Er ontbraken nog twee gasten.
          there lacked$_{plur}$ still two guests
          'Two guests were still lacking.'
     d.   Er verkochten twee dames koffie.
          there sold$_{plur}$ two ladies coffee
          'Two ladies were selling coffee.'
     e.   Er stierven veel patiënten.
          there died$_{plur}$ many patients
          'Many patients died.'

The same goes for German, except that German prefers a different construction for the verb of narrow existential being. German thus has no structural equivalent for the Dutch sentence (27a). The German way of saying what (27a) says will be shown in a moment. Examples (27b,c,d,e), however, are represented equivalently in German, the only difference being the use of an "it" and not a "there" existential:

(28)   a.   Es trafen zwei Fremde ein.
          it arrived$_{plur}$ two foreigners$_{nom}$
          'Two foreigners arrived.'
     b.   Es fehlten noch zwei Gäste.
          it lacked$_{plur}$ still two guests$_{nom}$
          Two guests were still lacking.'
     c.   Es verkauften zwei Damen Kaffee.
          it sold$_{plur}$ two ladies$_{nom}$ coffee$_{acc}$
          'Two ladies were selling coffee.'
     d.   Es tranken vier Jungen Bier.
          it drank$_{plur}$ four boys$_{nom}$ beer$_{acc}$
          'Four boys were drinking beer.'

   e. Es starben viele Patienten.
     it died$_{plur}$ many patients$_{nom}$
     'Many patients died.'

The German construction for the verb of narrow existential being uses the verb *geben* (give) instead of *sein* (be), and the thing said to be there is referred to by an NP in accusative case. The verb *geben* is always in the singular and takes the existential *es*. Similar constructions are also found in French (*il y a*), Spanish (*hay*), and Modern Greek (*échei*), which all use a form of the verb for 'have'. Overt accusative case is visible in German and Modern Greek:

(29)   a. Es gibt einen Presidenten / zwei Presidenten.
        it gives a$_{acc}$ president$_{acc}$ / two presidents$_{acc}$
     b. Échei éna próedhro / dhío proédhrous.
        (it)-has a$_{acc}$ president$_{acc}$ / two presidents$_{acc}$

Both mean 'There is a president' and 'There are two presidents', respectively. By analogy, one may surmise that French (*il y a*) and Spanish (*hay*), which also fail to agree in number, likewise assign accusative case, although these languages lack overt case endings. (Overt case would be manifest in clitics, but cliticization of pronominal accusatives is impossible in existential sentences, as the subject/object of an existential sentence has to be comment and is therefore always accented.) French also has a variant of impersonal *il y a* for certain intransitive verbs, mainly of coming and going, with the perfective auxiliary *être* (be), as in *Il est arrivé deux étrangers* (Two foreigners have arrived), with the verb *est arrivé* in the third-person singular despite the plural subject term.

   Modern Greek, moreover, has a construction with the verb *ipárcho* (exist, be available) and also with action verbs, without any overt existential morpheme, but the subject has to follow the verb. If we assume a zero *there* existential for these cases, just as a zero existential is assumed for *échei*, we may consider the following examples:

(30)   a. Ipárchi énas próedhros.
        (there) exists$_{sing}$ a$_{nom}$ president$_{nom}$
        'There exists (is available) a president.'
     b. Ipárchoune dhío próedhri.
        (there) exist$_{plur}$ two presidents$_{nom}$
        'There exist (are available) two presidents.'

    c. Chorépsane polí ánthropi
       (there) danced many$_{nom}$ men$_{nom}$
       'Many men danced.'

Italian, in contrast, uses the verb *essere* (be) for narrow existential being, which agrees in number. The existential is of the "there" type and is realized as the clitic *vi* or the more colloquial *ci*:

(31) a. Vi/ci è un presidente.
       there is a president
    b. Vi/ci sono due presidenti.
       there are two presidents

Since this construction is entirely congruent with that in which *vi* or *ci* is an anaphoric clitic for place adverbials—in which case (31a) means 'there is a president there'—and since in the "literal" place-adverbial sense there is room for first- and second-person subjects in the nominative case (*io* and *tu* are nominatives):

(32) a. Vi/ci sono io.
       there am I$_{nom}$
       'I am there.'
    b. Vi/ci sei tu.
       there are you$_{nom}$
       You are there.'

it seems reasonable to conclude that *un presidente* and *due presidenti* of (31a,b), respectively, are also nominatives.

    Unless one accepts a zero *there* existential for Italian, as in Chomsky (1995:274) and as has been done above for Modern Greek, Italian lacks an existential construction with action verbs, just like English. Cases like (33a,b) are deceptive in that they involve the anaphoric *vi/ci*, as in (32a,b), as appears from the necessary addition of the place anaphor *there* in the English translation. Sentence (33c), on the other hand, can again be interpreted as a true existential construction with the verb *accadere* (happen), which is a verb of coming into being.

(33) a. Vi/ci lavoravano due uomini.
       there worked$_{plur}$ two men$_{plur}$
       'Two men worked there.'

    b. Vi/ci ballavano i migliori ballerini.

        there danced$_{plur}$ the best dancers$_{plur}$

        'The best dancers danced there.'

    c. Vi/ci accadde un incidente.

        there happened an accident

        'An accident happened.'

Dutch and German have a so-called impersonal passive, which does not occur in English—unless one wishes to regard (36b) as an impersonal passive. Impersonal passives take the existential *er* (there) in Dutch and *es* (it) in German. In principle, Dutch and German impersonal passives are limited to action verbs, excluding process verbs, and do not allow for any argument NP-terms to go with the verb, beyond the dummy *er* or *es*. The syntax of these impersonal passives is to some extent accounted for by considering Dutch *er* or German *es* to be a quasi-NP inserted as a dummy subject term to satisfy syntactic surface structure constraints. Dutch examples are given in (34), German examples in (35). Note that (34c) and (35c) are not ungrammatical but semantically deviant (marked by the exclamation mark), perhaps even jocular, owing to the fact that 'die' is not an action but a process verb. The occurrence of the impersonal passive imposes an action interpretation on the verb for 'die', which may strike some as funny.

(34) a. Er werd toen vaak gedanst in dit lokaal.

        there was then often danced in this hall

        'There was often dancing going on in those days in this hall.'

    b. Er werd veel gelachen.

        there was much laughed

        'There was a lot of laughing.'

    c. !Er wordt hier niet gestorven.

        there is here not died

        '!There will be no dying going on here.'

(35) a. Es wurde damals oft getanzt in diesem Lokal.

        it was then often danced in this hall

        'There was often dancing going on in those days in this hall.'

    b. Es wurde viel gelacht.

        it was much laughed

        'There was a lot of laughing.'

    c. !Es wird hier nicht gestorben.

       it is here not died

       '!There will be no dying going on here.'

Whether impersonal passives should be regarded as a special form of existential sentences is moot. If they are, one must assume existential quantification over action events, not entities, and thus of a higher order. But no rule machinery is available in any theory of grammar to link up surface structures with semantic or logical analyses containing that sort of quantification. Moreover, it must then be assumed, given the different status of the (e)-sentences in (27) and (28) on the one hand, and the (c)-sentences in (34) and (35) on the other, that the class of verbs that allow for ordinary first-order existential *er/es*-insertion is different from the class of verbs that allow for impersonal passives.

The MP appears to be straying into the area of impersonal passives with the example (36a) (1995:155):

(36) a. *There was decided to travel by plane.

      b. It was decided to travel by plane.

The correct form is (36b), with *it* as dummy subject. The explanation given (p. 155) for the ungrammaticality of (36a) rests on the fact that the existential *there* lacks an associated NP that is in control of number agreement. Or in MP terminology: "These properties are rather naturally explained on the assumption, deriving from F[ull] I[interpretation], that the expletive [=existential] is an LF affix, with its associate adjoining to it." The unclarity of the notion of "an LF affix" has already been commented on (section 2.2.2), but apart from that, it must be considered odd that the corresponding impersonal passive in Dutch is fully grammatical:

(37) Er werd besloten per vliegtuig te reizen.

     there was decided by plane to travel

     'It was decided to travel by plane.'

This is odd because if F[ull] I[interpretation] requires an NP associate for English *there*, it should do the same for Dutch *er*.

For Dutch it is natural to treat (37) as an impersonal passive, licensed by the absence of an NP argument to the main (action) verb. Whether the same goes for its German counterpart (38) is not clear:

(38)   Es wurde beschlossen, mit dem Flugzeug zu reisen.
       it was decided with the plane to travel
       'It was decided to travel by plane.'

There is good reason to regard (38) as an impersonal passive, just as in Dutch, but it may also be considered to be a case of extraposition and *it*-insertion, an analysis that is precluded for Dutch on account of the "there"-type existential *er*. This brings us back to (36b): is this a case of impersonal passive in English, presumably only allowed with a non-NP subject term (*to travel by plane*), or is it a case of *it*-insertion and extraposition, as the standard analysis has it?

We do not know, but questions of this nature do present themselves to grammarians, theoretical linguists, and semanticists. It is reasonable to expect of any theory of grammar that it provides at least some insight into the different categories involved, and that it treats examples with even more than the normally required care and subtlety as long as the various categories involved do not stand out clearly. Unfortunately, however, next to nothing about all this is found in the MP, its concerns being largely limited to the tenability of proposals to do with Move, the Minimal Link Condition, feature checking, and similar aspects of the MP. The result is a disturbingly rough and blinkered way of handling example sentences. While an account is sought for existential constructions exclusively in terms of the inordinately constrained MP theory, obvious facts fall by the wayside and absurd word combinations that would not disturb any regular theory of grammar become problematic for the MP. Thus, an absurd sentence like (39) is considered "a perennial troublemaker" (1995:372):

(39)   *There is believed there to be a man in the room.

We shall see in a moment that a more sober analysis of existential *there* easily excludes such strange combinations on the grounds that they cannot be generated by the existing machinery in any case. This point will be taken up again shortly.

Despite the many uncertainties, there appears to be a fairly simple mechanism for the syntactic generation of existential sentences with a "there" or an "it" type existential, as long as they are restricted to first-order quantification over entities. This mechanism can be sketched as follows. Take the sentence:

(40)   There is a man in the room.

Consider it to be derived from an underlying structure $_S$[be – $_{NP}$[a man] – $_{PP}$[in the room]]. Assume a cyclic insertion rule inserting $_{NP}$[there] before $_{NP}$[a man], conditioned by the latter being existentially quantified. Finally, let the newly inserted $_{NP}$[there] be treated as subject term.

This treatment is simple and general, though the conditions for its application are unclear. It appears to apply not only in English but also in Dutch, German, and Icelandic to all existential constructions with a verb for 'be' (not to the *have/give* type existential constructions of (29)). The differences with respect to Dutch, German, Icelandic, and other languages reside not in the rule of *there*-Insertion, but in the lexical semantic restrictions that apply to the embedded matrix verb.

This also accounts for scope phenomena in existential constructions, an aspect not mentioned in the MP. The sentences (41a,b) differ in possible scope readings:

(41)   a.   There seems to be a man in the room.
       b.   A man seems to be in the room.

Sentence (41a) can only mean 'It seems that there is a man in the room', with the existential quantifier under *seem* and consequently a nonspecific reading for *a man*. Sentence (41b), in contrast, is ambiguous between a large and a small scope reading for the existential quantifier and is thus either about a specific man or about the appearance of the presence of a nonspecific man. How this difference is to be expressed in Chomskyan LF is not made clear, as such facts are not discussed.

The explanation of these scope differences is not far to seek. In a semantic structure where the existential quantifier takes scope over *seem*, *there*-Insertion is not possible since the verb *seem* is of the wrong kind: *there*-Insertion is allowed only when the matrix verb is a verb of "being" (in a wide sense), and *seem* does not satisfy that description. But if the existential quantifier takes scope over *be*, as in 'seem [∃x:man [be in the room(x)]]', *there*-Insertion is permitted, since the matrix verb *be* is of the right kind. Therefore, when *there*-Insertion is found, the existential quantifier must be interpreted, in English, as standing directly over the S-structure with the verb *be*.

It is now also clear why (39), quoted earlier from Chomsky (1995:372), must be ungrammatical and is not at all the "perennial troublemaker" it is made out to be. The passive *is believed* functions precisely the way *seem* does in (41), so that two possible versions exist, the second being ambiguous as to the scope of *a man*:

(42)   a.   There is believed to be a man in the room.
       b.   A man is believed to be in the room.

Only one existential quantifier can be involved, since there is only one indefinite NP, *a man*, and English has no impersonal *there*-passives. Nor does English have any form of *there*-copying.[11] Therefore, (39) cannot have a legitimate semantic source, and the grammar will simply never come up with such a sentence. A thinkable and less far-fetched sentence like (43) is ungrammatical because the passive predicate *be believed*, like its active counterpart *believe*, but unlike the passive *be decided*, is a subject raiser, which means that the embedded (quasi-)subject *there* must be raised to the position of matrix subject, as in (42a):

(43)   *It is believed there to be a man in the room.

It seems fairly obvious that the MP treatment of existential *there* constructions misses important points of syntax and semantics and will forever be struggling with "perennial troublemakers," without touching on the real questions. What linguists want to find out is how language works, and through language, how parts of the mind work. There is nothing in the MP that could possibly contribute to a better understanding of how *there*-constructions work, and, by extrapolation, how language works. The MP analysis of *there*-constructions tells us everything about the MP but nothing about language. The real questions are not about whether *there* lands in the specifier position of some Agr projection, or whatever, but are to do with finding the simplest system of getting all the syntactic and semantic facts right. It does not seem that the MP has brought any of these questions nearer a solution.

---

11. Paul Postal (personal communication) pointed out that (American) English does have sentences like:

(i)   There looks/*look like there is a flaw in his argument.
(ii)   There *looks/look like there are flaws in his argument.

These involve a form of *there*-copying, along with a copying of agreement features.

What is needed is, first, an unbiased and factually adequate survey of available data across a sufficiently large variety of languages. On the basis of such a survey, together with the formulation of an empirical (causal) question, a classification or categorization can be established, allowing for provisional taxonomic generalizations. At this point, scientific creativity becomes essential: one has to hope for an insight that makes all the data fall into place with the help of a hopefully simple set of rules and principles. Clearly, creative insights of that nature are driven by theoretical positions already taken and suggesting new applications. The success rate of the theory as a whole will then either be boosted or decline according to the success of new applications to hitherto unexplored data complexes.

In the case of existential *there* constructions, the MP loses out considerably. There is no survey of facts, just a limited amount of ad hoc sampling. As a result, there is no preliminary, taxonomic categorization or classification, and no data-based generalizations. All we have is a series of, mostly tentative, proposals meant to deal with the incidental examples presented. And none of these proposals touches on any of the real questions or takes into account what is immediately suggested by an adequate preliminary collection or inspection of data.

8.4 Conclusion

The sum total of this chapter could not be more negative. The MP does not emerge as a serious theory of grammar or language, based as it is on flimsy general premises, an unsound methodology, unclear formulations and ideas, and a fatal scarcity of data. Every single element in the MP, to the extent that it was not taken over from elsewhere, has turned out to be badly researched, vaguely presented, or insufficiently tested. At the same time, the MP aims at an unusually ambitious goal: one strictly regimented grammar for all languages, organized according to rigid structural principles. None of the proposals, however, has been subjected to anything like sufficient testing against possible crucial counterexamples or complications. On the contrary, disconfirming or complicating evidence is taken into account only in an incidental and unsystematic way. But mostly it is disregarded, assigned to non-core ("stylistic") components of the grammar, or declared to be insufficiently "idealized." Worse, the machinery that has been invented is centrally characterized by features, such as persistent raising, that are unmotivated by linguistic facts and thus empirically vacuous, while centrally important real facts found in the languages of the world remain unaccounted for.

A particularly embarrassing aspect of the MP is the contrast between, on the one hand, its insistence on universal parameters with values selected by each individual language, and, on the other, the complete absence of any serious research into universal linguistic properties. This is the more painful, since some syntactically central parameters are easily visible to an unprejudiced eye. For example, as shown in section 8.1.1, it does seem that languages that distinguish between finite and nonfinite verb forms allow for just two forms of raising in their infinitival complementation system: (a) SR or the raising of the embedded subject-NP to the position of its own S, which then becomes VP and is moved one position to the right, or (b) PR or the raising of the embedded V to the position of the higher V, to which it is adjoined to form a right-branching or left- branching V-cluster, whereby the complement S-node disappears and remaining material is reattached higher up. Unfortunately, however, the MP is hamstrung by its self-imposed a priori formal restrictions, thus becoming its own worst enemy.

Some phenomena that do not fit the MP framework have been considered here, but numerous other widespread grammatical phenomena can be cited for which the MP is unable to provide a solution. One only has to think of conjunction reduction phenomena, cliticization phenomena, which have proved problematic for any theory of grammar so far, adverb placement, quantifier floating, and others could easily be added, such as secondary case assignment (for example, the emergence of datives under PR, as discussed in section 8.1.1). There is nothing in the MP that might be taken to be conducive to a better understanding of such phenomena.

REFERENCES

Achard, Michel. 1998. *Representation of Cognitive Structures: Syntax and Semantics of French Sentential Complements*. Berlin: de Gruyter.

Akmajian, Adrian. 1970. On deriving cleft sentences from pseudocleft sentences. *Linguistic Inquiry* 1.2:149–168.

Arbib, Michael A. 1987. Modularity and interaction of brain regions underlying visuomotor coordination. In J. L. Garfield (ed.), *Knowledge Representation and Natural Language Understanding*. Cambridge, Mass.: MIT Press, 333–363.

———. 1989. *The Metaphorical Brain 2: Neural Networks and Beyond*. New York: Wiley.

Baker, Carl L. 1991. The syntax of English *not*: the limits of core grammar. *Linguistic Inquiry* 22.3:387–429.

Baker, Mark C. 1988. *Incorporation: A Theory of Grammatical Function Changing*. Chicago: University of Chicago Press.

Baptista, Marlyse. 2000. Verb movement in four Creole languages: a comparative analysis. In J. McWhorter (ed.), *Language Change and Language Contact in Pidgins and Creoles*. Amsterdam/Philadelphia: John Benjamins, 1–33.

Barwise, Jon. 1981. Scenes and other situations. *Journal of Philosophy* 78:369–397.

Barwise, Jon, and Robin Cooper. 1981. Generalized quantifiers and natural language. *Linguistics and Philosophy* 4.2:159–219.

Beauzée, Nicolas. 1767. *Grammaire générale, ou exposition raisonnée des éléments nécessaires du langage, pour servir de fondement à l'étude de toutes les langues.* (2 vols.) Paris: J. Barbou. References in this volume to modern edition: B. E. Bartlett (ed.), Stuttgart: Frommann-Holzboog, 1974, 2 vols.

Bech, Gunnar. 1983. *Studien über das deutsche Verbum infinitum.* (2nd ed.) Tübingen: Niemeyer.

Bickerton, Derek. 1981. *Roots of Language.* Ann Arbor: Karoma.

Bloomfield, Leonard. 1933. *Language.* New York: Henry Holt.

Botha, Rudolf P. 1989. *Challenging Chomsky: The Generative Garden Game.* Oxford: Blackwell.

———. 1997a. Neo-Darwinian accounts of the evolution of language: 1. Questions about their explanatory focus. *Language and Communication* 17.3:249–267.

———. 1997b. Neo-Darwinian accounts of the evolution of language: 2. Questions about complex design. *Language and Communication* 17.4:319–340.

———. 1998a. Neo-Darwinian accounts of the evolution of language: 3. Questions about their evidental basis, logic and rhetoric. *Language and Communication* 18.1:17–46.

———. 1998b. Neo-Darwinian accounts of the evolution of language: 4. Questions about their comparative merit. *Language and Communication* 18.3:227–49.

———. 1999. On Chomsky's "fable" of instantaneous language evolution. *Language and Communication* 19.3:243–257.

———. 2003. *Unravelling the Evolution of Language.* Oxford: Elsevier.

Buffier, Claude. 1714 (1709). *Grammaire françoise sur un plan nouveau, pour en rendre les principes plus clairs et la pratique plus aisée, contenant divers traités sur la grammaire en général, sur l'usage, sur la beauté des langues et sur la manière de les apprendre, sur le style, sur l'orthographe.* Paris: Pierre Witte.

Catchpole, Clive K. 1994. Bird song. In R. E. Asher and J. M. Y. Simpson (eds.), *The Encyclopedia of Language and Linguistics.* Oxford: Pergamon, 360–366.

Chomsky, Noam. 1964a. *Current Issues in Linguistic Theory* (=Ianua Linguarum, series minor 38). The Hague: Mouton.

———. 1964b. On the notion "rule of grammar." In J. A. Fodor and J. A. Katz (eds.), *The Structure of Language: Readings in the Philosophy of Language.* Englewood Cliffs, N.J.: Prentice Hall, 119–136.

———. 1965. *Aspects of the Theory of Syntax.* Cambridge, Mass.: MIT Press.

———. 1966. *Cartesian Linguistics: A Chapter in the History of Rationalist Thought.* New York: Harper and Row.

————. 1972. *Studies on Semantics in Generative Grammar* (=Ianua Linguarum, 107). The Hague: Mouton.

————. 1988. *Language and Problems of Knowledge: The Managua Lectures.* Cambridge, Mass.: MIT Press.

————. 1990. Topic ... Comment: on formalization and formal linguistics. *Natural Language and Linguistic Theory* 8.1:143–147.

————. 1995. *The Minimalist Program.* Cambridge, Mass.: MIT Press.

————. 1998. *Linguagem e mente: pensamentos atuais sobre antigos problemas* (=Language and mind: current thoughts on ancient problems. Part I and Part II. Lectures presented at the Universidade de Brasîlia, 1996). Brasilia: Editora Universidade de Brasîlia. (Page references are to the English text as sent from MIT.)

————. 2000. *New Horizons in the Study of Language and Mind.* Cambridge: Cambridge University Press.

————. 2002. *On Nature and Language.* Edited by Adriana Belletti and Luigi Rizzi. Cambridge: Cambridge University Press.

Chomsky, Noam, and Howard Lasnik. 1977. Filters and control. *Linguistic Inquiry* 8.3:425–504.

Cutler, Anne, and Charles E. Clifton. 1999. Comprehending spoken language: a blueprint of the listener. In Colin M. Brown and Peter Hagoort (eds.), *The Neurocognition of Language.* Oxford: Oxford University Press, 123–166.

Eco, Umberto. 1995. *The Search for the Perfect Language.* Oxford: Blackwell.

Eisenberg, Peter, Hermann Gelhaus, Hans Wellmann, Helmut Henne, and Horst Sitta. 1995. *Duden Grammatik der deutschen Gegenwartssprache.* (5th ed.) Mannheim: Dudenverlag.

Feyerabend, Paul K. 1975. *Against Method: Outline of an Anarchistic Theory of Knowledge.* London: NLB.

Fodor, Jerry A. 1983. *The Modularity of Mind.* Cambridge, Mass.: MIT Press.

Fodor, Jerry A., Thomas Bever, and Merrill Garrett. 1974. *The Psychology of Language: An Introduction to Psycholinguistics and Generative Grammar.* New York: McGraw-Hill.

Freidin, Robert. 1997. The minimalist program: a review article. *Language* 73.3:571–582.

Freidin, Robert, and Jean-Roger Vergnaud. 2001. Exquisite connections: some remarks on the evolution of linguistic theory. *Lingua* 111.9:639–666.

Gould, Stephen J. 1997. *Dinosaur in a Haystack.* London: Penguin.

Gruber, Jeffrey S. 1965. Studies in lexical relations. Ph.D. diss., MIT. (Published as *Lexical Structures in Syntax and Semantics.* Amsterdam: North-Holland, 1976.)

Harris, Randy A. 1993. *The Linguistics Wars.* New York: Oxford University Press.

Harris, Zellig S. 1951. *Methods in Structural Linguistics.* Chicago: University of Chicago Press.

Hauser, Marc D., Noam Chomsky, and W. Tecumseh Fitch. 2002. The faculty of language: what is it, who has it, and how did it evolve? *Science* 298(November):1569–1579.

Heidolph, Karl E., Walter Flämig, and Wolfgang Motsch. 1981. *Grundzüge einer deutschen Grammatik*. Berlin: Akademie-Verlag.

Hinrichs, Erhard W., and Tsuneko Nakazawa. 1994. Linearizing AUXs in German verbal complexes. In J. Nerbonne, K. Netter, and C. Pollard (eds.), *German in Head-Driven Phrase Structure Grammar* (Stanford Monographs in Linguistics). Stanford: CSLI Publications, 11–37.

Horn, Laurence R. 1985. Metalinguistic negation and pragmatic ambiguity. *Language* 61.1:121–174.

Huck, Geoffrey J., and John A. Goldsmith. 1995. *Ideology and Linguistic Theory: Noam Chomsky and the Deep Structure Debate*. London: Routledge.

Huxley, Thomas H. 1880. *The Crayfish: An Introduction to the Study of Zoology*. London: Kegan Paul.

Jackendoff, Ray. 1997. *The Architecture of the Language Faculty* (=Linguistic Inquiry Monograph 28). Cambridge, Mass.: MIT Press.

———. 2002. *Foundations of Language: Brain, Meaning, Grammar, Evolution*. New York: Oxford University Press.

Johnson, David E., and Shalom Lappin. 1997. A critique of the minimalist program. *Linguistics and Philosophy* 20:273–333.

———. 1999. *Local Constraints vs. Economy* (Stanford Monographs in Linguistics). Stanford: CSLI Publications.

Johnson-Laird, Phil. 2003. The psychology of understanding. In A. Sanford (ed.), *The Nature and Limits of Human Understanding: The 2001 Gifford Lectures at the University of Glasgow*. Edinburgh: T&T Clark, 1–46.

Joseph, Brian. 1990. On arguing for serial verbs (with particular reference to Modern Greek). In B. D. Joseph and A. M. Zwicky (eds.), *When Verbs Collide: Papers from the 1990 Ohio State Mini-Conference on Serial Verbs* (= Working Papers in Linguistics 39). Columbus: Ohio State University, Department of Linguistics, 77–90.

Katz, Jerrold J., and Jerry A. Fodor. 1963. The structure of a semantic theory. *Language* 39.2:170–210.

Katz, Jerrold J., and Paul M. Postal. 1964. *An Integrated Theory of Linguistic Descriptions*. Cambridge, Mass.: MIT Press.

Kempen, Gerard, and Ed Hoenkamp. 1987. An incremental procedural grammar for sentence formulation. *Cognitive Science* 11:201–258.

Kempson, Ruth, Wilfried Meyer-Viol, and Dov Gabbay. 2001. *Dynamic Syntax: The Flow of Language Understanding*. Oxford: Blackwell.

Kornai, András, and Geoffrey K. Pullum. 1990. The X-bar theory of phrase structure. *Language* 66.1:24–50.

Kuno, Susumo. 1987. *Functional Syntax: Anaphora, Discourse and Empathy.* Chicago: University of Chicago Press.

Labov, William. 1969. Contraction, deletion, and inherent variability of the English copula. *Language* 45.4:715–762.

———. 1972. *Sociolinguistic Patterns.* Philadelphia: University of Pennsylvania Press.

———. 1980. The social origins of sound change. In W. Labov (ed.), *Locating Language in Space and Time.* New York: Academic Press, 251–265.

———. 1994. *Principles of Linguistic Change.* Vol. 1. Oxford: Blackwell.

Lakoff, George. 1971. On generative semantics. In D. D. Steinberg and L. A. Jakobovits (eds.), *Semantics: An Interdisciplinary Reader in Philosophy, Linguistics and Psychology.* Cambridge: Cambridge University Press, 232–296.

Langacker, Ronald W. 1991. *Foundations of Cognitive Grammar.* Vol. 2: *Descriptive Application.* Stanford: Stanford University Press.

Lenerz, Jürgen. 1998. Review of Chomsky (1995a). *Beiträge zur Geschichte der deutschen Sprache und Literatur* 120.1:103–111.

Levelt, Willem J. M. 1989. *Speaking: From Intention to Articulation.* Cambridge, Mass.: MIT Press.

———. 1999. Producing spoken language: a blueprint of the speaker. In Colin M. Brown and Peter Hagoort (eds.), *The Neurocognition of Language.* Oxford: Oxford University Press, 83–122.

Levine, Robert D. 2002. Review of Uriagereka (1998). *Language* 78.2:325–330.

Lieberman, Philip. 1984. *The Biology and Evolution of Language.* Cambridge, Mass.: Harvard University Press.

Marr, David. 1982. Vision: *A Computational Investigation into the Human Representation and Processing of Visual Information.* San Francisco: W. H. Freeman.

May, Robert. 1977. The grammar of quantification. Ph.D. diss., MIT.

McCawley, James D. 1967. Meaning and the description of languages. *Kotoba no Uchu* 2:10–18; 38–48; 51–57.

———. 1968. Lexical insertion in a transformational grammar without deep structure. *Papers from the Fourth Regional Meeting, Chicago Linguistic Society.* Chicago: Linguistics Department, University of Chicago, 71–80.

———. 1970. English as a VSO-language. *Language* 46.2:286–299.

———. 1972. A program for logic. In D. Davidson and G. Harman (eds.), *Semantics of Natural Language.* Dordrecht: Reidel, 498–544.

———. 1973. *Grammar and Meaning: Papers on Syntactic and Semantic Topics.* Tokyo: Taishukan.

———. 1980. Review of Newmeyer (1980). *Linguistics* 18.9/10:911–930.

Miller, George A. 1991. *The Science of Words*. New York: Scientific American Library.

Murray, Stephen O. 1994. *Theory Groups and the Study of Language in North America: A Social History*. Amsterdam/Philadelphia: John Benjamins.

Newmeyer, Frederick J. 1980. *Linguistic Theory in America: The First Quarter-Century of Transformational Generative Grammar*. New York: Academic Press.

Peters, P. Stanley, and Richard W. Ritchie. 1973. On the generative power of transformational grammars. *Information Sciences* 6:49–83.

Piattelli-Palmarini, Massimo. 1989. Evolution, selection and cognition: from 'learning' to parameter setting in biology and the study of language. *Cognition* 31:1–44.

Pinker, Steven, and Paul Bloom. 1990. Natural language and natural selection. *Behavioral and Brain Sciences* 13:707–727; 765–784.

Pollock, Jean-Yves. 1989. Verb Movement, Universal Grammar, and the structure of IP. *Linguistic Inquiry* 20.3:365–424.

Popper, Karl R. 1945. *The Open Society and its Enemies*. London: Routledge & Kegan Paul.

———. 1959. *The Logic of Scientific Discovery*. London: Hutchinson.

Postal, Paul M. 1972. The best theory. In P. Stanley Peters (ed.), *Goals of Linguistic Theory*. Englewood Cliffs, N.J.: Prentice Hall, 131–170.

———. 1974. *On Raising: One Rule of English Grammar and Its Theoretical Implications*. Cambridge, Mass.: MIT Press.

———. 2004. *Skeptical Linguistic Essays*. New York: Oxford University Press.

Pullum, Geoffrey K. 1989. Topic . . . Comment. Formal linguistics meets the Boojum. *Natural Language and Linguistic Theory* 7.1:137–143.

———. 1996. Nostalgic views from Building 20. *Journal of Linguistics* 32:137–147.

Quine, Willard V. O. 1960. *Word and Object*. Cambridge, Mass.: MIT Press.

Radford, Andrew. 1997. *Syntax: A Minimalist Introduction*. Cambridge: Cambridge University Press.

Raposo, Eduardo. 1987. Case theory and Infl-to-Comp: the inflected infinitive in European Portuguese. *Linguistic Inquiry* 18.1:85–109.

Reichenbach, Hans. 1947. *Elements of Symbolic Logic*. London: Macmillan.

Richter, Michael. 2000. Verbkonstruktionen im Deutschen. Eine transformationelle Analyse syntaktischer Erscheinungen innerhalb des deutschen Verbsystems im Rahmen der semantischen Syntax. Ph.D. diss., Nijmegen University.

Rosenbloom, Paul C. 1950. *The Elements of Mathematical Logic*. New York: Dover.

Ross, J. Robert. 1967. *Constraints on Variables in Syntax*. Ph.D. diss., MIT. (Published as *Infinite Syntax!* Norwood, NJ: Ablex, 1986.)

Russell, Bertrand. 1905. On denoting. *Mind* 14:479–493.

Schachter, Paul. 1974. A non-transformational account of serial verbs. *Studies in African Linguistics*. (Suppl. 5): 253–270.

Seuren, Pieter A. M. 1972. Predicate Raising and dative in French and sundry languages. Unpublished paper, Magdalen College, Oxford. (Circulated by Linguistic Agency University Trier. Published as chapter 7 in Seuren 2001.)

———. 1973. The comparative. In F. Kiefer and N. Ruwet (eds.), *Generative Grammar in Europe*. Dordrecht: Reidel, 528–564.

———. 1985. *Discourse Semantics*. Oxford: Blackwell.

———. 1988. Presupposition and negation. *Journal of Semantics* 6:175–226.

———. 1990. Verb Syncopation and Predicate Raising in Mauritian Creole. *Linguistics* 28.4:809–844.

———. 1996. *Semantic Syntax*. Oxford: Blackwell.

———. 1998. *Western Linguistics: An Historical Introduction*. Oxford: Blackwell.

———. 2000. Presupposition, negation and trivalence. *Journal of Linguistics* 36.2:261–297.

———. 2001. *A View of Language*. Oxford: Oxford University Press.

———. 2003. Verb clusters and branching directionality in German and Dutch. In Seuren and Kempen, 247–296.

Seuren, Pieter A. M., and Herman Chr. Wekker. 1986. Semantic transparency as a factor in Creole genesis. In P. Muysken and N. Smith (eds.), *Substrata versus Universals in Creole Genesis: Papers from the Amsterdam Creole Workshop, April 1985*. Amsterdam/Philadelphia: John Benjamins, 57–70.

Seuren, Pieter A. M., Venanzio Capretta, and Herman Geuvers. 2001. The logic and mathematics of occasion sentences. *Linguistics and Philosophy* 24.2:531–595.

Seuren, Pieter A. M., and Gerard W. Kempen (eds.). 2003. *Verb Constructions in German and Dutch*. Amsterdam/Philadelphia: John Benjamins.

Townsend, David J., and Thomas G. Bever. 2001. *Sentence Comprehension: The Integration of Habits and Rules*. Cambridge, Mass.: MIT Press.

Travis, Charles. 1981. *The True and the False: the Domain of the Pragmatic*. Amsterdam/Philadelphia: John Benjamins.

Uriagereka, Juan. 1998. *Rhyme & Reason: An Introduction to Minimalist Syntax*. Cambridge, Mass.: MIT Press.

Van der Does, Jaap, and Michiel van Lambalgen. 2000. A logic of vision. *Linguistics and Philosophy* 23.1:1–92.

Weinreich, Uriel, William Labov, and Marvin I. Herzog. 1968. Empirical foundations for a theory of language change. In W. P. Lehmann and Y. Malkiel (eds.), *Directions for Historical Linguistics: A Symposium*. Austin: University of Texas Press, 95–188.

Wells, Rulon S. 1947. Immediate constituents. *Language* 23.1:81–117.

Zwart, Jan-Wouter. 1998. The Minimalist Program. Review article. *Journal of Linguistics* 34:213–226.

INDEX

accent, 169–70, 174–76, 178, 181, 184
  nuclear, 178 n.3
accommodation, 93
Achard, Michel, 108
adequacy, levels of, 113–14
Akan, 217
Akmajian, Adrian, 178
Akuapem, 217
algorithm, 48–49, 151–55
  derived, 49, 154–55
  primitive, 49, 154
analysis, semantic. *See* SA
analysis-by-synthesis, 84–85
anaphora, 94–95
anchoring, contextual, 93–94
animal communication, 86
Arbib, Michael, 15, 47
argument structure, 39, 87–88, 91,
  157–58, 165, 207, 209
Aristotle, 10, 125
arithmetic, 49
Arnauld, Antoine, 27 n.4

articulation, double, 80, 157–58
auxiliary system, 207–10, 214
auxiliation, 214

Baker, Leroy, 204 n.7
Baker, Mark, 14, 200 n.4, 201
Bambara, 204
Baptista, Marlyse, 204 n.7
Barwise, Jon, 47, 104
Beauzée, Nicolas, 5, 54–55
Bech, Gunnar, 200 n.5, 213
behaviorism, 48–49, 62, 118, 132,
  152–3
Bellarmine, Robert, 107
Belletti, Adriana, 107
Bever, Thomas, 85, 107
Bickerton, Derek, 144 n.3
Block, Ned, 27 n.5
Bloom, Paul, 27 n.5, 76 n.3
Bloomfield, Leonard, 3, 12, 54, 153
Botha, Rudolf, 16, 63–64, 73, 76
  n.3, 130